Queer Battle Fatigue

This book engages with the concept "queer battle fatigue," which is the everyday exhaustion that LGBTQIA+ people and communities often experience from anti-queer norms and values. Contributors express how this concept is often experienced across spaces and places, from schools to communities.

Queer Battle Fatigue is one way to express the everyday exhaustion that LGBTQIA+ people and communities often feel, which is a result of sociopolitical and cultural anti-queer norms and values. In this volume, contributors think about how queer battle fatigue hits bodies and their multiple ways of being, knowing, and doing. Chapters describe how such violence flows from early childhood experiences to universities and across community spaces. Contributors also describe how people and communities resist and refuse anti-queer norms and values, carving out pathways to live, love, and have joy despite everyday oppressions. From calling on Black queer ancestors, to using Science, Technology, Engineering, and Mathematics (STEM) education as a safe space, to artistic representations of identities, the chapters in *Queer Battle Fatigue* ask readers to consider how to disrupt and deconstruct anti-queer norms while also engaging in the many beautiful forms of queer joy as an act of resistance.

Queer Battle Fatigue will be a key resource for academics, researchers, and advanced students of education, qualitative research, queer theory and gender studies, educational research, and curriculum studies. The chapters included in this book were originally published as a special issue of *International Journal of Qualitative Studies in Education*.

Boni Wozolek is currently serving as the inaugural Director of Diversity, Equity, and Inclusive Excellence at Penn State University, Abington College, where she is also an Associate Professor.

David Lee Carlson is Full Professor in the Mary Lou Fulton Teachers College at Arizona State University.

Queer Battle Fatigue
Education, Exhaustion, and Everyday Oppressions

Edited by
Boni Wozolek and David Lee Carlson

LONDON AND NEW YORK

First published 2024
by Routledge
4 Park Square, Milton Park, Abingdon, Oxon OX14 4RN

and by Routledge
605 Third Avenue, New York, NY 10158

Routledge is an imprint of the Taylor & Francis Group, an informa business

Chapter 1 © 2024 Boni Wozolek and David Lee Carlson
Chapters 2–8 © 2024 Taylor & Francis

All rights reserved. No part of this book may be reprinted or reproduced or utilised in any form or by any electronic, mechanical, or other means, now known or hereafter invented, including photocopying and recording, or in any information storage or retrieval system, without permission in writing from the publishers.

Trademark notice: Product or corporate names may be trademarks or registered trademarks, and are used only for identification and explanation without intent to infringe.

British Library Cataloguing in Publication Data
A catalogue record for this book is available from the British Library

ISBN13: 978-1-032-55302-3 (hbk)
ISBN13: 978-1-032-55303-0 (pbk)
ISBN13: 978-1-003-43002-5 (ebk)

DOI: 10.4324/9781003430025

Typeset in Myriad Pro
by Newgen Publishing UK

Publisher's Note
The publisher accepts responsibility for any inconsistencies that may have arisen during the conversion of this book from journal articles to book chapters, namely the inclusion of journal terminology.

Disclaimer
Every effort has been made to contact copyright holders for their permission to reprint material in this book. The publishers would be grateful to hear from any copyright holder who is not here acknowledged and will undertake to rectify any errors or omissions in future editions of this book.

Contents

Citation Information vi
Notes on Contributors viii

1 Anti-Queerness as Educational Norms: Tracing the Contours of Queer Battle Fatigue 1
   Boni Wozolek and David Lee Carlson

2 Trans Faculty and Queer Battle Fatigue: Poetic (Re)Presentations of Navigating Identity Politics in the Academy 7
   Sean Robinson

3 Embracing Queer Heartache: Lessons from LGBTQ+ Intergenerational Dialogues 24
   Karen Morris, Adam J. Greteman and Nic M. Weststrate

4 Queer Black Joy in the Face of Racial and Queer Battle Fatigue 39
   Reagan P. Mitchell

5 STEM as a Cover: Towards a Framework for Queer Emotions, Battle Fatigue, and STEM Identity 56
   Mario I. Suárez, Andrea M. Hawkman, Colby Tofel-Grehl, Beth L. MacDonald, Kristin Searle, David F. Feldon, Taryn Sommers and Evelynn Foley-Hernandez

6 Curricula of Oppressions: Queering Elementary School Norms and Values 76
   Boni Wozolek and Samantha Antell

7 Embodied failure: Resisting Gender and Sexuality Erasures in K-12 Schools 89
   Darla Linville

8 Illegible and Illiterate in Honduras: Research in a Transnational Setting as a Queer from the Global North 103
   Kate E. Kedley

Index 118

Citation Information

The following chapters were originally published in the *International Journal of Qualitative Studies in Education*, volume 35, issue 9 (2022). When citing this material, please use the original page numbering for each article, as follows:

Chapter 2
Trans faculty and queer battle fatigue: poetic (re)presentations of navigating identity politics in the academy
Sean Robinson
International Journal of Qualitative Studies in Education, volume 35, issue 9 (2022), pp. 911–927

Chapter 3
Embracing queer heartache: lessons from LGBTQ+ intergenerational dialogues
Karen Morris, Adam J. Greteman and Nic M. Weststrate
International Journal of Qualitative Studies in Education, volume 35, issue 9 (2022), pp. 928–942

Chapter 4
The Art of Ridicule: Black Queer Joy in the Face of the Fatigues
Reagan Patrick Mitchell
International Journal of Qualitative Studies in Education, volume 35, issue 9 (2022), pp. 943–959

Chapter 5
STEM as a cover: towards a framework for Queer Emotions, Battle Fatigue, and STEM identity
Mario I. Suárez, Andrea M. Hawkman, Colby Tofel-Grehl, Beth L. MacDonald, Kristin Searle, David F. Feldon, Taryn Sommers and Evelynn Foley-Hernandez
International Journal of Qualitative Studies in Education, volume 35, issue 9 (2022), pp. 960–979

Chapter 6
Curricula of oppressions: queering elementary school norms and values
Boni Wozolek and Samantha Antell
International Journal of Qualitative Studies in Education, volume 35, issue 9 (2022), pp. 980–992

Chapter 7
Resisting embodied failure: Queer and trans adult allies welcoming queer and trans youth
Darla Linville
International Journal of Qualitative Studies in Education, volume 35, issue 9 (2022), pp. 993–1006

Chapter 8
The illegible and illiterate researcher in Honduras: Research in a transnational setting as a queer from the Global North
Kate E. Kedley
International Journal of Qualitative Studies in Education, volume 35, issue 9 (2022), pp. 1007–1021

For any permission-related enquiries please visit:
www.tandfonline.com/page/help/permissions

Notes on Contributors

Samantha Antell, Penn State University, Abi1ngton College, Abington, USA.

David Lee Carlson, Mary Lou Fulton Teachers College, Arizona State University, Tempe, AZ, USA.

David F. Feldon, Instructional Technology and Learning Sciences, Utah State University, Logan, UT, USA.

Evelynn Foley-Hernandez, Chaos Learning Lab, Logan, UT, USA.

Adam J. Greteman, School of the Art Institute of Chicago, Visual Critical Studies, Chicago, IL, USA.

Andrea M. Hawkman, School of Teacher Education and Leadership, Utah State University, Logan, UT, USA.

Kate E. Kedley, College of Education, Rowan University, Glassboro, NJ, USA.

Darla Linville, Department of Advanced Studies & Innovation, Augusta University, Augusta, GA, USA.

Beth L. MacDonald, College of Education, Illinois State University, Normal, IL, USA.

Reagan P. Mitchell, School of the Arts, University of North Carolina, Winston-Salem, NC, USA.

Karen Morris, School of the Art Institute of Chicago, Visual Critical Studies, Chicago, IL, USA.

Sean Robinson, School of Education and Urban Studies, Morgan State University, Baltimore, MA, USA.

Kristin Searle, Instructional Technology and Learning Sciences, Utah State University, Logan, UT, USA.

Taryn Sommers, Chaos Learning Lab, Logan, UT, USA.

Mario I. Suárez, School of Teacher Education and Leadership, Utah State University, Logan, UT, USA.

Colby Tofel-Grehl, School of Teacher Education and Leadership, Utah State University, Logan, UT, USA.

Nic M. Weststrate, Department of Educational Psychology, University of Illinois at Chicago, IL, USA.

Boni Wozolek, Penn State University, Abington College, Abington, USA.

Anti-Queerness as Educational Norms: Tracing the Contours of Queer Battle Fatigue

Boni Wozolek and David Lee Carlson

Queerness can be understood as a radical act of resistance and refusal rooted in the margins. One only need to recall images of ballroom culture (Baker-Pitts & Martin, 2021) as it existed alongside the acquired immunodeficiency syndrome (AIDS) epidemic and a lack of sociopolitical support or, more recently, beautiful images of couples celebrating the opportunity for their relationship to finally be legally affirmed by the U.S. government (Pierceson, 2014) to see how the margins are always already productive bloom spaces, teeming with both resistance and hope. Each act of resistance and refusal can be understood as engaging in a process of carving out and redefining the contours of queer spaces across sociopolitical landscapes. What is created despite the wake (Sharpe, 2016) of violence are spaces of possibilities: places of love, spaces of hope, and innumerable shimmering affects (Ahmed, 2010). Within the productive tensions that undergird queer(ed) spaces of possibilities, it is important to note that such places are as much about how they are hegemonically identified as they are about how people find their identities within them (Blair, 2016; Love, 2017; Mayo, 2017). Queer Battle Fatigue (QBF), or the exhaustion that LGBTQIA2S+ people and communities feel and experience that result from consistently surviving anti-queer aggressions (Wozolek et al., 2015), often emerges within the tensions between how one identifies and how they are identified by others. QBF is also produced as people and communities work to create bloom spaces of possibility against ongoing emotional and physical violence.

Much like critical geographers mapping the sociopolitical norms and values that are etched into the contours of spaces and places (e.g., Helfenbein, 2021; Massey, 2005), this edited volume emphasizes how queer(ed) cartographies reverberate with both oppressions and possibilities (Halberstam, 2005). Specifically, the contributors consider narratives that are too often formed and informed by QBF, and the polyphony of affects that are co-constituted in, and often despite, violence. There are many significant ways to describe how anti-queer hostilities are expressed, from places of employment (Sears, 2019) to social spaces (Adeyemi et al., 2021). This volume, however, focuses on the entanglements of anti-queer aggressions across educational contexts[1] as they are unpacked through qualitative research methodologies.

The focus on education is important because, as we write this introduction, queer youth make up 40% of the homeless youth population (Hail-Jares et al., 2021), self-harm and suicide rates continue to rise among LGBTQIA2S+ communities (Gnan et al., 2019), and trans/nonbinary women of color face ongoing and unchecked violence across the globe (Lenning et al., 2021). These normalized acts of violence are happening while schools across the United States face yet another rise of proposed, and increasingly passed, set of legislative barriers designed to keep any dialogue about queerness and race out of schools. In other words, while LGBTQIA2S+ folx, people of color, and those with minoritized intersectional identities experience daily violence, they simultaneously watch laws be proposed an enacted that delegitimize their very existence through schools.

Eve Kosofsky Sedgwick (1994) once described the knowledge of these realities as "indelible, but not astonishing, to anyone with a reason to be attuned to the profligate way this culture has of denying and despoiling queer energies and lives" (p. 1). For Boni, as a queer woman of color who has spent over a decade teaching and researching K-12 schools, the words "indelible, but not astonishing" deeply resonate with her personal experiences (e.g., Wozolek, 2018a), and with daily atrocities she witnessed queer youth encounter at school (e.g., Wozolek, 2018b). Similarly, David's experience as a queer man who has spent nearly two decades thinking about how Western epistemologies have been violently built on the backs of queer people by "denying and despoiling queer energies and lives" and living in the possibilities of "what if?" returning to Sedgwick's dialogue, it comes of no surprise to the voices heard in this book that schools are designed for and controlled by the White cishetero patriarchy (Gilbert, 2014; McCready, 2019; Whitlock, 2013) in ways that (un)intentionally dampen and destroy queer energies and lives.

The contributors to this volume are therefore not surprised by anti-queer aggression. Rather, this is a collection of scholars and activists who use their available space to resist and refuse such violence. This book also addresses the many ways that these scholars' indefatigable work and engagement with QBF has created spaces of possibility across places, from their personal experiences to the co-creation of experiences for young people in schools. In this issue, qualitative research is but one vehicle that authors use to think with and about those tangled up (Nespor, 1997) in the many forms of normalized anti-queer violence in educational spaces and places. At the intersections of education, qualitative research, and QBF, this edited volume serves as a dedication to those lives that have been diminished, despoiled, or lost. Additionally, this book is meant to signal active resistance to the QBF that engenders and maintains anti-queer norms and values across contemporary educational contexts.

The landscapes of schools that excuse and justify the despoiling of queer lives do not, as many scholars have documented (e.g., Bracho & Hayes, 2020; Halberstam, 2011; Meiners, 2016; Nespor, 1997; Woodson, 1933), exist in a vacuum. Rather, they are in constant circulation with broader sociopolitical and cultural values. What students learn through voices amplified in schools, as well as the bias that swells from the normalized silencing of marginalized perspectives, spills from classrooms and corridors, and into communities (Gumbs, 2016; Nespor, 1997). Or, as Carter G. Woodson (1933) argued regarding the proliferation of racism and physical violence against Black people and communities that is connected to schools: "Why not exploit…or exterminate a class that everybody is taught to regard as inferior?" (p. 3). Perhaps, it is no surprise that queer bias[2] and racism prevalent in the curriculum buttresses broader anti-queer and racist sociopolitical values, often condoning community violence against LGBTQIA2S people, people of color, and those with intersecting identities.

One way to theorize the exhaustion that emerges from these aggressions is through Barad's (2007) discussion of intra-actions. Barad uses the delineation between inter- and intra-actions is significant when describing how agency and subjectivities materialize from within events between bodies—whether human or nonhuman—not outside them. Take, for example, the recent bans on teaching Critical Race Theory (e.g., House Bill 327 in Ohio, among others across the country) or LGBTQIA2S+ stigmatizing state laws (e.g., Alabama State Code § 116-40 A 2(c)(8)). One can say that enacting these laws are not just events but an intra-action of human and nonhuman parts. This includes human bodies, discourses on minoritized populations, racism, anti-queer bias, politics, news coverage, and other such factors. The bias entangled with this legislation therefore becomes a phenomena that is made and unmade through intra-actions between the surrounding events (e.g., protests, news coverage, and, too often, curricular shifts to accommodate the bills), and broader sociopolitical norms. Through intra-actions, bodies are brought together through political phenomena, yet these intra-actions also separate actors into new co-constituted subjects: people can become, at least temporarily, those who are pro- or anti-legislation, those impacted through physical proximity and those not directly affected, to name a few.

In this way, everyone in the United States, regardless of where they live, can be considered entangled with such legislation, although, certainly, not everyone directly interacts with it in any fashion they might recognize. While we have placed the above categories into false binaries to illustrate a point, there are infinite points between each of these positions and a multiplicity of ways that these positions can collapse into themselves. While it is quite possible that queer youth might not be in physical proximity to state houses, or have a voting voice, intra-actions occur regardless of their awareness or ability to formally participate. Finally, as Barad argues, regardless of whether one interacts with or is aware of intra-actions with the event, the ecology of the United States, and less broadly, individual states, intra-act with this legislation, therefore distributing responsibility for the matter produced within these intra-actions—namely, discourses, materials, and subject positions.

As bodies intra-act, the shuttling intensities that are affects, and their relations to agency (Rosiek, 2018), emerges. Ahmed (2010) describes affects as "what sticks, or what sustains or preserves the connection between ideas, values, and objects" (p. 29). QBF is one possible intensity that materializes from intra-actions, sticking on the body of the victim who endured violence and impacting the person who becomes empowered through violent intra-actions. QBF therefore becomes one possible connection between past, present, and future victims, aggressors, sociopolitical values, and iterations of violence. Here I am theorizing QBF not only as a product of normalized queer bias but also as a part of the process that binds normalized anti-queer aggressions. QBF is the messiness of the experiential, the unfolding of bodies into anti-queer worlds, the "drama of contingency" (Ahmed, 2010, p. 39) that touches and is touched by bodies as it is affectively sewn together and pulled apart by ordinary, everyday events.

This edited volume begins with Sean Robinson's essay on trans faculty. Using a poetic (re)presentation of qualitative research, Robinson artfully illustrates the boundaries and borders that many transgender individuals endure in higher education. Robinson's use of poetry to describe and analyze participant narratives can be understood as a much-needed response to the call for nuanced, creative ways for readers to engage with narratives of trans educators (e.g., Prendergast, 2009; Simmons, 2017) who have experienced QBF across contexts in higher education.

Robinson's work is followed by Karen Morris, Adam Greteman, and Nic Westrate's scholarship. This paper attends to the narratives that emerged from a partnership between LGBTQ youth at a community center, an art and design college, and a public research university. This collaborative ethnographic study foregrounds questions of heartache as participants' negotiated grief, anger, and other affects that emerged from QBF. The vulnerable exploration of heartache within queer spaces as a way to strengthen queer communities makes Morris, Greteman, and Westrate's work especially significant to resisting and refusing sociocultural contexts that normalize silencing queer voices and experiences.

Reagan Mitchell's paper on Queer Black joy compliment's Morris, Greteman, and Westrate's work in that it describes how joy can counter the very fear and grief that the previous paper engages. Using an analytical framework at the intersection of racial and QBF, Mitchell analyzes how the music and artistic representations of Sylvester and Big Freedia serve as a formal curriculum of Black Queer joy. This curriculum is a refusal of spirit murdering (Love, 2019) that is normalized in White, cishetero spaces and places. While outside of traditional "schooling," popular culture is a form of public pedagogy. By centering Slyvester and Freedia's narratives and work, Mitchell speaks back to the violent (re)productions of pain by explicating the power of Black joy.

Building on Mitchell's notion of Black Queer joy, Mario Su_arez, Andrea Hawkman, Colby Tofel-Grehl, Beth MacDonald, Kristin Searle, David Feldon, Taryn Sommers, and Evelynn Foley-Hernandez use data collected from queer youth who participated in a LGBTQþmaker camp in the Western United States to argue that STEM can be a tool to validate queer identities. The authors argue that with support, care, and respect, queer youth who participated in the program were able to articulate the violence they experienced while providing a space of creativity where youth could build capacity personal expression through STEM-related projects. The implications of this paper are not solely rooted in queer success but in an attention to how a justice-oriented curriculum should always already be entangled with the STEM field. Addressing several gaps in the field as it is related to STEM, queer youth, and rural contexts, this paper is significant in that it uniquely calls for STEM programs that foreground affects, queerness, and, by extension, queer excellence.

Continuing the previous article's attention to curricular change, Boni Wozolek and Samantha Antell's work uses narrative inquiry to explore the experiences of a 19-year-old bisexual college student as he reflects on events that occurred in elementary school that deeply shaped his ways of being, knowing, and doing. Wozolek and Antell use this participant's narrative to argue that elementary schools and teacher education programs should foreground the forms of curriculum—formal, enacted, hidden, and null—in order to support burgeoning queer identities in the classroom. The significance of Wozolek and Antell's work is that it serves as a call for teacher preparation, especially programs geared toward early childhood education, to include curriculum studies as a way to disrupt normalized silencing of LGBTQIA2Sþvoices and perspectives.

Wozolek and Antell's work is followed by Darla Linville's theoretical analysis of the Queer Art of Failure. Linville uses Halberstam's work to examine how institutions, and the adults who are embedded in these systems, consistently fail queer and trans youth. Linville argues that there are multiple points of failure, including questions of solidarity, rigid ideas and ideals of "success," and basic failure to create and maintain spaces and places of care in institutions. Attend to the opposite end of the educational spectrum from Wozolek and Antell's article, Linville powerfully argues that queer onto-epistemologies not only left underserved but placed in a system that is filled with experiences crafted for queer fatigue and failure. Questioning what a truly "safe space" might mean at an institution, Linville refuses normalized systems of failure that are too often "business as usual" in higher education.

Finally, Kate Kedley's ethnographic work situates personal experiences in Honduras as a queer person in a transnational, multilingual context. Although working closely with the LGBTQIA+ community in Honduras, Kedley explores the tensions that arise between perceived versus personal identity and the significance of queering narratives and research in ways that open, rather than limit, experiences and opportunities for queer people and communities in the Global South. Kedley's vulnerable sharing of personal experiences that include watching participants be murdered, experiences with smugglers, and other kinds of violence bravely unpacks the exhaustion that queer people can experience as researchers in research contexts, reminding readers of the tension between being authentic and questions of safety in the field.

Together, these articles tell a collective narrative about queerness as it touches and is touched by educational contexts, from classrooms to STEM clubs, to research contexts, to music, and to the academy. The significance of these papers is that they explore not only the pain and heartache of QBF but also affects like joy and hope. Weaving questions of race, class, and language with dialogues on genders and sexual orientations, this edited volume speaks not only to the heart of queerness in and across educational contexts but also it seeks to queer where and how we honor the lives of LGBTQIA2S+ people and communities. It is an intra-action of voices, perspectives, and stories.

The purpose is an intra-action where a space of resistance and refusal to anti-queer violence emerges to interrupt the despoiling of queer energies—from classrooms to communities.

Notes

1. The editors of this book define "educational contexts" broadly, recognizing that human bodies are always already in a state of learning. Further, defining education solely through schools and systems of schooling is a Western construction that is marginalizing across communities, but especially to communities of color that have defined educational contexts outside of Western constructions of "formal" learning.
2. Our use of the term "queer bias" is intentional and meant to move away from the use of "phobias" to describe anti-queer norms and values. Specifically, we are arguing that anti-queer bias goes beyond the construct of phobias, which can be written off as unconscious. Rather, such actions and beliefs, while sometimes implicit and unexamined, are not innate to human behavior.

Disclosure statement

No potential conflict of interest was reported by the author(s).

ORCID

Boni Wozolek http://orcid.org/0000-0003-4226-1439

References

Adeyemi, K., Khubchandani, K., & Rivera-Servera, R. (2021). *Queer nightlife*. University of Michigan Press.
Ahmed, S. (2010). Happy objects. In M. Gregg & G. J. Seigworth (Eds.), *The affect theory reader* (pp. 29–51). Duke University Press.
Baker-Pitts, C., & Martin, D. (2021). Realness with a Twist1: Gender creativity in the LGBTQ Ballroom. *Studies in Gender and Sexuality*, 22(3), 206–218.
Barad, K. (2007). *Meeting the universe halfway: Quantum physics and the entanglement of matter and meaning*. Duke University Press.
Blair, Z. (2016). Boystown. In E. P. Johnson (Ed.), *No tea, no shade: New writings in Black queer studies* (pp. 287–302). Duke University Press.
Bracho, C. A., & Hayes, C. (2020). Gay voices without intersectionality is White supremacy: Narratives of gay and lesbian teachers of color on teaching and learning. *International Journal of Qualitative Studies in Education*, 33(6), 583–592. https://doi.org/10.1080/09518398.2020.1751897
Gilbert, J. (2014). *Sexuality in school: The limits of education*. University of Minnesota Press.
Gnan, G. H., Rahman, Q., Ussher, G., Baker, D., West, E., & Rimes, K. A. (2019). General and LGBTQ-specific factors associated with mental health and suicide risk among LGBTQ students. *Journal of Youth Studies*, 22(10), 1393–1408. https://doi.org/10.1080/13676261.2019.1581361
Gumbs, A. P. (2016). *Spill: Scenes of Black feminist fugitivity*. Duke University.
Hail-Jares, K., Vichta-Ohlsen, R., Butler, T. M., & Byrne, J. (2021). Queer homelessness: The distinct experiences of sexuality and trans-gender diverse youth. *Journal of LGBT Youth*, 18, 1–25. https://doi.org/10.1080/19361653.2021.1990817
Halberstam, J. (2005). *In a queer time and place: Transgender bodies, subcultural lives*. NYU Press.
Halberstam, J. (2011). *The queer art of failure*. Duke University Press.
Helfenbein, R. J. (2021). *Critical geographies of education: Space, place, and curriculum inquiry*. Routledge.
Lenning, E., Brightman, S., & Buist, C. L. (2021). The trifecta of violence: A socio-historical comparison of lynching and violence against transgender women. *Critical Criminology*, 29(1), 151–172. https://doi.org/10.1007/s10612-020-09539-9
Love, B. (2017). A ratchet lens: Black queer youth, agency, hip hop, and the black ratchet imagination. *Educational Researcher*, 46(9), 539–547. https://doi.org/10.3102/0013189X17736520
Love, B. L. (2019). *We want to do more than survive: Abolitionist teaching and the pursuit of educational freedom*. Beacon Press.
Massey, D. (2005). *For space*. Sage.

Mayo, C. (2017). Queer and trans youth: Relational subjectivity, and uncertain possibilities: Challenging research in complicated contexts. *Educational Researcher*, 46(9), 530–538. https://doi.org/10.3102/0013189X17738737

McCready, L. T. (2019). Queeruptions, queer of color analysis, radical action and education reform: An introduction. *Equity & Excellence in Education*, 52(4), 370–372. https://doi.org/10.1080/10665684.2019.1705206

Meiners, E. (2016). *For the children?: Protecting innocence in a carceral state*. University of Minnesota Press.

Nespor, J. (1997). *Tangled up in school: Politics, space, bodies and signs in the educational process*. Lawrence Erlbaum.

Pierceson, J. (2014). *Same-sex marriage in the United States: The road to the Supreme Court and beyond*. Rowman & Littlefield.

Prendergast, M. (2009). "Poem is what?" Poetic inquiry in qualitative social science research. *International Review of Qualitative Research*, 1(4), 541–568. https://doi.org/10.1525/irqr.2009.1.4.541

Rosiek, J. L. (2018). Agential realism and educational ethnography. In D. Beach, C. Bagley, & S. Marques da Silva (Eds.), *The Wiley handbook of ethnography of education* (pp. 403–423). John Wiley & Sons, Inc.

Sears, J. T. (2019). *Lonely hunters: An oral history of lesbian and gay southern life, 1948-1968*. Routledge.

Sedgwick, E. K. (1994). *Tendencies*. Routledge.

Sharpe, C. (2016). *In the wake: On blackness and being*. Duke University Press.

Simmons, S. L. (2017). A thousand words are worth a picture: A snapshot of trans_ postsecondary educators in higher education. *International Journal of Qualitative Studies in Education*, 30(3), 266–284. https://doi.org/10.1080/09518398.2016.1254303

Whitlock, R. U. (Ed.). (2013). *Queer South rising: Voices of a contested place*. Information Age Press.

Woodson, C. G. (1933). *The miseducation of the negro*. Tribeca Books.

Wozolek, B. (2018a). Gaslighting queerness: GSAs, schooling, and teachers' education. *Journal of LGBT Youth*, 15(4), 319–338. https://doi.org/10.1080/19361653.2018.1484839

Wozolek, B. (2018b). In 8100 again: The sounds of students breaking. *Educational Studies: A Journal of the American Educational Studies Association*, 54(4), 367–381. https://doi.org/10.1080/00131946.2018.1473869

Wozolek, B., Varndell, R., & Speer, T. (2015). Are we not fatigued? Queer Battle Fatigue at the intersection of heteronormative culture. *International Journal of Curriculum and Social Justice*, 1(1), 1–35.

Trans Faculty and Queer Battle Fatigue: Poetic (Re)Presentations of Navigating Identity Politics in the Academy

Sean Robinson

ABSTRACT
Research on the experiences of trans* employees show that trans* individuals face disproportionate levels of harassment, discrimination, violence, and forms of aggression in the workplace. While broader organizational and workplace research exploring issues of trans* employees may be transferrable to higher education settings, higher education nevertheless has specific needs that make it distinctly different from non-higher education work environments. Although organizational scholars writing on workplace discrimination issues have offered recommendations for increasing trans-affirmation in workplace environments, little research has focused exclusively on trans* faculty on college and university campuses. Responding to calls for a nuanced understanding of trans* educators in more creative ways, this article (re)presents the experiences of six trans* identified post-secondary faculty in the format of a found poem that weaves together the voices of the participants into a collective narrative. When read through the lens of queer battle fatigue, the poem highlights the violence, marginalization, and forms of aggression experienced by trans* individuals that lead to feelings of exhaustion.

Within the past two decades, a number of scholars have documented the experiences of faculty with minoritized identities of sexuality and gender (MIoSG) working at colleges and universities in the United States.[1] Key areas of exploration have included issues of coming out in the classroom (e.g. Pryal, 2010), issues related to specific fields such as education (Sears, 2002) engineering and science (Bilimoria & Stewart, 2009), social work (LaSala et al., 2008), or general experiences related to campus culture and climate (DeVita & Anders, 2018; Garvey & Rankin, 2018; Jourian et al., 2015; Rankin et al., 2010; Robinson, 2019; Simmons, 2017; Vaccaro, 2012). While such organizational and workplace research has historically focused on those sexual identities that fall within the traditional LGBTQ acronym, the past few years have seen an increase in scholarship focused on the experiences of individuals whose minoritized identities are outside of the binaries, specifically those who hold trans*[2] identities.

At its broadest conceptualization, research demonstrates that LGBTQ employees' experiences are characterized by numerous challenges: markedly different rules of engagement and behavior; particular risks of harassment, violence, and discrimination; lower wages and career advancement; ongoing fear of losing one's job; and lack of health benefits or access to appropriate medical care both for oneself as well as to family or partners/spouses (e.g. Bowen & Blackmon, 2003; Sears & Mallory, 2014; Wingfield, 2010). In their research on the ways in which LGBTQ employees navigated expectations around family, Dixon and Dougherty (2014) found that "the traditional family is not merely a choice, but rather it is compulsory in that a composite of discursive expectations, unspoken rules, and organizational norms converge to create an expectation that workers will conform to the traditional family structure. Those who fail to conform are othered" (p. 7). Furthermore, they show that LGBTQ employees are "made invisible through day-to-day discourse that fails to acknowledge them, and when they do become visible, they are treated as a curiosity to be examined with scientific intensity" (p. 8). In this way, LGBTQ workers are both invisible and hypervisible, and are always at risk of being othered. According to Dixon and Dougherty, a threshold of acceptance exists, whereby an unseen and shifting line exists for which identities are privileged, what/who gets othered, and how organizational discourse and practices serve to police those identities. In their focused study of 45 trans* employees across numerous workplace environments, Mizock et al. (2018) found that trans* individuals faced transphobia in the workplace regarding lack of social support, workplace gender policing, personal safety threats, acquisition and advancement barriers, intersectional discrimination, intuited stigma, and lack of inclusive policy.

Although organizational scholars writing on workplace discrimination issues have offered recommendations for increasing trans-affirmation in workplace environments (Law et al., 2011), little research has focused exclusively on trans* faculty on college and university campuses (Jourian et al., 2015; Park, 2015; Pitcher, 2017; Robinson, 2018; Simmons, 2017). While higher education continues to grapple with policies and practices aimed at increasing diversity, equity, and inclusion of students, the same must be considered for faculty. An increasingly diverse and inclusive student body necessitates an increasingly diverse faculty body (Wright & Smith, 2015). However, as Bilodeau (2009) aptly points out, colleges and universities reinforce a heteronormative culture through the policing of gender binaries vis a vis gender norms and sex-segregated spaces; these practices and structures also serve to create a hostile environment for trans* individuals. As several scholars demonstrate, higher education environments are unwelcoming places to be for a majority of trans* individuals, and most campuses lack policies and services specific to the needs of trans* individuals, students, faculty, and staff alike (Dirks, 2016; Park, 2015; Seelman, 2014; Simmons, 2017). Trans* faculty experience a number of microaggressions, including unfair scrutiny, isolation, tokenism, stereotyping, and difficulties with fellow faculty, students, and administrators (Garvey & Rankin, 2018). Finally, as Pitcher (2017) found, trans* faculty also experience misgendering and mispronouning, are labeled as impossible people, and are hired specifically because they are trans*, thus being tokenized. As much of the literature shows, for trans* faculty, the negative consequences of hostile campus environments, where microaggressions and other forms of ostracizations exist, often result in lower self-esteem, depressive symptoms, more frequent binge drinking, negative emotions, being excluded from scholarly and professional networks, or fear of losing their job either through loss of contracts or denial of tenure and promotion (e.g. Garvey & Rankin, 2018; Nadal et al., 2016).

Taking to heart Nicolazzo et al.'s (2015) call for additional research "to explore trans* subjectivities, identities, and experiences in educational contexts" (p. 367) and Simmons's (2017) desire for research that offers a nuanced understanding of trans* educators in more creative ways, this article presents the experiences of six trans* identified post-secondary faculty in the format of a found poem (Butler-Kisber, 2018; Patrick, 2016; Prendergast, 2009) that weaves together the voices of the participants into a collective (re)presentation (Teman, 2010). Acknowledging the growing scholarship highlighting the way trans* faculty experience various forms of harassment, violence, assaults, and discrimination on college and university campuses, situating their experiences as real, relevant, and important offers the possibility of shaping a more inclusive campus climate and culture. Drawing upon Wozolek et al.'s (2015) conceptualization of queer battle fatigue offers a powerful lens through which to read and understand their experiences as presented in the poetic (re)presentation below.

Queer battle fatigue

Aimed at highlighting the intersectional nature of policies, practices, and academic contexts that serve to maintain marginalization of individuals with MIoSG (Collins, 1990; Crenshaw, 1991; Duong, 2012; McCall, 2005; Parent et al., 2013), Wozolek et al. (2015) proposed what they termed Queer Battle Fatigue (QBF), drawn from the work by Smith et al. (2006, 2007) on Racial Battle Fatigue (RBF). In their narrative research where they present stories by MIoSG individuals or allies from different educational contexts, Wozolek et al. demonstrate how heteronormative environments impact access and equity for MIoSG people when gender and sexuality are placed at the center. Similar to the effects of racial battle fatigue (e.g. emotional, psychological, and physiological distress; Smith et al., 2006, 2007; Sue et al., 2007), the effects of queer battle fatigue can be extrapolated to also include a negative impact on personal and professional achievements, inequitable access to goods or services, and limited opportunities for social mobility. Originally termed as microaggressions by Pierce et al. (1978) and reintroduced by Sue et al. (2007), these systematic exposures to various forms of psychosocial stressors (i.e. microaggressions) have also been shown to impact the long-term health and wellbeing of MIoSG individuals (e.g. Chang & Chung, 2015; Nadal et al., 2016; Platt & Lenzen, 2013). Recognizing the consequences of such exposure, queer battle fatigue (QBF) is used in this study to highlight how trans* faculty experience "exhaustion by simply being themselves ... regardless of whether they are out or closeted for their own protection" (Wozolek et al., 2015, p. 3).

As Wozolek et al. (2015) note, the conceptualization of queer battle fatigue is intentionally fluid and broad, avoiding a formal model or a formal set of postulates. This aligns with the basis of queer theory, upon which my original study was framed, which seeks to dismantle gender- and sex-based binaries, undo hierarchies, and serves as a site of contestation against social inequalities (Jagose, 1997). Queer battle fatigue, used in parallel with queer theory, pushes against heteronormativity, exposing and breaking down essentialist assumptions about gender and sexualities. Queer battle fatigue acknowledges the violence, marginalization, and forms of aggression experienced by MIoSG individuals that lead to feelings of exhaustion. Using queer battle fatigue as the starting point rather than the end point serves to "guide us to understanding a story but not to dimmish our ability to listen. Theories are there to be used, not to dictate us or shape our stories" (Kim, 2016, p. 77). If we attempt to fit the narratives by our research participants into the forms of particular theories, Kim (2016) contends we might do so "at the risk of missing the 'real, important' aspects of the stories" (p. 77). The poems presented here serve as a collective narrative, operating at the nexus between queer battle fatigue as theory and queer battle fatigue as experience, exposing those "sociocultural ceilings, norms, and values [that] create the structure through which individuals experience daily microaggressions that engender exhaustion for marginalized groups and individuals" (Wozolek et al., 2015, p. 10).

Methodology: (re)presenting identity through found poetry

Qualitative methodologies in general, and creative approaches in particular, are perfect forms of research to "engage with marginalized participants and their stories in a way that radically centers their reality, claims their experience as valid, and evokes an affective understanding among audiences" (Jen & Paceley, 2021, p. 66). One particular type of creative research is that of poetry, with various forms used to create and craft poetic (re)presentations. According to Leavy (2015), poetry "challenges the fact-fiction dichotomy and offers a form for the evocative presentation of data" (p. 78). She further contends that poems "can be understood as evoking a snippet of human experience that is artistically expressed as in a heightened state" (p. 78). Poetry is thus seen not just as a creative act or as just another way of representing data, but as a way of interpreting which can lead to deeper understanding of experiences (Brady, 2004). As Hirschfield (1997) portends, poetry is an ideal choice to present identity narratives: "Poetry can do what other forms of thinking cannot: approximate the actual flavor of life, in which subject and objective become one, in which conceptual mind and the inexpressible presence of things become one" (p. 32). Taking this further, Faulker (2009) maintains that "poetry defies singular definitions and explanations, it mirrors the slipperiness of identity, the difficulty of capturing the shifting nature of who we are and want to be, and resonates more fully with the way identity is created, maintained, and altered through our interacted narratives" (p. 100).

A particular form of poetry, described as both research poetry (Langer & Furman, 2004) and as found poetry (Butler-Kisber, 2018; Patrick 2016; Prendergast, 2009), is crafted directly from participants' own words in order to present a more focused narrative. Although considered a form of arts-based research methodologies, research/found poems have not always been accepted by all qualitative researchers due to their "creative" nature (Leavy, 2015). Taking the form and style of a more traditional fictional poem, the found poem (re)presents qualitative data and knowledge in a more artistic form rather than typical prose analytical presentation (Cousik, 2014). In found poetry, all of the content is "found" within the data provided by participants, in this case transcripts of interviews completed with individuals. The interview data used to craft the research poem here was drawn from a larger narrative study of 70 MIoSG faculty from across the United States. That study, and by extension, this poem, draws on Bruner's (1986) narrative mode of thinking, which relies on stories to understand the meaning of actions and experiences while incorporating feelings, goals, perceptions, and values to situate experience in ambiguous and complex ways. The interviews used to craft the poem here include six trans* identified faculty members each from a different institution, and representing diverse fields. Of the six faculty, one identifies as multiracial, five as white, one as an immigrant/refugee, and four offered that they were of lower-middle/working class backgrounds.

The crafting of my research poem aligns with the queer epistemology (Sullivan, 2003; Wiegman, 1995; Wilchins, 2004) that framed my broader narrative project, as it disrupts traditional ways of thinking and honors and amplifies the multiple voices, realties, and truths of the participants. Sullivan (2004) contends that the power of poetry is to "compress and render accessible" the results and to merge data and interpretation into a "single act, a single form" (p. 34). The development of the found poem below followed processes similar to Faulkner (2009) and Walsh Walsh (2006). I first read each transcript multiple times taking notes about the particular, individual narratives withing the larger story(ies) each person told, followed with memos about the recurring themes showing up across and within participants' stories. I then began to extract out those phrases, sentences, and segments of the conversations that related to the broad, holistic themes and narratives I identified across participants. Once I had completed this process for each interview, I placed similar segments from all participants into a single grouping or cluster. Once each thematic cluster was complete, I then parsed and culled each segment into smaller "chunks" while maintaining the essence of the narrative segment. I deleted those words that seemed extraneous within individual segments, leaving what I deemed those most significant, impactful, and important; no additional words were added by me. In the words of Prendergast (2009), this process required "intuitively sorting out words, phrases, sentences, passages that synthesize meaning from the prose" (p. 136). Following the approach by Teman (2010), I wove together the words, phrases and segments of participants into a unified whole, adding only line breaks, punctuation, and formatting in order to create the final poetic form; in this manner the poem stands as a collective voice highlighting the experiences and realities of trans* faculty. In its final form, the poem below "represents holistically what otherwise might go unnoticed" (Prendergast, 2009, p. 136).

By illuminating the experiences of trans* faculty here, this art-based (re)presentation can serve to expose and enhance our understanding of the lived reality of those with marginalized and minoritized identities. As a queer, gay, cisgender, white, male faculty member, I have both witnessed and experienced the violence, assaults, and discrimination that MIoSG face. The process of reading, deconstructing, and reconstructing the narratives of my participants took me beyond the traditional notion of merely looking for emerging themes across participant's stories, and allowed me to focus on the meaning making, tensions, vulnerabilities, queer battle fatigue, and moments of both crisis and reconciliation present for each individual; the final (re)presentation is thus based on my own understanding as both insider and outsider (Lorde, 1984).

The final form of the found poem allows for the (re)presentation of a collective narrative in a single space, whereby the many become one. In addition to amplifying and validating the experiences of trans* faculty, my aim in creating this found poem was also to legitimize the multiple ways of knowing and being, of knowledge-making and meaning-making within academia, and of engaging in a research process that is not always privileged in academic discourses (Bhattacharya, 2013). In an effort to honor the experiences presented in the poem here, and in order to avoid what Kim (2016) calls an epic closure, I make no final pronouncements or conclusions about the poem below, thus "allowing multiple voices or multiple interpretations to emerge, and yielding no final and complete truth" (p. 235). In this way, I invite readers to "engage as active witnesses...standing beside participants in their search for justice, recognition, healing, a better life (Prendergast, 2015, p. 683).

Trans faculty and queer battle fatigue: navigating identity politics in the academy

I. Of Identifying and Being

The point is not presenting as some *thing*, it's presenting
    As I am
    Who I am
I roll out of bed, get ready, go to the office
Given a safe environment....
    Many people know it – it's not like I am putting on a role
It's not to say I don't have any concerns, but mostly around the issue of safety...
In any space where there's more than one person,
    I have a shell that allows me to go about my business publicly
Sure, I've felt nervous about my physical safety at times being out,
    of having my name and picture on the front page of our local newspaper
    of having my identities attached to some story.
I'm not out to very many people on campus
    I hold it very close to my vest
I'm the only trans faculty that I know for miles
    Repercussions keep students and faculty from finding out
Fear of discrimination keeps me closeted
I don't have any protection at work on campus
    As gender queer and gender non-conforming and non-binary
    As a trans woman and a lesbian
    As a queer, trans man, married to a cisgender woman
    As queer and female partnered — trans partnered — gender nonconforming
    As trans with an asterisk — and pansexual
    As FTM – I like that it emphasizes both parts of my life — I am trans.
20 years post transition, of identifying and being...
Who I am is really fluid, changes day to day, and with who I am around
I get to negotiate my trans identity on my own terms
I often say I'm "half out"
Queer is a label I feel comfortable with –
    I think it's kind of nebulous –

    it's what I want it to mean
I didn't think about my queerness, because I'm out, until.... I showed up on campus
    It's a fairly homogenous campus
    I look a bit strange, but I'm white, so the general sentiment is, "*You belong here.*" But I am also a first-generation immigrant, a refugee.
It's always presumed I'm gay because my mannerisms are more feminine
I dress in the stereotypically, middle class, white way – business casual if you will
    Traditionally masculine attire, but I'm not read as particularly masculine
    I'm read as male, but not masculine–
        My hand gestures
        Speech
        Body language
        Movement
If I cared I would put on a more masculine persona – but it's a lot of effort
A lot of performativity that doesn't mesh with my identity.
I learned early on in transition that I was being read–
    consistently as male, but also
    fairly consistently as feminine
As a woman I was never read as a feminine woman
As soon as that switch flipped, strangers read me as male
    and all of that femininity I did possess seemed to be very e-x-a-g-g-e-r-a-t-e-d on a body that is considered male
I've always read as feminine and of course
The feminine is always associated with being gay on a male body.
I've become more comfortable
    making my students and other people around me
    uncomfortable
I enjoy the word *queer* - it makes older cis white men very uncomfortable
My identity has shifted
as I started to transition from more of an "I am a butch lesbian"
to start to pass as a cisgender straight man –
    although I have students who read me as gay
Yet, I feel uncomfortable occupying the space that isn't actually mine
    I'm *not* a cisman
Identifying queer and being out feels like a way to be more authentic
I am in a position of privilege — I am consistently read by everyone as a man
Yet operating in the world as a "dude" makes me very...
    ...uncomfortable...
        I don't identify
            as a man,
            as male
Part of my identities became invisible,
    So, to make the more visible I became more vocal about it
I try to clear up everything I possibly can
    I put my pronouns in my email.
Being trans is really important to me.
The point is not presenting as some *thing*, it's presenting
    Who I am
    As I am.

II. The Lavender Vita

To what extent do others know about me?
    I have a lavender vita – there is no way around that
    How others know me, read me, see me, I don't know...
My job search activities have been extremely problematic
My work is LGBT and trans, there's no hiding it
An application with a lot of research experience, a lot of papers, an NIH grant...
    But there's just a lack of response
My job search has been so *shitty*,
    yet I landed in a place that allows me to do the kind of work I do.

I once played academic job speed dating – 15-minute interviews that were
    Hell. On. Earth!
I was starting to transition, on T for several years
Interview questions that legally skirted the edges of being illegal –
    So, lesbians, huh? What's that like?
I rationalized my research agenda - gave an academic excuse –
    Well, this is an understudied population in the south…
        End. Of. Date!
I don't know what people actually thought about what I was telling them
We pick topics close to our heart
    I have a lavender vita – there is no way around that
    How others know me, read me, see me, I don't know.
On my job interview, one retiring faculty just couldn't help himself.
    Can we talk a few minutes? I know you have a few minutes before you have to go to dinner.
    I thought to myself, I am exhausted, it's 5 o'clock, my brain is a puddle, and you wanna talk to me?
We enter his office, he closes the door, sits down and says:
    I thought your job talk was interesting but I have to let you know personally I don't believe in it.
    I'm sorry?
    I am a Christian and I just don't believe in it.
Befuddled, my brain is a puddle
    I have 1400 queers in my sample
    they are all real people
    Your beliefs don't matter to me
I didn't tell anyone about that except my best friend that night
    This shit just happened to me!
I have a lavender vita – there is no way around that
    How others know me,
        read me,
            see me,
                I don't know.
For individuals not doing trans academic work, they will have:
    better interactions
    better career options
After working in an LGBT environment for years, where does one go?
    Limits on the places that will hire you,
    A pool of jobs much smaller than a lot of people
I was terrified about being out during my job interview process!
A backlog of applicants, budget cuts – I had 75 applications before I landed my TT job
"Minority health research" – they didn't ask and I didn't tell
    I (don't) have a lavender vita
    How others know me, read me, see me, I don't know…
But I'm estranged from my primary discipline, my primary field
The only jobs I get success in have been in…. public health
    I've applied to other departments for years, but empty responses come–
        We'll get back to you…
    I have a lavender vita – there is no way around that
How others know me, read me, see me, I don't know…
The job offer came!
    "Let me get back to you!" I said
I ran up and down the hall of my office, freaking. the. fuck. out!
    Googling the city for trans resources
    Finding trans stories and resources in town, on campus
That was a big sign that, hey, at least they're not clueless!
    They have a context for trans folks
It ended up being a good match between what I do and what they want me to do
I have a lavender vita – there is no way around that
How others know me, read me, see me, I don't know.
I was cautioned to not be out in my interviews
But it was a *personal* choice for me not to be totally out in my last interview
    Be cautious – so I *was* cautious
My research and publications are related to trans issues and experiences –

Google me, those are the first things that pop up
I'm guilty by association
  for writing on *these* topics
My blog – it's out there and could be used in a variety of ways
It doesn't come up with my students usually though—I teach composition and rhetoric
  I have a lavender vita – there is no way around that
  How others know me, read me, see me, I don't know ...
I came into my first faculty job as queer
  I was very politically savvy around LGBT issues
I was going to be tenured and promoted early – that coincided with my birthday
  I decided I was going to take the plunge
Literally the day after I got my tenure letter, I started taking my first testosterone injections
I have a lavender vita – there is no way around that–
  How others
  know me, read me, see me,
  I don't know.
I see what's gotten published, I see what's being presented ...
  There's a lack of interest in trans issues
It's OK as long as it's within narrow disciplines like gender studies
Going outside of that is problematic ....
To what extent do others know about me?
  I have a lavender vita – there is no way around that
  How others know me, read me, see me, I don't know ...

III. I am here to make you question things

I am a feminist
I am a liberal
This is what you get with me
I am here to make you question things
I am less likely to use power in the classroom
I am likely to sit in a circle and discuss things
We're going to talk about the messy stuff
My outness in the classroom depends on the class
I am a fly by the seat of your pants kind of person
It becomes obvious to students.
Day one – ask me anything you want
Shocked by my super short buzz cut and suit jacket–
  Can you tell us about your family?
What they really are asking is,
  Are you a homo?
Straight gender-conforming faculty don't think about this.
In class, early on I address it all, we talk race, gender, sexuality, class
The issues have become more of a question of:
  How do I interject LGBTQ issues into my classes?
  How can I properly talk about this with my students?
  What's it like when one's relationship might be unrecognized?
  Or if you are denied access to bathrooms?
I don't come out formally, but I bring myself in my experiences to the classroom
I am more likely to casually mention my sexuality, that I have a wife,
  making reference to situations in my life as part of teaching
I'm reluctant to discuss my gender in class – that goes to my fear –
  How will students respond to me then?
Straight gender-conforming faculty don't think about this.
I talk about gender in very different ways in the classroom
  I look at gender because of my own experiences
My focus is really rooted in personal experiences–analyzing and being critical of gender
It's so ingrained in everything I do, everything I write, in my teaching
I have this gender presentation
  that just doesn't fit with my life experiences
This is apparent to me because I'm interested in topics like SES, race, class, gender, but sometimes,

>   it's
>   really
>   exhausting

I show up to class and feel like ... I'm selling oppression to other people
What I'm living and what are other peoples' reality,
>   are two
>   very
>   different
>   things

Straight gender-conforming faculty don't think about this
I don't come out about my sexuality to my students,
>   But I have come out as trans

I'm intentional; It needs to be about content, not me
I did come out in one class because students said problematic stuff
>   *Trans people are like aliens! Oh my God, who would ever be trans?!*
>   *I just want to pause for a second and note that we don't need to talk about trans identities as if no one in the room might have that identity, because I am trans and we're talking about trans people as if they are foreign objects!*

Straight gender-conforming faculty don't think about this.
My identities come up most often when working with students
>   who disclose that they are LGBT,
>   or who I *suspect* of being LGBT

On this campus, where we don't have many supportive resources,
>   where I don't know other LGBT faculty or staff who are out,
>   where other faculty are not open of their LGBTQ identities,
>   it's critical for students to have role models

In every class, every term, there's at least one student ...
It's not *really* my job, but is the work I'm doing anyway ...
They seek me out – office hours or outside of class – to discuss issues they are going through
The student underground takes care of a lot of that conversation anyway,
>   I don't necessarily *have* to come out.

Straight gender-conforming faculty don't think about this.
When they have a student who is struggling,
>   they point them in my direction–
>>   *There is someone else on campus to whom you can speak about these issues. I don't know how to help you.*

I teach about micro aggressions
>   but I don't censor myself as part of it

I will talk some about things I've experienced
>   but I'm not the centerpiece

Straight gender-conforming faculty don't think about this.
We do our students a disservice if they leave the University
>   with the idea
>   they have never met
>   an LGBT person

It's part of my job to make students realize
>   things are not as black-and-white
>   as they think they are

I'm just astonished
>   by the number of students
>   that are so unfamiliar
>   with LGBT issues

We can assume students don't know anything
>   It's just not discussed
>   We have to be nice

We don't have this dialogue on campus
Straight gender-conforming faculty don't think about this.
Class evals are always a sensitive spot for us, for me
>   *Why are you pushing social justice?*
>   *Why so much emphasis on LGBT?*
>   *He talks about gay shit too much.*

Yet I was deeply closeted and totally scared

Straight gender-conforming faculty don't think about this.
LGBT is part of the social justice continuum –
It's important that I create and talk about braids of oppression and intersexuality
My goal is to normalize language
    I talk oppression across-the-board
    And make connections
    It's constant.
A daily challenge? How cute to dress each day!
Honestly, dressing is a big deal –
    I want to look professional –
        I want to look good –
            I want to look groomed
I feel like I am representing trans people in academia
I want to look good, but being who I am is a risk.
Straight gender-conforming faculty don't
Straight gender-conforming faculty don't think
Straight gender-conforming faculty don't think about this
    This
    This
This is what you get with me
I am here to make you question things.

IV. Me-search ≠ Research

My identity has absolutely everything to do with how I ended up doing research
    on physical and mental health issues in queer populations
I have to emphasize methods
    more than the population
    or the specific topic of my queer health concerns
But I speak the language of academia –
    on paper I can check the boxes people are interested in.
The question becomes, who should be teaching it, or talking about it?
Trans inclusion has been very limited outside of different silos
I see more work and emphasis on cis individuals than
Trans individuals in terms of who gets attention
    What role do trans people have about what is being researched?
    What is written?
    What is discussed?
I can't separate my research and scholarship from my own identity
I started researching and writing about trans issues around the time
I realized I was trans
    I was on my own transition journey
I never left that scholarship –
    the more interested I became, the more I read,
    the more I read, the more interested I became.
Traditionally academic – you need a nationally representative dataset,
if you don't have the most complicated quant analysis it isn't going to get published
    I have a very difficult time
I keep sending to journals and keep getting rejected because "It isn't a good fit"
    What a copout! What does that even *mean*? Because it's LGBT work?
The issue of course becomes that since I *am* part of the community I research,
my research is biased—it can't be empirical because I'm doing me-search.
Yes, trans scholars doing research on trans issues is considered me-search,
but there aren't other people really going to get the same depth of information
    if they aren't part of the community
Trans communities are really distrusting about outside researchers;
    there's historical bases for that.
We are told what sort of research we can and cannot do,
    what research is valuable
We are told that me-search is not OK
    Researching your own community is less empirical,

    holds more bias
Our research is devalued if we research *these* topics and issues.
It's controlled – the way it is for any marginalized community
I have published in all the LGBT journals I can
None of my LGBT work has gained traction,
there's a whole audience that doesn't get access to my work because of that.
Being trans has been an important part of my academic work and my activism
Yeah, I may do research on trans issues,
    It's just a piece of me like anything else
I just can't separate my research and scholarship from my own identity
But I speak the language of academia –
    on paper I can check the boxes people are interested in.

V. My Job and My Life are on the Line

My first year I jumped right in, being engaged in the University
But I was making up little white lies about myself
    Then, *Oh shit! I don't know how to answer that*!
How do I navigate these conversations and not out myself?
It became increasingly uncomfortable.
There is a culture of niceness
You have to make sure you're nice all the time!
If students had issues, or felt any type of way about how I present,
    about my identity, my classes,
    it just wasn't brought up
You don't talk about it, you don't say those things here.
First year I learned another faculty in his intro class was asked
    if they can talk about trans people for a bit
Well if you want to understand trans people, watch the Jerry Springer show.
He votes on my tenure file; he's very important to my case.
But I'm white, on a white campus, and that plays out in how I'm accepted
Yet students stare, trying to figure out my gender;
    when I look at them, when our eyes meet, they look away
You have to be nice here
You just don't name things here.
Just chatting with my colleague Samantha –
    You know I'm trans, right?
    Yea, we all know.
I gave her the, *what the fuck?* look
It was stressful and relieving at the same time
The next conversation was with my chair –
She acted surprised like she didn't know
    We are happy to have you, please let me know if there any concerns you have.
    We value you for who you are and what you bring…
Again stressful, but relieving.
Institutional social support is based on individuals reaching out to others
But on a campus that doesn't name "those things" as being an issue – forget it
    Gender neutral bathrooms? Forget it
    Housing? Doesn't exist. Forget it
Sure, institutional benefits exist –
    insurance, educational discounts,
    name change policies for some, but not for all
No institutional or structural changes that reflect *real* LGBT issues
    that the community needs exist here
Limited campus communication about events and activities
How *do* people communicate here?
Let's talk etiquette, like how to communicate with a trans person
That's not present at all in discussions at work
    Nor are bathroom conversations had
    Nor about things that my body needs to feel safe in an environment
Queerness is reaching a sense of normativity in some spaces

As queerness is normalized people cast trans people in that normalization,
    and it's not the case at all
Why can't you use a bathroom that your body feels safe in?
    Yeah, that's important to talk about.
My queerness is only allowed in spaces where people are able
    to look different and to be different and to read different
I haven't learned how to negotiate, to navigate as a queer person
    I sit far away from students,
        Don't touch them…
Other faculty hug their students
I don't want to put myself in a position where others feel weird
    That's not OK!
I'm very conscious — my job and my life are on the line!
Fourth-year, pre-tenure, on a campus
without gender identity in the non-discrimination policy
I was asked by a student to do a public talk about
how a "plus one" benefit package would benefit me personally
I couldn't do it – I supported the cause privately, but couldn't speak out publicly.
I love what I do and I'm really in love with my profession
    I want to make the world a better place!
It was hard when I started my medical transition
    I had colleagues that were supportive;
    and I lost colleagues at the same time
I had people that were my friends as a queer person
    who weren't willing to make that transition with me
I experienced microaggressions from a number of them
    You don't belong here
The comments eventually stopped but I would get rude stares;
    people kept mispronouning me
In classes I could feel the stares and those oddities
Eventually I would have to confront my colleagues
Having those talks with colleagues was difficult because it kept happening
Eventually I left
        I could never be seen as I needed to be seen.
My state is an at-will state, so there is no explicit protection, even for faculty
Any sort of dissent, any pushback, could jeopardize my job
I have to be careful about the things I'm doing
My activism takes a much quieter form,
    much more discrete than others
I mentor students – but can't be a physical body
    that helps students when they protest
I have to think about what I am jeopardizing by being involved
    with student organizations or protests
I avoid active involvement and disrupting the status quo
The obvious risks –
    Where am I going to feed myself from?
    Where is that money coming from?
    Will I be fired?
    Will I gain a negative reputation?
Where I work, everyone is so fucking nice – but is it real?
The work of caring – the unpaid work we as faculty and staff are providing,
the extra counseling and extra mentoring for students –
This burden falls disproportionately on marginalized scholars
It's work we are doing
    that takes substantial energy
    that is absolutely rewarding
    that other colleagues aren't doing and without the same emotional toll
        when they do this sort of work
It's hard to be one of the only resources for students
You feel obligated whether you want to or not
Burn out and the demands of moving forward

and moving along the tenure track
    cause people to not to want to engage with students in this way
Extra time and emotional commitment is one of the biggest challenges
    as an LGBTQ faculty member.
There's a paradox –
    working with students is huge and rewarding –
    but is incredibly draining –
    it is unrecognized and unpaid labor that is hard to sustain over the long term
That is the most rewarding part of my job –
    which is not really a part of my job!
You may be the only person a student can talk to –
    that's a taxing experience
If not us, then who, right? If not now, then when? That is one of my constant mantras.
The same year I got tenure, they added gender identity to the NDP
    Now I don't give two shits – you can't fire me because I'm trans!
That's the glorious thing about tenure –
    pissing people off while still doing your job
There's a constant battle in public of how political I can be
    and still be OK with the institution
I made a conscious decision to be out to show students:
    If you want to be in higher education,
    you can do that and be trans or queer or whatever.
We know inherently our jobs are never fully secure
A change in management,
    a change in the administration that causes a change in the culture
    can make us feel there is a hostile environment,
    where we are no longer safe
There's an inherent risk in being trans
We are always contingent faculty
Always contingent even if we're not in contingent positions
Nothing actually protects us from a hostile work environment if we are outed on our jobs.

VI. Coda

Being transparent in academia about being transgender is critical
Making sure I'm present and available
    I can never turn anybody away
Paying it forward in the sense that visibility is important
    Paying it forward – being out professionally
I just want to give back.
    It's my turn to give back.
        It's my turn. To give back.
            It's my turn. To give.
                It's my turn...

Postscript

The purpose of this article was to move beyond more traditional forms of data analysis and representation using poetic expression as a tool of narrative research exposing a deeper expression of individuals' stories to live by, in the spirit of sense making (Connelly & Clandinin, 1999). Richardson (1993) contends that poetic representation is an effective way to convey complexities of both expression and of identity making:

> Self-knowledge is reflexive knowledge. Poetic representation reveals the process of self-construction, deferrals and transformation, the reflexive basis of self-knowledge, the inconsistencies and contradictions of a life spoken as a meaningful whole... Poems can be experienced as both whole and partial; text and subtext. (p. 704)

Found poems, such as those presented here, invite readers to consider multiple layers of meaning and understanding, making it a valid form from which to understand the complexity of participants' storied lives. My hope is that the poetic (re)presentations here enable the reader to make meaning as they both provoke and evoke from within as readers consider the experiences of trans* faculty.

Research exploring workplace experiences has shown that MIoSG employees are confronted by a set of different and often implicit rules, feelings of isolation, fear of termination, and often different health care benefits, particularly for those who are trans* identified (Bowen & Blackmon, 2003; Wingfield, 2010). Bowen and Blackmon also found that a "spiral of silence" exists due to the "inability to fully express one's personal identity within the workgroup because of a negative climate of opinion towards a particular aspect of one's identity" (p. 1393). As a result, trans* individuals can experience invisibility and hypervisibility simultaneously, based on notions built around traditional male-female and masculine-feminine binaries, thus marking these individuals as alternative at best, and marginal at worse (Dixon & Dougherty, 2014). Trans* identified employees may face further marginalization and jeopardy at work when they bump up against and call out such cisnormativities that are present in the policies, practices, and rules of engagement in an organization; this creates a double bind for trans* employees whereby they have a diminished voice in their organization and also neglected in academic research (Spencer & Capuzza, 2015). Within my poetic (re)presentations, silence, erasure, invisibility, and hypervisibility were all present, in different forms, at different times, in different contexts; the emotional, physical, and psychological impact of these institutional and social dynamics are palpable in the narratives.

I do not intend to distill the narratives within the found poems into a set of common themes nor produce a final interpretation, which risks essentializing both identities and experiences; instead, my aim is to allow the space for multiple readings, inviting critical engagement with the narratives. Discussions about trans* issues and identities can be challenging and personal for everyone involved. In order to make our institutions more inclusive however, we must continue to consider the perspectives and experiences of trans* individuals. Creating change and shifts in institutional policies and practices that are welcoming, affirming, and inclusive is a non-linear and complicated process (Gonzalez, 2010). For this to happen, it is imperative that researchers, scholars, administrators, and policy makers alike engage in meaningful and applicable conversations about what constitutes a climate and culture of inclusion and actively work towards that. Only then can institutions truly be safer, healthier, and better work environments for everyone.

Notes

1. Consistent with scholars who use the term minoritized when referencing those whose identities have been consigned to lower status, visibility, and power (e.g. Benitez, 2010; Chase et al., 2014; Patton et al., 2015; Robinson, 2018), I use minoritized identities of sexuality and gender (MIoSG) rather than LGBTQ because choosing particular identities in the LGBTQ acronym excludes and normalizes groups of people. I do use versions of the LGBTQ acronym to honor names, titles, and terminology choices of other authors when appropriate.
2. Consistent with prior scholarship (e.g., Pitcher, 2017; Simmons, 2017; Tompkins, 2014), I use trans* as a way to encompass additional self-described identities including but not limited to trans, FTM, MTF, non-binary, gender non-conforming, and genderqueer, unless specifically referencing an individual and their personal identities. As seen in the poem later in this paper, the participants in this (re)presentation hold multiple identities along both gender and sexuality spectrums.

Disclosure statement

No potential conflict of interest was reported by the author(s).

ORCID

Sean Robinson http://orcid.org/0000-0002-2277-7633

References

Benitez, M. (2010). Resituating culture centers within a social justice framework: Is there room for examining whiteness? In L. Patton (Ed.), *Culture centers in higher education: Perspectives on identity, theory, and practice* (pp. 119–136). Stylus Press.

Bhattacharya, K. (2013). Voices, silences, and telling secrets: The role of qualitative methods in arts-based research. *International Review of Qualitative Research*, 6(4), 604–627. https://doi.org/10.1525/irqr.2013.6.4.604

Bilimoria, D., & Stewart, A. J. (2009). Don't ask, don't tell: The academic climate for lesbian, gay, bisexual, and transgender faculty in science and engineering. *National Women's Studies Association Journal*, 21(2), 85–103.

Bilodeau, B. (2009). *Genderism: Transgender students, binary systems, and higher education*. VDM Verlag.

Bowen, F., & Blackmon, K. (2003). Spirals of silence: The dynamic effects of diversity on organizational voice. *Journal of Management Studies*, 40(6), 1393–1417. https://doi.org/10.1111/1467-6486.00385

Brady, I. (2004). In defense of the sensual: Meaning construction in ethnography and poetics. *Qualitative Inquiry*, 10(4), 622–644. https://doi.org/10.1177/1077800404265719

Bruner, J. (1986). *Actual minds, possible worlds*. Harvard University Press.

Butler-Kisber, L. (2018). *Qualitative inquiry: Thematic, narrative and arts informed perspectives* (2nd ed.). Sage Publications.

Chang, T. K., & Chung, Y. B. (2015). Transgender microaggressions: Complexity of the heterogeneity of transgender identities. *Journal of LGBT Issues in Counseling*, 9(3), 217–234. https://doi.org/10.1080/15538605.2015.1068146

Chase, M. M., Dowd, A. C., Pazich, L. B., & Bensimon, E. M. (2014). Transfer equity for "minoritized" students: A critical policy analysis of seven states. *Educational Policy*, 28(5), 669–717. https://doi.org/10.1177/0895904812468227

Collins, P. H. (1990). *Black feminist thought: Knowledge, consciousness, and the politics of empowerment*. Routledge.

Connelly, F. M., & Clandinin, D. J. (1999). *Shaping a professional identity: Stories of educational practice*. Teachers College Press.

Cousik, R. (2014). Research in special education: Using a research poem as a guide for relationship building. *Qualitative Report*, 19(26), 1–16.

Crenshaw, K. (1991). Mapping the margins: Intersectionality, identity politics, and violence against women of color. *Stanford Law Review*, 43(6), 1241–1299. https://doi.org/10.2307/1229039

DeVita, J., & Anders, A. (2018). LGTQ faculty and professionals in higher education: Defining allies, identifying support. *College Student Affairs Journal*, 36(2), 63–80. https://doi.org/10.1353/csj.2018.0016

Dirks, D. A. (2016). Transgender people at four Big Ten campuses: A policy discourse analysis. *The Review of Higher Education*, 39(3), 371–393. https://doi.org/10.1353/rhe.2016.0020

Dixon, J., & Dougherty, D. S. (2014). A language convergence/meaning divergence analysis exploring how LGBTQ and single employees manage traditional family expectations in the workplace. *Journal of Applied Communication Research*, 42(1), 1–19. https://doi.org/10.1080/00909882.2013.847275

Duong, K. (2012). What does queer theory teach us about intersectionality? *Politics & Gender*, 8(03), 370–386. https://doi.org/10.1017/S1743923X12000360

Faulker, S. L. (2009). *Poetry as method: Reporting research through verse*. Taylor & Francis.

Garvey, J. C., & Rankin, S. (2018). The influence of campus climate and urbanization on queer spectrum and transspectrum faculty intent to leave. *Journal of Diversity in Higher Education*, 11(1), 67–81. https://doi.org/10.1037/dhe0000035

Gonzalez, J. A. (2010). Diversity change in organizations: A systemic, multilevel, and nonlinear process. *The Journal of Applied Behavioral Science*, 46(2), 197–219. https://doi.org/10.1177/0021886310367943

Hirschfield, J. (1997). *Nine gates: Entering the mind of poetry*. Harper Collins.

Jagose, A. (1997). *Queer theory: An introduction*. NYU Press.
Jen, S., & Paceley, M. S. (2021). Capturing queer and trans lives and identities: The promise of research poems to inform stigma research. *Stigma and Health*, *6*(1), 62–69. https://doi.org/10.1037/sah0000282
Jourian, T. J., Simmons, S. L., & Devaney, K. C. (2015). "We are not expected": Trans* educators (re)claiming space and voice in higher education and student affairs. *TSQ: Transgender Studies Quarterly*, *2*(3), 431–446. https://doi.org/10.1215/23289252-2926410
Kim, J. H. (2016). *Understanding qualitative inquiry*. Sage.
Langer, C. L., & Furman, R. (2004). Exploring identity and assimilation: Research and interpretive poems. *Forum Qualitative Sozialforschung/Forum: Qualitative Social Research*, *5*(2), Art. 5. http://nbn-resolving.de/urn:nbn:de:0114-fqs040254
LaSala, M. C., Jenkins, D. A., Wheeler, D. P., & Fredriksen-Goldsen, K. I. (2008). LGBT faculty, research, and researchers: Risks and rewards. *Journal of Gay & Lesbian Social Services*, *20*(3), 253–267. https://doi.org/10.1080/10538720802235351
Law, C. L., Martinez, L. R., Ruggs, E. N., Hebl, M. R., & Akers, E. (2011). Trans-parency in the workplace: How the experiences of transsexual employees can be improved. *Journal of Vocational Behavior*, *79*(3), 710–723. https://doi.org/10.1016/j.jvb.2011.03.018
Leavy, P. (2015). *Method meets art: Arts-based research practice* (2nd ed.). The Guilford Press.
Lorde, A. (1984). *Sister outsider*. The Crossing Press.
McCall, L. (2005). The complexity of intersectionality. *Signs: Journal of Women in Culture and Society*, *30*(3), 1771–1800. https://doi.org/10.1086/426800
Mizock, L., Riley, J., Yuen, N., Woodrum, T. D., Sotilleo, E. A., & Ormerod, A. J. (2018). Transphobia in the workplace: A qualitative study of employment stigma. *Stigma and Health*, *3*(3), 275–282. https://doi.org/10.1037/sah0000098
Nadal, K. L., Whitman, C. N., Davis, L. S., Erazo, T., & Davidoff, K. C. (2016). Microaggressions Toward lesbian, gay, bisexual, transgender, queer, and genderqueer people: A review of the literature. *Journal of Sex Research*, *53*(4-5), 488–508.
Nicolazzo, Z., Marine, S. B., & Galarte, F. J. (2015). Introduction [Special issue]. *TSQ: Transgender Studies Quarterly*, *2*(3), 367–375. https://doi.org/10.1215/23289252-2926360
Parent, M. C., DeBlaere, C., & Moradi, B. (2013). Approaches to research on intersectionality: Perspectives on gender, LGBT, and racial/ethnic identities. *Sex Roles*, *68*(11–12), 639–645. https://doi.org/10.1007/s11199-013-0283-2
Park, P. (2015). Transgendering the academy: Transforming the relationship between theory and praxis. In J. C. Hawley (Ed.), *Expanding the circle: Creating an inclusive environment in higher education for LGBTQ students and studies* (pp. 83–104). SUNY Press.
Patrick, L. D. (2016). Found poetry: Creating space for imaginative arts-based literacy research writing. *Literacy Research: Theory, Method, and Practice*, *65*(1), 384–403. https://doi.org/10.1177/2381336916661530
Patton, L. D., Harper, S. R., & Harris, J. (2015). Using critical race theory to (re)interpret widely studied topics related to U.S. higher education. In A. M. Martinez-Alem'an, B. Pusser, & E. M. Bensimon (Eds.), *Critical approaches to the study of higher education: A practical introduction* (pp. 193–219). Johns Hopkins University.
Pierce, C., Carew, J., Pierce-Gonzalez, D., & Willis, D. (1978). An experiment in racism: TV commercials. In C. Pierce (Ed.), *Television and education* (pp. 62–88). Sage.
Pitcher, E. N. (2017). 'There's stuff that comes with being an unexpected guest': Experiences of trans* academics with microaggressions. *International Journal of Qualitative Studies in Education*, *30*(7), 688–703. https://doi.org/10.1080/09518398.2017.1309588
Platt, L. F., & Lenzen, A. L. (2013). Sexual orientation microaggressions and the experience of sexual minorities. *Journal of Homosexuality*, *60*(7), 1011–1034.
Prendergast, M. (2009). "Poem is what?" Poetic inquiry in qualitative social science research. *International Review of Qualitative Research*, *1*(4), 541–568. https://doi.org/10.1525/irqr.2009.1.4.541
Prendergast, M. (2015). Poetic inquiry, 2007-2012. *Qualitative Inquiry*, *21*(8), 678–685. https://doi.org/10.1177/1077800414563806
Pryal, K. R. (2010). Intimate pedagogy: The practice of embodiment in university classrooms. *Assuming Gender*, *1*(2), 62–77. https://doi.org/10.18573/ipics.45
Rankin, S., Weber, G., Blumenfeld, W., & Frazer, S. (2010). *2010 State of higher education for lesbian, gay, bisexual, & transgender people*. Campus Pride.
Richardson, L. (1993). Poetics, dramatics, and transgressive validity: The case of the skipped line. *The Sociological Quarterly*, *34*(4), 695–710. https://doi.org/10.1111/j.1533-8525.1993.tb00113.x
Robinson, S. (2018). Hiding in plain sight: Early career experiences of a non-binary faculty member. *Women & Language*, *41*(1), 110–127.
Robinson, S. (2019). Gender & sexual minority faculty negotiating 'a way of life': Friendships, networks, and social supports within the academy. In D. Carlson & N. Rodriguez (Eds.), *Foucault, friendships, and education* (pp. 77–90). Palgrave.
Sears, B., & Mallory, C. (2014). Existence and impact. In C. M. Duffy & D. M. Visconti (Eds.), *Gender identity and sexual orientation discrimination in the workplace* (Chapter 40, pp. 1–19). Bloomberg BNA.

Sears, J. T. (2002). The institutional climate for lesbian, gay, and bisexual education faculty: What is the pivotal frame of reference? *Journal of Homosexuality, 43*(1), 11–37. https://doi.org/10.1300/J082v43n01_02

Seelman, K. L. (2014). Recommendations of transgender students, staff, and faculty in the USA for improving college campuses. *Gender and Education, 26*(6), 618–635. https://doi.org/10.1080/09540253.2014.935300

Simmons, S. L. (2017). A thousand words are worth a picture: A snapshot of trans* postsecondary educators in higher education. *International Journal of Qualitative Studies in Education, 30*(3), 266–284. https://doi.org/10.1080/09518398.2016.1254303

Smith, W. A., Allen, W. R., Danley, D. G. (2007). "Assume the position…you fit the description": campus racial climate and the psychoeducational experiences and racial battle fatigue among African American male college students. *American Behavioral Scientist, 51*(4), 551–578. https://doi.org/10.1177/0002764207307742

Smith, W. A., Yosso, T. J., & Solórzano, D. G. (2006). Challenging racial battle fatigue on historically White campuses: A critical race examination of race-related stress. In C. A. Stanley (Ed.), *Faculty of color: Teaching in predominately white colleges and universities* (pp. 299–327). Anker Publishing.

Spencer, L. G., & Capuzza, J. C. (2015). *Transgender communication studies: Histories, trends, and trajectories.* Lexington Books.

Sue, D. W., Capodilupo, C. M., Torino, G. C., Bucceri, J. M., Holder, A. M. B., Nadal, K. L., & Esquilin, M. (2007). Racial microaggressions in everyday life: Implications for clinical practice. *American Psychologist, 62*(4), 271–286. https://doi.org/10.1037/0003-066X.62.4.271

Sullivan, A. M. (2004). Poetry as research: Development of poetic craft and the relations of craft and utility. *Journal of Critical Inquiry into Curriculum and Instruction, 5*(2), 34–36.

Sullivan, N. (2003). *A critical introduction to queer theory.* New York University Press.

Teman, E. D. (2010). Now, he's not alive. *Qualitative Inquiry, 16*(8), 611–611. https://doi.org/10.1177/1077800410374036

Tompkins, A. (2014). Asterisk. *TSQ: Transgender Studies Quarterly, 1*(1–2), 26–27. https://doi.org/10.1215/23289252-2399497

Vaccaro, A. (2012). Campus microclimates for LGBT faculty, staff, and students: An exploration of the intersections of social identity and campus roles. *Journal of Student Affairs Research and Practice, 49*(4), 429–446. https://doi.org/10.1515/jsarp-2012-6473

Walsh, S. (2006). An Irigarayan Framework and Resymbolization in an Arts-Informed Research Process. *Qualitative Inquiry, 12*(5), 976–993. https://doi.org/10.1177/1077800406288626

Wiegman, R. (1995). *American anatomies: Theorizing race and gender.* Duke University Press.

Wilchins, R. (2004). *Queer theory, gender theory.* Alyson Publications.

Wingfield, A. H. (2010). Are some emotions marked "whites only"? Racialized feeling rules in professional workplaces. *Social Problems, 57*(2), 251–268. https://doi.org/10.1525/sp.2010.57.2.251

Wozolek, B., Varndell, R., & Speer, T. (2015). Are we not fatigued? Queer battle fatigue at the intersection of heteronormativity culture. *International Journal of Curriculum and Social Justice, 1*(1), 1–35.

Wright, T. E., & Smith, N. J. (2015). A safer place? LGBT educators, school climate, and implications for administrators. *The Educational Forum, 79*(4), 394–407. https://doi.org/10.1080/00131725.2015.1068901

Embracing Queer Heartache: Lessons from LGBTQ+ Intergenerational Dialogues

Karen Morris, Adam J. Greteman and Nic M. Weststrate

ABSTRACT
In this article, we reflect on the role of heartache during the first 2 years of *The LGBTQ+ Intergenerational Dialogue Project*. The project—a partnership between an LGBTQ+ community center, an art and design college, and a public research university—brings together racially, socioeconomically, and gender diverse cohorts of LGBTQ+ young (18–26 years old) and older adults (62–81) for dialogue, creative collaboration, and shared dinners. The project was conceived as a collaborative ethnographic pedagogical experiment in which participants became partners in research, education, and community formation. We quickly realized that heartache would be central to our journey together, as we navigated this rare opportunity for LGBTQ+ intergenerational contact. Grief, anger, and pain generated through interactions between LGBTQ+ people can be surprising, and especially weighty, components of Queer Battle Fatigue. It is necessary, we argue, to explore the heartache we experience within queer spaces as a pedagogical tool with which to strengthen queer communities.

The heartaches of "queer"

Queer joy gave way to heartache by the second meeting of the *The LGBTQ+ Intergenerational Dialogue Project*. We, the three co-authors and project facilitators (ranging in age from 36 to 45 years old at the time), were sitting in a circle with 15 LGBTQ+ young adults (18–26 years old) and 15 LGBTQ+ older adults (62–81 years old), eagerly discussing our collective hopes and dreams for the first year of our intergenerational experiment. The atmosphere felt ebullient, as younger and older LGBTQ+ folks—members spanning generations who rarely interact—employed terms such as "queer" and "family" to describe the new community we were creating. Ric, a 75-year-old Italian-American gay man who had been listening quietly, suddenly spoke up to express his discomfort with the group's use of the word "queer."[1] "I don't like it," he said emphatically. "Queer, faggot, homo—that's what the NYPD called us." Ric did not want to be associated with a group that described itself as queer.

Many of the younger participants, ourselves included, were taken aback. We knew that the term was a reclaimed pejorative, but had not realized the violence it might still perpetuate against members of our community today. Our (abstract) understanding of queer's historicity came up against the embodied feelings such a word provokes in those whose relationship to the word came about in the 1950s and 1960s. Having "you queer" hurled at you and used derisively is not, as we learned, easily forgotten despite a reclamation project within activist and academic circles and popularity within entertainment media.

Sometime later in the meeting, after our conversation had meandered away from Ric's comment towards other topics, Marti Smith, a 74-year-old self-proclaimed "Midwestern farm girl and non-separatist lesbian," pointed out participants' continued use of the word "queer":

> I grew up fighting the word queer. Younger people using the word is offensive less because the word is offensive, and more because it shows a lack of listening .... A perfect example is that Ric said he found the term really offensive and then it was passed around like you [young people] never heard him say that .... Maybe context doesn't matter, maybe it's wrong for you to use queer at all. Think about who you're with.

Arlo, a 26-year-old white transgender man, responded with a shaking voice:

> I identify very strongly with the word queer. It's an umbrella term and it feels safe. I need to prioritize myself over other people in this situation. I *need* that word to describe myself. I know this is a hard stance. But it's what I need to do.

Don Bell, a 71-year-old gay black retired academic who grew up on South Side of Chicago, jumped into the fray in an attempt to mediate as tensions arose in the room:

> Now, I'm of the same generation as Ric, and I also recognize that there are other experiences. For some people of our generation, queer was a declaration of independence. Queer could get you suspended, bashed, sent to Vietnam, killed, when I was young ... I could have lost my job, my children. I was coming out in a dangerous time and place. But queer has evolved into a collective term. We've got to find a way to accept that, just accept it. And, at the same time, it's really important for people [today] to know what queer meant in 1971. People of my age will not be here for much longer .... Often, collective terms don't express the diversity within groups.

This early foundational moment highlighted the importance and challenge of connecting across generations in order to create education rooted in LGBTQ+ histories and experiences. This is necessary work given the reality that schools remain one of the last institutional bastions of homo-and-transphobia to deny access to such conversations. The hostile legacies of schooling and society are written on the bodies and minds of LGBTQ+ people across generations (Lugg, 2016). Schools, as central institutions in socialization and cultural production, were and continue to be sites that deny and suppress LGBTQ+ presence (Blackburn & Pascoe, 2015; Woodford et al., 2017).

A central challenge of these exclusionary legacies is generational. Generation after generation of LGBTQ+ students have been and are denied access to LGBTQ+ histories and knowledges; left to fend for themselves as they age into adulthood. A key component to this problem is that LGBTQ+ young people have, more often than not, lacked access to LGBTQ+ adults through which such histories and knowledges can be transmitted (Blount, 2005; Graves, 2009). To counter this lack of access, opportunities for sustained engagement across LGBTQ+ generations are necessary to learn from and with one another.

The LGBTQ+ intergenerational dialogue project

For many years, we (a lesbian anthropologist, a gay philosopher, and a gay developmental psychologist) have been struck by the disconnect of our LGBTQ+ college students from the LGBTQ+ histories, cultures, and people who came before them. At the same time, we have learned from LGBTQ+ older adults how forgotten and isolated they feel from LGBTQ+ communities they helped to create. In 2019, we partnered with an LGBTQ+ community center in our area to launch an intergenerational pedagogical project that brings together racially, socioeconomically, spiritually, and gender diverse cohorts of LGBTQ+ young and older adults for dialogues, collaborative creative work, and shared dinners. We wanted to explore what would happen if members of these different generations—who rarely interact—were brought together repeatedly over a sustained period of time. The importance of this endeavour deepened as we came to realize that many of our students had never imagined their own futures past 40 years old and were not even sure if many LGBTQ+ folks lived beyond that age.

In this article, we reflect on the role of heartache in the first 2 years of the project in which 52 younger and older adults, and 4 student research assistants, participated. Approximately half of the participants were undergraduate and graduate students enrolled at an art and design school in Chicago, and half were older adults who participate in the Senior Services Program at the LGBTQ+ community center. All participants, co-facilitators, and research assistants identified in some way as LGBTQ+. The majority of our older participants lived in Rainbow Land,[2] one of only eight residential facilities serving low-income LGBTQ+ older adults in the United States. Our participants were socioeconomically, racially, spiritually, and gender diverse. About half identitied as women, more than a third as gender expansive (nonbinary, queer, and/or transgender), and a third as people of color. More than half qualified as low-income and food insecure.

We quickly realized, in the first few months, that a very queer form of heartache would be central to our collective journey together, that there would be more heartache to come along the way, and that heartache would be intertwined with and, often, the source of great joy. For most of us, this project was our first time within an exclusively LGBTQ+ educational space, and hopes were high.[3] Our hearts ached at the moment, during our second meeting, in which we realized that our casual and frequent use of the term "queer" provoked a sense of exclusion, and a traumatic return of queer bashing, for some of the older adults in our group. In ensuing conversations, "youngers" and "elders" (as participants began referring to themselves and each other) wrestled with a word informed, yes, by theory but also by bodies of knowledge, particularly, the knowledge borne out of physical bodies encountering words in different ways and times.[4] Queer's contemporary efficiency, expansiveness, and seeming inclusiveness became problematized for what it covers over, clothed in a form of radicality. Should we, as a group, an emerging community, use the word at all? How should we refer to ourselves so that we are inclusive and mindful of how words, as Toni Morrison taught us, have power? Cruz, a 22-year-old Latinx self-identified queer student, complicated the picture, noting that for them "queer was the word that first allowed me to feel at home." Queer could not simply be banished from our mouths because queer had different stories to tell, different things to do, and these emerged from different contexts and conditions. These contexts and conditions were not liberated from homophobia or transphobia, but had changed the relation to the word and its aftereffects.

Such aftereffects implicated the emotional labor that comes into play as generations meet across shared but also different experiences. Our students pointed out, numerous times along the way, this emotional labor and its requirement for meaningful, sustained engagement across LGBTQ+ generations. Talking across difference, and "staying in the room," when things get difficult, as Rankine (2020) argued, can render us vulnerable to emotional pain, anguish, sadness, grief, anger, and feelings of rejection (p. 151).[5] Yet, as we illustrate in the following sections, we have learned through these dialogues how generative heartache can be for LGBTQ+ people and communities.

As we began the second year of the project, Rain Shanks, a newly joining 26-year-old Latinx lesbian student who had heard about our previous conversations around "queer," asked the group is everyone felt okay if she and her peers used the word. "Or," she continued, "would you prefer if we don't use the word"? Ric, who a year before had bravely expressed his strong aversion to "queer," shocked many of us by responding:

> It's okay. I'm okay with the word queer now because they [the younger participants] showed me it can be good.

In our ensuing discussion, it became clear that our collective heartache around "queer," felt and interrogated in a year's worth of discussions, had yielded something new. For Ric and several of the elders, learning about younger generations' reclamation of the slur felt freeing, and empowering. For many of the younger participants, the experience of being confronted in a very personal way with the violence of a term they casually threw around prompted them to think critically about their positionality within a history and a community. We decided, as a group, that "queer" can be both complicated and useful. Many of us (including the authors) now make strides to be thoughtful, and deliberate, when we invoke the term. In this article, we use queer as an adjective and a noun where we think it fits (or as a way to reference ways the term is used by others in scholarship and popular culture). But we avoid writing about "queers" as an amorphous category that makes claims at universality, except when invoking how it is used by others.

Through *The LGBTQ+ Intergenerational Dialogue Project*, we explore how education might be harnessed to cultivate, rather than suppress, LGBTQ+ people and community. In the following sections, we explore the role of heartache within this work. We begin by describing the collaborative ethnographic framework of our methodology and the evolution of the project over the past two years. Next, we unpack the idea of heartache as a pedagogical tool that can teach and transform us in affective ways that often are not available in other forms of learning. A section on intergenerational grieving explores the potential of witnessing loss to strengthen a marginalized community. In the final two sections, we explore feelings of "unrequited love" within queer communities and spaces and argue for the transformative potential of embracing heartache within queer education.

"Peering into each other's' hearts": collaborative ethnographic experimentation

From the very beginning, *The LGBTQ+ Intergenerational Dialogue Project* has been a grand, constantly evolving, glorious experiment through which participants create a new form of queer studies informed by embodied histories and their complex interactions (Morris & Greteman, 2021). We employ an ethnographic approach that centers collaborative exploration with community members (Rabinow & Stavrianakis, 2013). Ethnography, an immersive qualitative method conducted with relatively small subject populations over long periods of time, is generative for this work as it allows for in-depth and sustained engagement with subjects as they (and we) unpack complex legacies that have limited intergenerational contact in order to build an intergenerational LGBTQ+ community. As researchers, we actively participate in the communities and processes we are studying and draw just as much on our sensory and emotional experiences as our more intellectual observations. "Deep hanging out," as Clifford (1996) called it, is a practice often cited as the cornerstone of ethnographic fieldwork that adds depth and rigor to more formal methods such as participant observation, interviews, material and archival research, and note-taking (p. 56). It captures what Gusterson (2008) has described as the "improvisational quality of fieldwork, the confusing overlap between informal street corner conversation and the serious inquiry embodied in ethnographic fieldwork, and the profound level of understanding of the other for which ethnography aims through apparently casual methods" (p. 93).

Similar in many ways to participatory action research (McIntyre, 2008), ethnographic experimentation creates space for collaborative innovation. Rather than entering into and studying field sites that already exist, researchers venture into the collaborative production of venues for knowledge creation that turn the field into a site for inquiry (Estalella & Sánchez Criado, 2017). Together we create, study, and modify this experimental project of queer pedagogy. This methodological approach challenges epistemic injustice within research by "destabilizing hierarchies of expertise" (Biehl & Locke, p. xii).[6] Put differently, it places LGBTQ+ participants alongside the researchers as collaborators and co-creators in generating knowledges and practices rooted in LGBTQ+ experiences.

Anthropologists of education have noted the potential of collaborative ethnography to function as a form of pedagogy (Marcus, 2008). It is physical, emotional, and sensory work centered around personal interaction as a means of learning about both ourselves and others. Campbell and Lassiter (2010), for instance, have written about the success of *The Other Side of Middletown*, an ethnography of African American history in Muncie, Indiana, collaboratively researched by a team of faculty, students, and community participants. The project served as "a collaborative experience, as well as experiment, with teaching and learning in which students, faculty, and community members engaged the project in multiple roles as co-teachers, co-learners, and, eventually, as co-citizens" (p. 380). In a similar fashion, undergraduate students at the University of Pennsylvania who worked with local high school students on an ethnographic film project as part of an "experimental" film cass noted, in their own words, the role of collaborative ethnography "as a pedagogic process centered around excavating one's own biases even as they [participants] learn about those whom they are in conversation with" (Kelly et al., 2017, p. 147).

Storytelling has emerged as central to our collective approach to research, education, and community formation. Listening to LGBTQ+ people telling stories offers an affective way to discover (and recover) the people and histories that evade us. It helps to fill gaps in knowledge, and foster empathy across differences.[7]

We structured the first year of the project (the 2019–2020 academic year) as a series of themed dialogues followed by informal conversation over shared meals. Participants committed to active participation for at least 4–9 months to allow time for relationships and trust to grow.[8] Initially, we (the facilitators) chose the ice-breaking activities and topics for our themed dialogues. Yet the plan was to work towards a model in which participants worked together to select topics, and plan and lead discussions. As evidenced in our interrogation of the word "queer," almost immediately, participants' differences in experience, identification within the umbrella category of "LGBTQ+," and perspectives emerged. Participants began to focus a significant amount of time in our dialogue meetings on questions of who we were as a group, what participants wanted the project to be and do, how to talk across differences within the group, and what folks found important to talk about in future dialogues. These conversations offered incredible insight into how participants understood LGBTQ+ identities and communities, what they valued as important for LGBTQ+ people, their dreams for LGBTQ+ futures, and their perspectives on racial, socioeconomic, and generational divides within LGBTQ+ communities. All dialogues were documented with video and audio-recording, ethnographic note-taking by student research assistants, and fieldnotes written by the facilitators. When the COVID-19 pandemic necessitated moving the project (and its documentation) to Zoom, several older participants initiated "informal" meetups in the weeks in between our "formal" (themed) dialogues. These meetings continued into the summer (beyond the timeframe we had initially envisioned).

As we planned for the second year of the project, participants assessed, as a group, the first year, and ways they would like to see the project develop. Participants also responded individually to surveys that asked them to reflect on the project (and their own experience within it), and share suggestions for the second year. As we (the facilitators) analyzed the data collected from the first year of the project, discussed our own experiences and what we had learned, and reflected on the thoughts and suggestions of participants, we zeroed in on the work the project was doing as a radical educational model for countering legacies of epistemic injustice that continue to oppress and divide LGBTQ+ people (Greteman et al., 2021). We had, from the beginning, envisioned the project as an educational one. Yet we learned from those participating in the project the depth of their feelings of loss at being denied access to knowledge about LGBTQ+ histories, identities, and communities. Most of our participants had never received any formal education, or had any significant access to sources of information, about LGBTQ+ people and histories.

We designed the second year of the project (2020–2021) to push back at the erasure and suppression of LGBTQ+ people and histories within education (broadly defined), and experiment with an embodied pedagogical approach that brings generations together to teach each other, and together learn about our "people." More than half of the participants from the project's first year elected to continue on with the project in its second year, and we welcomed a new cohort of 13 students and 9 elders. In response to suggestions from students in the first year, we created and co-taught a course entitled *Generating Queers* for students joining the project in its second year. The course allowed students to better fit their participation into their academic schedules and receive college credit. The course structure alternated between seminars (with assigned readings, films, and podcasts on LGBTQ+ social movements, histories, and issues) and themed intergenerational dialogues in which students and elders discussed their personal experiences with, knowledge of, and perspectives on the topics engaged in the assigned materials. We left the syllabus open so that participants could determine the topics we would engage during the second half of the semester. The pairing of "academic" learning with embodied, dialogic discovery brought a great deal more depth, nuance, and understanding to topics such as the HIV/AIDS pandemic, LGBTQ+ social movements, LGBTQ+ aging, and queer radical care networks. For their final class assignment, students worked with elders in small groups on creative projects (a blog, an audio piece, an art book, a visual anthology, and a virtual roadtrip) that explored the topic of "queer joy." Participants decided to focus on queer joy as a way to counter negative representations of LGBTQ+ lives in media and public culture.

As the project has evolved, participants have come to understand their role in this ethnographic experiment as more than research subjects, but rather as "epistemic partners that define the imaginary and plot of our own inquiries'" (Holmes & Marcus, 2008, p. 83). Early on, several younger participants ruefully observed that "the majority of the students are not cisgender, and the majority of the seniors are cisgender" (excerpt from a student's ethnographic fieldnotes). Their advocacy for the inclusion of more transgender and nonbinary elders resulted in a shift in our ongoing recruitment practices. Participants determined the topics of themed dialogues (most recently gender expansiveness and nonbinary identities, lesbian cultural shifts, media represetentations of LGBTQ+ folks over time, race and racial reckoning in LGBTQ+ communities, and disability). Small groups of participants with special interests in the topics at hand planned and led each dialogue. Lindsey Lascaux, a long-time participant in the project, built our website, a process which involved countless group conversations. The website (generationliberation.com) has served as a constantly evolving collaborative project as well as a site of inquiry and analysis. Grant-seeking to cover the costs of shared meals, participant research assistants, and materials has become a dynamic "family" affair, with participants suggesting funding resources, writing testimonials and letters of support for inclusion in grant applications, mourning each rejection letter, and celebrating each success. Recent news that we would need to wait ten months to receive word on a large grant application was met with collective groans as Marti exclaimed, "Tell them I might be dead by then!"

As we reflect on the project as a whole, we find that the moments of shared heartache have often been the moments in which we, as a community, have progressed. The act of storytelling (described in more detail in the following section) has often caused grief and sadness for both the project's storytellers and listeners. Yet storytelling is consistently folks' favorite (and most anticipated) part of our dialogues. Learning through heartache is an incredibly difficult task. It requires a cultivation of empathy—an approach beautifully described by activist and educator Loretta Ross (2020) as "peering into each other's hearts"—through which we witness others' pain and take it on as part of our collective queer history.

Heartache as a pedagogical tool (or, what We can learn through heartache)

"I think everyone who does gay and lesbian studies," Eve Sedgwick (1993) noted, "is haunted by the suicides of adolescents." (p. 1). This was a motivation, in Sedgwick's work, for the *then* just emerging realms of scholarship that *now* invariably falls under the labels of "gay and lesbian" or "queer" or "trans" studies. Writing in the early 1990s, Sedgwick continued, "to us, the hard statistics come easily: that queer teenagers are two to three times likelier to attempt suicide, and to accomplish it, than others" (p. 1). Little has changed by way of these hard statistics as teenagers—queered by sexuality, queered by gender, queered by how genders and sexualities intersect with race, geography, ability, and more—continue to experience violence, exclusion, and ostracism that contributes to the still unacceptable high rates of youth suicide (Kosciw et al., 2020; Meyer et al., 2021). Heartache, we might suggest, is a founding affect—an underlying bodily sensation—of gay, lesbian, queer, and trans studies.

Yet, what queer theorists writing in the early years didn't, perhaps couldn't, point out yet were the (coming) realities of LGBTQ+ "elders," and what "hard statistics" would illuminate about their experiences and lives. This oversight may be, in part, understood given realities that, amidst the genocidal consequences of the HIV/AIDS pandemic on queer populations, the ability to imagine growing "old" was unfathomable to a range of scholars and activists encountering the pandemic. It may, as well, have to do with the reality that intergenerational contact across LGBTQ+ communities was uncommon, particularly in the academy, contributing to the invisibility of challenges that faced LGBTQ+ individuals beyond childhood and adolescence. However, decades later—amidst the continued realities of the HIV/AIDS pandemic—LGBTQ+ people have aged and in aging represent what we might recognize as the first out-and-proud population of elders who are facing new challenges as they age into and beyond retirement (Ramirez-Valles, 2016). Many have lived their lives openly as LGBTQ+ since their teens or early twenties. Others have come out to themselves and others later in life. Today's elders were the young activists who agitated within the Gay Liberation Movement, publicly celebrated gay pride, and demanded change through ACT UP. They made us visible by being visible despite the repercussions many faced for such an act. Now, because of the systemic inequality which has shaped their lived experiences, the majority of LGBTQ+ older adults are low-income, live alone with minimal support systems, and are more likely to struggle with mental and physical health issues than their cisgender heterosexual peers (Emlet, 2016; Fredriksen-Goldsen et al., 2015).

LGBTQ+ folks aging into and beyond retirement makes manifest that we are everywhere, including across the lifespan. And while we might be everywhere, the ability for us to meet across generations within educational spaces is still quite limited and fraught.

We did not intend initially to explore heartache, especially in a project that has brought so much joy to its members. But it kept coming up in our dialogues and informal interactions. Participants brought grief, pain, sadness, and loss with them into the project—much of it related, we found, to what Wozolek et al. (2015) have described as Queer Battle Fatigue. In turn, new forms of heartache were generated through the cultivation of intergenerational relations. The anger, disappointment, and discomfort that participants felt within an exclusively LGBTQ+ space came as a surprise to many. Queer spaces are often imagined as, and cultivated to be, spaces where LGBTQ+ people can get away from Queer Battle Fatigue (Wozolek et al., 2020, p. 225). *The LGBTQ+ Intergenerational Dialogue Project* proved not to be an airtight refuge from the "implicit and explicit aggressions [assault, verbal harassment, feeling unsafe] LGBTQ people and their allies encounter daily that contribute to a cartography of queer exhaustion" (Wozolek et al., 2015, p. 12). The dialogues exposed divisions, discrimination, and suppression within LGBTQ+ communities. Yet, at the same time, participants told us the project gave them hope, pleasure, and pride. One student observed:

> I have found better language to articulate myself with, I have a fuller sense of LGBT history grounded in wonderful stories, I am a more confident person, I have a better idea of how activism actually works, I've finally been able to envision my own future, and I now have a real community I belong to.

While our initial reaction is often to avoid that which causes us pain, we have learned through this project the pedagogical value of opening up, and exploring, our aching hearts as a way to heal them.

Our exploration of the "queer heartache" within LGBTQ+ intergenerational dialogues offers a lens through which to think about forms of Queer Battle Fatigue at play within queer spaces and between LGBTQ+ people, and their intersections with Queer Battle Fatigue experienced in primarily cisgender, heteronormative spaces. Embracing queer heartache within queer spaces can help to bridge divides within LGBTQ+ communities and empower individuals of all ages within them.

Grieving generations

In a chapter on queer feelings, the lesbian feminist scholar Sara Ahmed (2004) reflected on the impact of exclusions of "queer losses" from public cultures of grief (p. 157). She wrote:

> It is because of the refusal to recognize queer loss (let alone queer grief) that it is important to find ways of sharing queer grief with others.... To support others as grievers – not by grieving for them but allowing them the space and time to grieve – becomes even more important when those others are excluded from the everyday networks of legitimation and support. The onoing work of grief helps to keep alive the memories of those who have gone, provide care for those who are grieving, and allow the impressions of others to touch the surface of queer communities (p. 161).

In the second year of the project, we began incorporating "storytelling hours" into our dialogue meetings. These sessions helped uncover and navigate queer losses and grief related to HIV/AIDS, aging, and youth experiences with violence and exclusion in ways that we could not have predicted.

Our move to storytelling hours emerged organically the week that our intergenerational dialogue focused on the HIV/AIDS pandemic. The previous week, students in our class had watched a documentary, listened to a podcast chronicling one person's experience, and read several written pieces on histories of HIV/AIDS. Before our dialogue meeting, we (the facilitators) reached out to several elders in the project who had previously mentioned personal connections to the topic and asked if they would be willing to share a 6–8 min story. We ended up with enough volunteers to fill an hour with stories. Ric described his abandonment by his family as a gay teenager living in New York in the 1960s, being taken in by a gay uncle, and being diagnosed as HIV+ in the 1980s. Ric watched his friends and, eventually, his uncle die until he had no one left. Ron, a white 62-year-old gay man who was usually a quiet presence in our conversations, began crying as he recounted the moment he was informed about his own diagnosis, and realized that his life was over. George, a 65-year-old Filipino gay man who usually likes to joke around and make folks laugh, recalled how he gave away all of his possessions in the month after his diagnosis as he prepared to die. Christina, a 62-year-old Chicana lesbian, recounted the horror and fear her community felt as they watched young men in their neighborhood disappear. Marti, the 74-year-old Midwestern lesbian who had first challenged our younger participants over their use of the word "queer," described the time she had spent as a volunteer "angel of death" who helped console young men dying alone and convince them to sign "do not resuscitate" orders in the AIDS ward of the hospital where she volunteered. Marti talked about the guilt she has carried for decades after she decided to withdraw from this role and her activism within the HIV/AIDS crisis due to exhaustion and emotional trauma. Several of the older HIV+ members of the group thanked Marti for what she had done and reassured her that she should not feel guilty for honoring her own need for self-care.

When we first began *The LGBTQ+ Intergenerational Dialogue Project*, we (the facilitators) did not realize that the majority of the older men participating had been HIV+ for decades. For our students, this news came as a shock. As they listened to the stories told by elders they had come to know in a more light-hearted way, the process of learning about the suffering their fellow participants had endured was heart-breaking.

Heartache, we have learned, can be generated (created a new, rather than simply shared) through intergenerational exchange. Elders' engagement with youngers often engendered sadness and a sense of loss as they learned how much younger queer-identifying folks do not know about the experiences of earlier LGBTQ+ generations. Ric, who shared his story of losing his friends and uncle to AIDS, was disheartened to find that many of our students knew very little about the HIV/AIDS pandemic. Many students shared his dismay as they came to realize how much knowledge about LGBTQ+ peoples and histories—both sad and joyful—they had been denied. That dismay often turned to anger: anger at their own loss, and anger from learning what LGBTQ+ people have been subjected to and lost at different moments in time and in different places. Several elders who live at Rainbow Land like to recount to newly-joining project participants the history of the building that now offers a safe haven to low-income LGBTQ+ seniors. For decades, the building housed the neighborhood's police station that played an active role in the harassment and persecution of LGBTQ+ people. George, who was once employed at the police station (while hiding his sexuality), described to us the cells (located in what is now the kitchen) in which butch women, transgender women, and gay men were held. Ric shared how surreal it felt to see police at Pride parades today, when only a few decades before they were a source of terror for LGBTQ+ people; this true still.

Perhaps the most distressing thing that we (the facilitators) and our younger participants have learned is the dire situation of many LGBTQ+ elders today. Over a year into the project, we all watched Stu Maddux's *Gen Silent*, a 2010 documentary that follows six older adults in Boston as they navigate the difficult terrain of aging while LGBTQ+. *Gen Silent* showed us the harsh reality of many LGBTQ+ elders who are making the difficult decision to go back "in the closet" when they can no longer live independently and must enter nursing homes. Many of the students in our project cried as they watched scenes depicting a transgender woman, in great emotional and physical pain, dying alone and scared as her estranged family members refused her pleas to visit.

During our intergenerational dialogue that followed the film, the elders in the group acknowledged the reality, in their own lives, of the challenges it depicted. Roger, a cheerful 63-year-old white gay man from the South who sometimes wears a tiara (either as a headpiece or a necklace) during our meetings, recounted losing his husband of 30 years and, at the same time, their house, dog, and access to their bank account because they weren't in his name. Roger spent time on friend's couches and in homeless shelters before finding his way to Rainbow Land. He described the informal home health care networks that he and other residents of Rainbow Land have formed to care for one another in the absence of family and financial support. Each day, Roger helps a friend change his incontinence underwear and bathe. Don, the retired academic who had attempted to mediate our earlier conversations about "queer," later relayed to one of the facilitators that "ending up in a nursing home is worse than death" for him and many others. Don plans to die at Rainbow Land, so he will never have to move to a nursing facility.

The multiple layers of trauma carried by the first "out" generation has been overwhelming for younger project participants to take in. Yet this transgenerational sharing of trauma has gone both ways. For many older participants, including the facilitators who have been teaching college-aged LGBTQ+ students for years, perhaps the greatest heartache has come from the discovery that our younger participants have not found it easier, or safer, to be LGBTQ+ than we have. We thought things were better (not perfect, but better than what we'd experienced) for LGBTQ+ youth today, given the progress in LGBTQ+ civil rights and increased societal acceptance (as suggested by a proliferation of LGBTQ+-friendly TV shows, and "out" LGBTQ+ youth influencers on social media). We found out that over half of our younger participants are not out to their families, many grew up never knowing an LGBTQ+ person and thinking they were "the only one" in their community, and several had been victims of sexual abuse. Shauna, a Black bisexual student, was trying to figure out how to reconcile her identity with her family's deep religious beliefs. Emerald Pitts, a 23-year-old nonbinary student from a small town in Missouri, found participating in what they playfully termed our "very gay project" just as scary as it was exciting.

The COVID-19 pandemic brought our individual challenges and loss into high relief. Many of our students were forced to return home, and we watched them through Zoom as they sat in their childhood bedrooms and tried to muffle our queer conversations so their parents wouldn't hear. Kathleen, a 21-year-old self-proclaimed "dyke," spoke to us in hushed tones while she listened through earbuds and furtively glanced at the door for any signs of parental presence. The elders who lived in Rainbow Land were on lockdown for months with little to no in-person contact. Many spoke of their appreciation of the staff who left meals outside of their doors. Don worried that he might sound like a "dirty old gay man" when he ruefully observed that "no one has touched me in months." The group's collective decision to move to more frequent (weekly) meetings during the pandemic was an active response by the community that had formed to meet the needs of its most vulnerable members for connection and a space in which to share and witness loss.

Lovesickeness: unrequited love in queer communities and spaces

Just as the dialogues have fostered connection between LGBTQ+ folks who would usually never meet, they have, at the same time, reopened wounds caused by inequity, discrimination, and exclusion within the LGBTQ+ community. A dialogue in Spring 2021 brought such wounds to the forefront. Playfully deemed "Lesbian Week," the dialogue set out to focus on lesbian identities, histories, and cultures. Tensions quickly began to arise in the small group planning session when it became clear that the younger and older folks had very different ideas about what we should talk about. Connie, a 67-year-old white lesbian, wanted to talk about "disappearing lesbians." Lesbians, she insisted, are disappearing as younger generations eschew the label and women-only lesbian spaces such as bars and music festivals have shut down due to financial instability, sexism, and struggles over the exclusion of transgender women.

For Connie, the dialogue was a chance to mourn the history and culture she and many of her "lesbian boomer" friends feel have been devalued within the LGBTQ+ community (especially by cisgender gay men) and now forgotten. Yet, for some of the younger lesbian-identified folks planning the dialogue, Connie's strongly-voiced concerns felt transphobic and divisive. In addition they did not, much to Connie's dismay, share her sense of loss over lesbian spaces. One of the younger lesbians decided not to share a personal story during our lesbian-themed dialogue as she feared she was not "lesbian enough." In the end, our lesbian-themed dialogue felt respectful and constructive while also, at the same time, tense. People with very different identities and histories were engaged and speaking up. As we explored the sometimes contentious history between lesbians and transgender women, Danie, a 69-year-old transgender woman who had transitioned later in life, bravely spoke up to acknowledge and validate the immense loss that Connie and other aging lesbians felt. By the end of the dialogue, we hadn't solved anything—indeed, many participants felt that the conversation was nowhere near finished. But we were talking about and across our divides. "Wow," Danie observed, "we never would have been able to have this conversation a year ago."

Lesbian Week has been one of many moments in the project in which participants, excited to "come together" as a community, have had to grapple with a very queer form of battle fatigue triggered by violence, discrimination, and suppression within LGBTQ+ communities. Our discussions brought up for some folks their own conflicted feelings about, disappointment in, and feelings of alienation from LGBTQ+ communities. There is pain and resentment at not feeling acknowledged, or understood, as one would like within a community that is purportedly supposed to be "ours."

Many participants, especially younger ones, entered the project with imaginaries of a queer utopic safe space in which fellow "queers" would understand and support them without question or need for explanation of their identification. The shock at having one's pronouns and gender identity alternatively ignored, questioned, or misconstrued could be disarming. At the end of the first year, Julian, a 26-year-old nonbinary Taiwanese student, decided to write an open letter to students joining for the second year in an effort to prepare them for the challenges that would likely arise:

> I am writing to you because I think it is important for you to know that to join the Dialogue group is akin to gaining a large and diverse family where everyone comes from very different cultural-temporal backgrounds.... Some of you may enter the group assuming that because the phrase 'LGBTQ+' is in the title that this would be a safe space for yourself, much as I had. But as I have come to learn, everyone's definition of 'safe' can be wildly different... I ask you to engage with uncomfortable topics if you feel the desire to, as I am trying (and sometimes failing) to do as well. After all, my belief is that these are the key moments that further meaningful dialogue that will most likely have lasting effects on us and our worldviews, which is another whole reason why we gather together despite all of the outside-wordly obstacles.

As community, trust, fondness, and personal relationships have grown so, too, has a queer form of lovesickness. As we dare to be optimistic about queer commnunities and spaces, we are often met with the realities of all that these spaces (and in this case, this project) cannot be or do.

For many of us, this project has been our first time within an exclusively LGBTQ+ educational space. The work has necessitated the opening of hearts, a willingness to be vulnerable as we listen to others, and a commitment of time and emotional labor. Many participants have used the word "love" to describe their feelings about the project and their fellow participants. It can be especially difficult, then, to feel at times that one's love is unrequited. Abbe, an 81-year-old minister, noted wistfully that it had become clear to her that the group did not want to discuss spirituality—a topic that was so important to her. Don was heartbroken at what he felt was the shallowness and lack of understanding expressed by fellow participants in our dialogue about race and racism within LGBTQ+ communities. Lindsey, our 29-year-old web designer, shared their hesitancy to discuss gender expansiveness with the group because "it's been so disheartening and hurtful in the past when people haven't responded in the way I would hope for a community that's gotten to know each other so well." At the same time, a quiet divide has seemed to emerge between LGBTQ+ elder participants with a long history of activism and elders who have only recently come out or transitioned.

The term "family" has been a contested one within our intergenerational dialogues, and some participants' hopes for newfound "queer family" difficult to realize. Louis, a 72-year-old Black bisexual poet, invoked the term "family" repeatedly in our very first meeting to describe the new community and relationships we were forming with this project. His description of the importance, to him, of "feelings of inclusion, love, being brought into a family" was met with snaps, nods of agreement, and smiles from younger and older participants. Kathleen, our student note-taker at the time, wrote in her notes "I teared up a bit." Some students, excited about their burgeoning relationships with some of the elders, have jokingly expressed their wish that the elders could adopt them. Yet others have shared privately with us, the facilitators, their discomfort with the use of the word "family" to describe our group. They already have family, some students told us, and family relationships could be fraught and rooted in hierarchy which they didn't want to recreate with elders. Mid-semester, we decided to incorporate readings by Kath Weston (1997) on histories of LGBTQ+ kinship and "families we choose" into our course content to help younger participants contextualize others' evocations of family. This history was new to many of our students, and they were drawn to Weston's description of kin networks in San Francisco during the first decade of the HIV/AIDS crisis. At the same time, most did not feel a desire to create kinship with fellow project participants.

The lovesickness and heartache generated through our dialogues draws attention to the salience of Queer Battle Fatigue produced *within* LGBTQ+ communities and queer spaces. Not only can Queer Battle Fatigue be a product of interactions between LGBTQ+ people, it can, at times, feel even more hearbreaking than that which is produced within predominantly cisgender, heteronormative spaces. There is immense heartache in both (re)discovering, and experiencing anew, division, animosity, inequity, and lack of understanding between the letters of LGBTQ+. Over the last two years, we (the facilitators) have felt emotionally torn when tensions arise between participants, or folks find dialogues upsetting, even as we acknowledge the pedagogical value of these moments. Yet both younger and older participants in the project have shown that while "peering into each other's hearts" often causes heartache, it can also feel incredibly rewarding for members of a community that is strikingly divided along lines of race, gender, class, sexuality, and age.

Conclusion: lonely hearts club (or, healing aching hearts)

As small intergenerational groups of students and elders explored their own experiences with "queer joy" for their final projects in fall 2020, a pattern emerged. Stories of queer joy almost always involved heartache. Heartache plays a central role within the most joyful of our queer experiences, because they are queer. The exhilaration of falling madly in love for the first time with a boy, or stepping out into the world as a woman is tempered with the simultaneous pain—truly a dagger in our hearts—of not being able to share this feeling with loved ones and have it celebrated. The affirmation we feel in our relationships with chosen family is often directly related to its absence within our families of origin. This is what makes certain forms of joy "queer."

This multi-layered heartache interwoven with joy is at the center of our collaborative work, as are the inevitable loss and failure within it. Heartaches were never too far from joy, allowing all participants, in complex and sometimes fraught moments, to express their grief, to experience grief in relation to others stories, but to also move alongside such grief to encounter various forms of queer joy.

The intersection of heartache and joy could be felt on 2 July 2021 when members of *The LGBTQ+ Intergenerational Dialogue Project* met in person for the first time since the pandemic had begun. There was a birthday cake and lots of hugs. As our reserved afternoon slot on the outdoor terrace of the LGBTQ+ community center came to a close, George proposed we adjourn to a leather bar around the corner. A caravan of LGTBQ+ folks ranging in age from 22 to 79, some holding hands, others navigating the bumpy sidewalk with canes and walkers, made their way into the dimly lit space, pushing tables together to form a lopsided circle. It felt heart-warming to see folks of such different ages, gender identities, sexualities, and socioeconomic and racial positionalities - folks who had, over the last two years, both argued with and comforted each other—express such joy in coming together. At some point, Emerald, who had travelled over six hours from their hometown for the occasion, yelled "shots! We're doing tequila shots! Who's in?" Fox, a 22-year-old transgender man who had just graduated, admitted "I've never done them. I don't know how!" Marti reassured Fox, saying "come on, I'll teach you." Much laughter ensued at the "truly intergenerational learning" going on as Marti and Ric walked Fox through the steps of salting his hand ("not yet, not yet!" Marti corrected when Fox licked his hand too soon) and readying the lime slice before the group, in unison, drank their shots.

The conversation eventually turned to a slightly tipsy intergenerational discussion of gender—the ongoing "hot button" topic of our dialogues that has often provoked strife. Marti admitted that she still did not "get nonbinary." The younger people "stayed in the room" and talked openly and honestly. One asked Marti "does it matter if you get it? Maybe it doesn't. As long as you get that we get it." "Yeah," replied Marti. "I just *want* to get it." It was a moment of profound empathy and, for many of us, a resuturing of hearts.

Just as this project creates (or renews) heartache for all of us involved, it simultaneously heals our aching hearts. As we learn about our histories and communities through each other, we find ways to counter both the heartache we experience from living as queer people in an overwhelmingly non-queer world, and the heartbreak caused by divisions within LGBTQ+ communities. Kathleen found positive lesbian role models and mentors who delighted in her decision to start identitfying as a "butch dyke." Rain marveled at her feeling of being accepted by older adults for who she really is, and talking with them about things (queer sex, love, and politics) she would never be able to discuss with elders in her own family. LGBTQ+ elders who have felt forgotten by the generations that followed them have felt their hearts warm at finding, as Danie expressed it, "these younger people want to hear from us - they are hungry for it."

We have found joy in our differences, in interacting with folks within the LGBTQ+ umbrella with whom we would usually never connect, and recognizing the unique heartaches that different folks (lesbian, gay, nonbinary, transgender, queer, black, brown, white, religious, etc.) within the LGBTQ+ population bring to the table and cause for one another. We have each in our own way, we think, strengthened our sense of value and belonging within the LGBTQ+.

At times along the way, however, as the emotional labor required for participation in this grand experiment at times felt overwhelming, we wondered: Can queer heartache kill you? Does it make us stronger? We have found, through this experience, that it is necessary to embrace queer heartache for a liberatory approach to queer education. The heartache is already there, in queer spaces and communities. Yet we often do not have the chance to collectively sit with the pain and discomfort as Ahmed (2004) pointed out.

We see queer heartache as generative as both a theoretical framework and pedagogical tool, and its engagement as a powerful way to strengthen queer people and our communities. Queer heartache opens up the nuances of Queer Battle Fatigue by articulating the fatigue we experience through interactions *within* the LGBTQ+ community, and the ways that fatigue relates to our interactions with non-queers. It reminds us that we cannot think and write about "queers" as a category in discussions about LGBTQ+ experiences of fatigue, joy, and trauma without complicating it.

Heartache, we have found, is an embodied, empathic form of learning. "Discomfort," anthropologist Camille Frazier (2021) observed, "produces visceral reactions that can lead to reflection, and in this reflection is the capacity for political action" (p. 3). Queer heartache is a mode of investment, of caring and feeling things deeply, and wanting to effect change for the better.

Notes

1. In this article, we use a combination of pseudonyms and real names for project participants based on their individual preferences.
2. Rainbow Land is a pseudonym for the senior living facility.
3. And an institutionally sanctioned educational space, to boot!
4. Early on, participants began using the terms "younger" and "elder" which led to thinking about and through the use and problems with such terms. A general agreement to the words "younger" and "elder" was landed on to capture the two age groups broadly represented. This agreement is not without complications.
5. Reflecting on an especially tense conversation around race and politics in the shadow of the 2016 presidential election, Rankine writes "I learned early that being right pales next to staying in the room" (p. 151).
6. Epistemic injustice, a concept coined by feminist philosopher Miranda Fricker (2007) gets at the ways marginalized groups are unjustly treated as knowing subjects. This occurs when a member of a marginalized group is given a deflated level of credibility by a hearer, what Fricker called testimonial injustice. It also occurs at a prior stage when a member of a marginalized group lacks access to interpretive resources for making sense of their experiences, termed by Fricker as "hermeneutical injustice."
7. Our use of storytelling as method takes up an established approach to countering erasure and legacies of epistemic injustice imposed on marginalized populations. Storytelling can provide a way to construct counter-narratives vis-à-vis dominant narratives that oppress or erase certain peoples and histories and legitimize the experiences and perspectives of some over others (Bamberg & Andrews, 2004; Johnson, 2008; McLean & Syed, 2015, Tuhiwai-Smith, 1999).

8. For our work, participants recognized both the usefulness and falsity of "generation" talk. There is something to having been born at a particular time, but such a time is complicated by other variables such as race, gender identity, economic class, geography (urban vs rural vs suburban) and so forth. Time may be a particular arbiter, but other factors can connect people across time that generate different relationships. Our dialogues have thus never centered on generations in any traditional sense (Boomers, Gen Xers, Millennials, etc.)

Disclosure statement

No potential conflict of interest was reported by the author(s).

ORCID

Karen Morris http://orcid.org/0000-0001-9381-9194
Adam J. Greteman http://orcid.org/0000-0003-0115-3386
Nic M. Weststrate http://orcid.org/0000-0001-5272-472X

References

Ahmed, S. (2004). *The cultural politics of emotion*. Routledge.
Bamberg, M., & Andrews, M. (2004). *Considering counter-narratives: Narrating, resisting, making sense*. John Benjamins Publishing Company.
Blackburn, M., & Pascoe, C. J. (2015). K-12 Students in schools. In G. Wimberly (Ed.). *LGBT Q issues in education: Advancing a research agenda*. (pp. 89–104). American Educational Research Association.
Blount, J. (2005). *Fit to teach: Same-sex desire, gender, and school work in the twentieth century*. SUNY Press.
Campbell, E., & Lassiter, L. (2010). From collaborative ethnography to collaborative pedagogy: Reflections on the other side of middletown project and community-university research partnerships. *Anthropology & Education Quarterly*, 41(4), 370–385. https://doi.org/10.1111/j.1548-1492.2010.01098.x
Clifford, J. (1996). Anthropology and/as travel. *Etnofoor*, 9(2), 5–15.
Emlet, C. A. (2016). Social, economic, and health disparities among LGBT older adults. *Generations*, 40(2), 16–22.
Estalella, A., & Sánchez Criado, T. (2017). *Ethnographic experimentation: Other tales of the field*. Anthropology for Radical Optimism. https://allegralaboratory.net/post-1-ethnographic-experimentation-other-tales-of-the-field-collex/
Frazier, C. (2021). Positionality and the transformative potential of discomfort. *City and Society*, 33(1). https://doi.org/10.1111/ciso.12386
Fredriksen-Goldsen, K. I., Kim, H.-J., Shiu, C., Goldsen, J., & Emlet, C. A. (2015). Successful aging among LGBT older adults: Physical and mental health-related quality of life by age group. *The Gerontologist*, 55(1), 154–168. https://doi.org/10.1093/geront/gnu081
Fricker, M. (2007). *Epistemic injustice: Power and the ethics of knowing*. Oxford University Press.
Graves, K. (2009). *And they were wonderful teachers: Florida's purge of gay and lesbian teachers*. Urbana, IL: University of Illinois Press.

Greteman, A. J., Morris, K., & Weststrate, N. M. (2021). Countering Epistemic Injustice: The Work of Intergenerational LGBTQ+ Dialogues. *Studies in Art Education, 62*(4), 408–413. https://doi.org/10.1080/00393541.2021.1975492

Gusterson, H. (2008). Ethnographic research. In A. Klotz & D. Prakash (Eds.), *Qualitative methods in international relations.* Palgrave Macmillan. https://doi.org/10.1057/9780230584129_7

Holmes, D. R., & Marcus, G. E. (2008). Collaboration today and the re-imagination of the classic scene of fieldwork encounter. *Collaborative Anthropologies, 1*(1), 81–101. https://doi.org/10.1353/cla.0.0003

Johnson, E. (2008). *Sweet tea: Black gay men of the south–An oral history.* University of North Carolina Press.

Kelly, L., Raheel, N., Shen, J., & Shankar, A. (2017). Anthropology, film, pedagogy, and social change: Reflections from an experimental course. *American Anthropologist, 119*(1), 147–153. https://doi.org/10.1111/aman.12827

Kosciw, J. G., Clark, C. M., Truong, N. L., & Zongrone, A. D. (2020). *The 2019 National School Climate Survey: The experiences of lesbian, gay, bisexual, transgender, and queer youth in our nation's schools.* GLSEN.

Lugg, C. *US Public Schools and the Politics of Queer Erasure.* Palgrave MacMillan (2016).

Marcus, G. (2008). Collaborative options and pedagogical experiment in anthropological research on experts and policy process. *Anthropology in Action, 15*(2), 47–57. https://doi.org/10.3167/aia.2008.150205

McIntyre, A. (2008). *Participatory action research.* SAGE Publications, Inc.

McLean, K. C., & Syed, M. (2015). Personal, master, and alternative narratives: An integrative framework for understanding identity development in context. *Human Development, 58*(6), 318–349. https://doi.org/10.1159/000445817

Meyer, I. H., Russell, S. T., Hammack, P. L., Frost, D. M., & Wilson, B. (2021). Minority stress, distress, and suicide attempts in three cohorts of sexual minority adults: A U.S. probability sample. *PloS One., 16*(3), e0246827. https://doi.org/10.1371/journal.pone.0246827

Morris, K., & Greteman, A. (2021). Generating Queers.Anthropology News Online, April.

Rabinow, P., & Stavrianakis, A. (2013). *Demands of the day: On the logic of anthropological inquiry.* University of Chicago Press.

Ramirez-Valles, J. (2016). *Queer aging: The gayby boomers and a new frontier for gerontology.* Oxford University Press.

Rankine, C. (2020). *Just Us: An American Conversation.* Minneapolis, Minnesota: Graywolf Press.

Ross, L. (2020). How to call people in (Instead of Calling Them Out). *Ten Percent Happier with Dan Harris.* [Podcast]. https://podcasts.apple.com/us/podcast/how-to-call-people-in-instead-calling-them-out-loretta/id1087147821?i=1000505631002

Sedgwick, E. K. (1993). *Tendencies.* Duke University Press.

Tuhiwai-Smith, L. (1999). *Decolonizing methodologies: Research and Indigenous Peoples.* Zed Books.

Weston, K. (1997). *Families we choose: Lesbians, gays, and kinship.* Columbia University Press.

Woodford, M. R., Weber, G., Nicolazzo, Z., Hunt, R., Kulick, A., Coleman, T., Coulombe, S., & Renn, K. (2018). Depression and attempted suicide among LGBT Q college students: Fostering resilience to the effects of heterosexism and cisgenderism on campus. *Journal of College Student Development, 59*(4), 421–438. https://doi.org/10.1353/csd.2018.0040

Wozolek, B., Bettez, S. C., Coloma, R. S., & Kelly, H. (2020). The Queer Love Project: AESA, fatigue, and building the body of an organization. *GLQ: A Journal of Lesbian and Gay Studies, 26*(2), 223–226. https://doi.org/10.1215/10642684-8141746

Wozolek, B., Varndell, R., & Speer, T. (2015). Are we not fatigued? Queer Battle Fatigue at the intersection of heteronormative culture. *International Journal of Curriculum and Social Justice, 1*(1), 1–35.

Queer Black Joy in the Face of Racial and Queer Battle Fatigue

Reagan P. Mitchell

ABSTRACT
Queer Black joy is the grand ridiculer creating possibilities for organisms to collaborate, fracture, rock with, and throw shade. In this paper, the collective analytical frameworks of racial and Queer battle fatigue are brought together to consider the implications for Queer Black communities in light of the simultaneous disparagements created through normalized violent collectives of heteronormative, cisgender White supremacist ideologies. As exemplars of Queer Black joy, an analysis of the embodiments and music from disco innovator Sylvester and New Orleans bounce artist and "Queen Diva" Big Freedia are examined to consider the ways in which they enacted Queer Black joy in the public sphere, simultaneously in connection with the witnessing ways in which their Black Queer joy was and is attacked. In conclusion, Black Queer joy is situated as an enlivenment to embolden qualitative research lenses in the equity imagining/building project for the overall eradication racial and Queer battle fatigue.

The counter to Queer Black joy is fear. Fear assumes multitudes of forms when addressing attempts to suppress Black joy in Queer communities. While discourse around the ways in which fear impacts Queer Black communities is often partitioned along the fault lines of either race or queerness, the attacking conscripts countering Queer Black joy must always be discussed within a continuum. In some spaces fear of Queer Black joy emerges from notions of Black authenticity, absence of analyses of cultural capitol, White supremacy, and economic disparagement, this is not by any means an exhaustive list. However, these hegemonic apparatuses are the problems plaguing the Queer Black communities' survival and quality of life. My concern is the fear sustained and projected and from the aforementioned problematic ideological constructs. The fatigue experienced in regard to anti-Queer Blackness is discussed along a partisan, those Queer or Black. However, it is important to situate these discussions interwoven because when considering Queer Black queer communities, policy (or in this U.S. administration, the constant reversal and/or dissolving of policy) renders differing realms and depths of oppression for Queer Black communities which is an attack on Queer Black joy (Story, 2020).

The development of the analytical frameworks of racial battle fatigue and the latter, queer battle fatigue, to discuss the effects of violent agendas rooted in anti-Blackness and Queerness situated at the intersections of these identities has been necessary and timely. Furthermore, these frameworks must be utilized together in considering the broader disparagement of complexities Queer Black communities face in relation to the violence inflicted upon them from the spectrum of Black heteronormative/cisgender to White Queer ideologies (Smith et al., 2007; Wozolek et al., 2015). In addressing this violence, I am most concerned with Queer Black joy. In this discussion, I situate the attacks on Queer Black bodies as a broader mobilized violence rooted in the repression, attack, and fear of Black Queer joy.

Queer Blackness is the joying factor. In Queer Black imagining, realized through the realms of the arts, survivance, ridicule, and sustenance, there is a collective discourse of joying (Vizenor, 1994). However, this joying is not only about the translating joy exclusively within Queer Black communities. Rather this sense of joying radiates beyond the community. An example of this Queer Black joying is exemplified in the Madonna's 1990 song and video "Vogue." In the video, Madonna and ensemble perform the dance movements derived from the ballroom scene. It is important to note is that the release of this video/song aided in elevating voguing beyond the improvised ballroom spaces. However, the problematic misconception is that Madonna creating voguing. Yet, what can be realized from Madonna et al. and voguing is the overall radiance of joying bequeathed to her through Queer Blackness. Yet, what happens when Queer Black joy is presented in the context of fear?

The violence imposed upon Queer Black communities is a repression/attack/fear of Queer Black joy formulating a complicatedness in framing the battle fatigues. Thus, to consider the battle fatigues generated through the anti Queer Blackness on the community is simultaneously as an attack on Queer Black joy. Therefore, when addressing the constant denials of freedoms and equity to Queer Black communities is the overall denial of their pleasure and happiness (Brown, 2017, 2019; Taylor, 2018). This is realized in the psychological to the material as witnessed with the 2020 murders of Black transwomen Riah Milton and Dominique "Rem'Mie" Fells.

Acknowledgement of the Black radical imagination is necessary to get open and set intimately with how the radical joying the Queer Black imagination has gifted neighboring communities in light of the erasure of Queer Black folx (Kelley, 1994/1996). The overall concern in inquiring about the Queer Black imagination addresses attacks on Queer Black joy while considering simultaneously how analyses of Queer Black Battle fatigue function in light of honoring and protecting Queer Black joy in violent contexts.

This paper examines survivance enacted through Queer Black joy in the face of its attackers, those being but not limited to: heteronormative/cisgendered violence, White supremacy, and classism (Vizenor, 1994). While Queer Black joy is constantly called on to joy, the constant irony lies in the love and/or cooption of the expressions. In a similar sentiment around the consuming of Black culture through the marketized absorption of aesthetics (i.e.-music, dance, fashion, etc.) there is an intensification of this consumption when considering the meanings of consumption of expressions from Queer Black communities.

I start my discussion with unpacking meaning of "spirit murdering" in the context of fearing Queer Black joy (Love, 2019). Spirit murdering, coined by Bettina Love (2019), is the acknowledgement of the practices utilized to repress the dreams and livelihoods of oppressed communities. With considering the spirit murdering, I will address this in light of one of the most oppressive and damaging mantras, "Don't tell the family business." I take issue with this ideal because of the encouragement of repression promoted. Yet, the analysis of the connection of "spirit murdering" and "not telling the family business" contextually allows for unpacking the constructs of battle fatigue in the context of Black Queer communities. I follow with of an analysis of late disco artist Sylvester[1] and their 1978 song and video "You Make Me Feel (Mighty Real)" along with interview segment from the 31 December 1986 performance of "Someone Like You" on the nationally syndicated talk show, The Late Show with Joan Rivers. In the analysis of Sylvester, I am interested in how they engage the radical Queer Black imagination to develop joy in addition to considering the points of Queer Black battle fatigue is addressed. Afterwards, I come to New Orleans, LA bounce artist, Big Freedia and their 2014 song and video, "Explode" along with interview segments. My inquiries of Big Freedia's song and overall affect in the selected interview segments are the same as the aforementioned ones presented for Sylvester. However, in the penultimate section discussion I will bring Sylvester and Big Freedia closer together in comparison to consider the function of the Queer radical Black imagination; their confrontations with Black Queer battle fatigue; and the broader implications for Queer Black joy.

The selection of Sylvester and Freedia as of the exemplars of Queer Black Joy in this discussion come as a result of their public critiques of cisheteropatriarchical, White supremacist, and Black heteronornormative violence. Both Sylvester's and Freedia's unapologetic expressions of Black Queer Joy nationally and globally are the refusals to be silenced. Furthermore, the scope of their influence in regard to their popularity as artists simultaneously translates and is translated into their elevation as cultural icons. For Sylvester, their contributions expanded beyond the disco genre to eventual disclosing their status as having AIDS and being an AIDS activist prior to their ancestral assent. For Freedia, aka "The Queen Diva" like Sylvester, their accomplishments extend beyond the New Orleans bounce music scene to national and global statuses. As witnessed with Freedia's cameos and acknowledgement as an influence from such luminaries Beyoncé Knowles, Byron Otto "Mannie Fresh" Thomas, and Tarriona "Tank" Ball, Freedia is a cultural influence. Thus, when Freedia states that they are "bring[ing] all walks of life together through the power or ass" referencing twerking, they are considering modalities of community and coalition building developed in Queer Black/Femme communities and further injected into public discourse as witnessed when a Big Freedia show pops off and everybody is out there shaking that ass. Altogether, Sylvester and Big Freedia develop as cultural icons as a result of their Black Queer joy and further normalize it in national and global discourses. They both exemplify of the power of Black Queer joy to liberate self and in this public liberation also be able to aid the broader community finding the possibility to be liberated as well.

Killing me softy (this ain't no Roberta Flack): spirit murdering through not telling the family business

"Don't tell the family business." This is an ancient and still ever toxic mantra sometimes uttered throughout chosen and blood families. Collectively, the message is toxic in that it simultaneously puts forth advocacy of respectability politics along with suppressing narratives around abuse occurring within families. The toxicity of this message is immeasurable. It is the secrecy which murders the spirit. It is the secrecy which interrupts and other cases murders the possibilities of relational developmental health within families chosen and blood on communal scales (Helfenbein, 2010). Thus, when broaching the tensions bequeathed through the collective of queer and racial battle fatigues, they also reside in the entangled generational resonances of an "Don't tell the family business" ethos builds a false/complicated/problematic web of misplaced responsibility on the bodies of those repressed in families. I say nothing new in this chronicling, yet it is important raise the issue of not telling the family business in reference to Queer Battle fatigue. This is not to recklessly vilify every family, nuclear and/or chosen, however it is equally reckless to not acknowledge that the curricular implementation of such ideologies takes place in spaces deemed familial (Gershon, 2020; Young, 2016). I raise this premise in light of considering the necessity of how equity must assume, maintain, and engender a temporal ethos whereby the toxic mis-associations with equality is debunked. Equity after all is the reflexive inquiry into the complexity of needs for individuals and/or collectives need to survive. However, inquiry into equity pertains to a realization that mere survival is not the benchmark of existence. Existence, in the context in equity is infused with an inquiry regarding how the quality and joy must be the preeminent tension which thrives the survival. This is why the discourses Bettina Love and the collective, living and ancestral, sustaining a discourse critiquing base level survival is essential. Thus, to "not tell the family business" is a point of fatigue infiltration and in the cases of Queer and Racial Battle fatigue, it is witnessed in governing apparatuses of White supremacy ranging from the state sanctioning and supported murdering and erasure of Black queer folx to witnessing the very problematic ways in which cispatriarchal heteronormative violence ideologies have functioned in Black nationalist discourses, rationalizing the incurrence of the Queer spectrum in Black diasporic communities to rape and whiteness. I would go further to assert that it is this embodying and consistent re-embodying of this limited ethos with survival as the benchmark generates the collective repression of marginalized voices in in ways of thinking outside the familial. Furthermore, when the notion is allowed to ferment, it transforms into exclusivity. It is the panoptic construct "Don't tell the family business" which leaves those under a broader umbrella of shame in which silence is one the conscripts (Foucault, 1977). This is but one part of the engine of Queer and Racial battle fatigue. The collective of shaming from within the family and the transformation of it into a self-sustaining shaming locus. I am not placing blame on the victim, but I want to be sure to lay out one of the ways in which the seeds of Queer and racial battle fatigue are spread.

Thus, coming back to Love's discourse of "spirit murdering" in relation to Queer and Racial battle fatigue, for Queer Black folx it is an ethos spirit murdering always occurring at state to community levels which makes the discussion/analysis/elevation/overall doing and acknowledgement of Black Queer joy most timely. In the following section, I will look to Queer Black joy in relation singer Sylvester James. I start with analysis of their most popular 1978 song and video "You Make Me Feel, Mighty Real" in addition to discussing an interview Joan Rivers conducted with Rivers on "The Late Show" in 1986 post performance of the song "Someone Like You."

Affirmation: Sylvester on realness

You make me feel, mighty real. (James, 1978)

Sylvester's song 1978 song "You make me feel, mighty real" is a song of affirming their Queer self or rather selves. In the lyrics, Sylvester describes a romantic engagement that starts at the club on the dance floor and progresses back to their home. While the engagement Sylvester chronicles might be denoted as simply a hook up, it is much more. This engagement Sylvester has with the unnamed and nongendered accomplice is about realness. Sylvester's feeling of realness is discovered through the generative romantic bond they share. One context of this realness is about the eroticism and arousal their collective is generating. During Sylvester's lyric they proclaim that the selected lover "Love me like, you should." Thus, Sylvester is proclaiming their right to be romantically respected and satisfied (Brown, 2019). Sylvester's utilization of "love" encompasses varieties of intercourse simultaneously with call to honoring the embodied selves. The mantra "you make me feel, mighty real" doubles as a reclamation from Sylvester about of how their lover is causing sexual arousal in connection to feeling of safety and respect. Additionally, "you make me feel, mighty real" opens up the other inquiry about if Sylvester was feeling seen and acknowledged through the connection with another club attendee, did they not feel "mighty real" before this encounter? Does the club function as a liberative space for a community members deemed unreal by the outer community of comprised of a cisheteropatriarical ethos? An ethos which performs the multidisciplinary violence of the battle fatigues further enlivening spirit murdering countering the realness Sylvester desires. While the lyric provides the richness, I would will now move to addressing 4:27 the video that accompanies this song.

The opening of the video shows three disco balls surrounded by miscellaneous lights all with a red tint. While the song depicts an encounter in a dance club, the opening image elevates the club to an intergalactic engagement. The space of the club is dimly lit excluding the red tinted light which is constant in the video obscuring the colors of the objects it hits. The following scene is a side view of the lower torso to upper thigh region, one placed behind the other engaged in a gyrating motion. The shot then pans out to reveal five individuals (that might be read as female) which engage in a dance routine before Sylvester descends the stair case illuminated by the flickering red lights.

The space the video is filmed appears as club and outer space. There is a Black speculative fictive element which queers the line between the reality and the imaginative. This aesthetic spatial production incites a sense of liberation not available prior to entrance into the space. The production of intergalactic imagery resonates similarly to Sun Ra's discussion of outer space as the ultimate liberatory place (Szwed, 1997).

Ra situated the intergalactic in reference to acknowledging Black folx as being seen as myths. For him, myth straddles two distinct meanings. Thus, when Ra referred to Black folx as myths, he was describing the sub-human treatment afforded to their beingness. However, Ra's reference to Black folx as myths is also an acknowledgement of the magic and mysticism he sees Black folx as embodying (Pickens, 2019).

For Sylvester, like Ra, the video is a mythological creation/imagining of a liberative space. It is not merely a club; it is a space where the radical Black imagination is free to flow and explore without ostracization for reclaiming its realness (Kelley,) Additionally, the video pushes the boundaries of realness. In listening the Sylvester recite and enact, "you make me feel, mighty real" there follows a series of shapeshifting from Sylvester to drive their point home.

The video shows six different outfit changes from Sylvester. I see the changes as being about something much larger than a shift in scenery. These outfit changes combined with Sylvester recitation of "you make me feel, mighty real" articulate a series queerings via shape shifting. While Sylvester's development of feelings is verbalized via the relationship to the love interest, shapeshifting through outfit changes serves to reveal the selves making the feeling of realness. More specifically, if you, the possible courter, desires me (Sylvester), are you able to "make me feel, mighty real"? Realness being the exciting of Sylvester's passions but also, can you the courter, be loving of all the queered permutations of how I understand my realness. Let us look at some of the outfits shifts/shapeshifts in Sylvester proclaims their realness.

Both Afro-Surrealism's and Afro-Futurism's mysticism reside in the call to communities within the Chocolatized spectrum to dream (Miller, 2012). The dreaming in turn is the doing through with the discovery lies in the simultaneity of the possibilities. It is the dreaming of the possibilities intersecting with notions of the impossible with cultivates a sense of freedom and agency in the Chocolatized communal spectrum which exists uniquely in the sense that these communities must take the most impossible hand and in turn make it work. Furthermore, whether it is looking at spirituals like "Follow the Drinking Gourd" sang by Black folx enslaved on U.S. soil to imagine freedom and therefore becoming free through the imaginary in connection with discovering ways to free their bodies from bondage to witnessing the ways in which economic disparagement severely limits access to foods choice which has resulted in many traditions subsumed into national food ways, ala BBQ. At the core of these radical moves of Black folx discovering liberation has always been the imagination. Thus, it is through radical refusal to never stop dreaming whereby alternative meanings and pathways to liberation have been discovered. This is the ethos witnessed when watching Sylvester's "You Make Me Feel (Mighty Real)" video, an individual unafraid to unapologetically dream in public spheres as a way to discover agency and liberation.

In the video, Sylvester changes outfits 6 times in 4:27. However, the outfits are disclosures depicting the complexity of the self. Sylvester's statement, "You make me feel, mighty real" is a mantra affirming the changes in outfits as outward proclamations of their embodied selves. Additionally, the mantra situates the discovery of their realness as being spoken into existence through a relationship with another in which the feeling of realness was developed collective sentiment. A chronicling of Sylvester's shapeshifts starts with a black head to toe outfit. In detail, the outfit contains black boots with spurs, a black leather jacket and pants with a black chiffon top. The second shape shift, Sylvester is dressed head to toe in a white single-breasted single button suit and is carrying a white fan.

The white fan is a carryover from the Black church. Contextually, the fan was a component to cool the body in response to catching the spirt immitted from the preacher's sermon. The fan, in the hands of the church usher, often women, was also a component to aid cooling the spirit-stricken attendee. Therefore, Sylvester's utilization of the fan can be understood as queering the representations of space and place. It is not a coincidence being that they discussed learning and developing their craft of singing in the Black church. In Sylvester's hands, the fan is both a queering of religious historically rigidly gendered a secular space and place.

In Sylvester's 3rd shapeshift they are wearing a sequin turban and top. The top has one tassel adorning the lower section of both sleeves along with black leather pants, again with a white fan which follows through as adornment for the 4th and 5th shapeshifts. In the 4th shapeshift, Sylvester is wearing a gold sequin kimono influenced garb, a black chiffon top, and matching gold material tied in a draping fashion around the waist. The penultimate shapeshift presents Sylvester wearing another kimono influenced garb composed of what appear to be a combination of purple, black, silver sequins over a black chiffon top. Sylvester's last shape shift comes back to their first look.

Altogether, Sylvester is able to exist in an environment in which radical Queer Black joy thrives. Their six outfit/shapeshifts in conjunction the relationship they are having with the person of interest becomes an affirmation of all the expressions of self. Sylvester's realness is not questioned nor denied which spells a thriving of their spirit in addition to being a point whereby they are able to avoid chiding by the club community in the hypothetical discourse of the family business. In the club, to tell the family business is a healing process absent of the shame as opposed to outside the club as representing a violent silencing spatial zone in which the family business is to never be revealed.

In the following section I will discuss Sylvester's appearance on the "Late Show" with Joan Rivers as the host. In the post-performance interview segment Sylvester incidentally outs his partner. Rivers aids in further intensifying the outing, absent of Sylvester's consent, in addition to violently and rigidly framing Sylvester's identity. While Rivers is a friend of Sylvester, this exchange also speaks to the realms of queer and racial battle fatigue in relation to being an ally vs. an accomplice (Gershon, 2020).

Queer Black Joy surveilled: panoptic gazes on sylvester

The interview segment from Sylvester's 31 December 1986 performance of "Someone Like You" on the nationally syndicated talk show, Late Show with Joan Rivers presents a point in which surveillance of Queer Black Joy is witnessed (McKittrick & Woods, 2007; Moten, 2003; Rivers, 1986; Sharpe, 2016). The interaction between Sylvester and Rivers, speaks of the nuanced ways in which surveillance of Queer Black joy functions regarding marginalized bodies, Queer Black bodies, in this context, surveil themselves along with how other bodies surveil Queer Black bodies (Browne, 2015). While I do not see Rivers' interaction entirely being rooted in malintent, I do not think this removes the harm put forth in her statements. Simultaneously, Sylvester's surveillance of self is witnessed through discussion of slippages in their discussion with Rivers. What is witnessed with Sylvester is a variation of code switching in the context of Black Queerness, rooted in the repression of intimacy and relationship status. This is in no way an indictment on Sylvester's character. Often as a Queer Black body, there is a necessity to operate with series of codeswitches rooted both in Blackness and Queerness. Furthermore, while the dream might be to live Black, loud, and unapologetically proud, the material circumstances of living in a climate infused with violent heteronormativity, anti-Blackness, and classism put foremost the necessity to survive. However, in the spirit of Bettina Love, I do not think that survival is the stopping point in living life. Considering the Sylvester's circumstances of being Queer, Black, expressing joy openly, and joying the public sphere, what are they contending with in the interview with Rivers? I will address this inquiry with attention to two transcribed sections of the interview.

Sylvester walks over to Joan Rivers and they hold each other's hands. Sylvester then gives her a kiss on the right cheek walks over to Rivers' co-host and shakes his hand before sitting down in the chair closest to Rivers. Rivers' co-host offers Sylvester water which Sylvester does not see because they promptly engage in a conversation with Rivers who hands them a glass of water. Below is one of the conversational streams.

> Rivers: Happy New year
>
> Sylvester: Happy New Year to you
>
> Rivers: And what are your new year's resolutions?
>
> Sylvester: I'm gonna stop drinking
>
> Rivers: Yeah but that's water, so that's ok. Look at your jewelry (gasps)
>
> Sylvester: That's my wedding set.
>
> Rivers: That's your wedding set? All right. Who are you married to?
>
> Sylvester: (gasps, laughs, and smiles) To Rick.
>
> Rivers: (*smiles and laughter from her and the audience cheers. Rivers releases Sylvester's hand and sits up right*) Good.
>
> Sylvester: You know....(puts hands up and over face in surprise of the announcement of their public declaring their marriage to another man.) Oh God, I'm sorry, You know?....
>
> Rivers: What?
>
> Sylvester: Rick's parents are watching.
>
> Rivers: Well... (looks directly into the camera) surprise!
>
> Sylvester: (full-bodied laugh)
>
> Rivers: You're telling me they didn't know Rick was living with you? How long are you together with Rick?
>
> Sylvester: 2 $\frac{1}{2}$ years.
>
> Rivers: Well, and what's his last name?
>
> Sylvester: (laughs and rocks away from Rivers)
>
> Rivers: What's Rick's last name?
>
> Sylvester: Cranmer.
>
> Rivers: Rick, Rick?
>
> Sylvester: Cranmer.
>
> Rivers: Rick Cramer
>
> Sylvester: (corrects Rivers) Cranmer. (spells it out) C-R-A-N, Cran-mer
>
> Rivers: (looking around to camera and audience) Rick Cranmer's parents, now if you looked in your closet 10 years ago you wouldn't shocked.

In this part of the interview, Sylvester is moves from the performer's spot to the interviewee's spot. The subject matter is discovered in Rivers' gawking at Sylvester's jewelry to which Rivers focuses her attention and gesture towards their rings. Sylvester simply says, "That's my wedding set." Rivers asks who Sylvester is married to, to which they say, "To Rick." Sylvester's response is an affective signal to Rivers denoting, "come on you already know my story." However, the difference is that this conversation might have been one or an occurrence in which Rivers is already privy to this information, judging by Sylvester's response. This interaction between Rivers and Sylvester articulates a space of intimacy they have, in which, off-screen, both parties might otherwise more comfortably disclose with substantial depth. However, in the context of the a widely syndicated late night talk show, the discussion being presented regarding Sylvester's marital status to a male in light of being read as male is a reminder to surveil themselves. This is indicated when Sylvester, uninhibited, reminds Rivers they are married to Rick Cranmer and then promptly apologizing. Sylvester's apology marks a surveilled awareness that Cramner's parents are not aware, or willfully non-accepting, that they are an intimate exclusive union. Thus, Sylvester is carrying a continuum of survival baggage based in the realms of: (1) Maintaining the secrecy of their union (2) Maintaining the secrecy of Cranmer's identity and sexual orientation (3) Suppression of relationships to sustain their realness (4) Blackness. Altogether, Sylvester and River's interaction is an example of how politics are mapped onto bodies articulating the specific and rigid directions of how they are able to move. For, Sylvester, a Queer, Black, gender-fluid being, this functions as a "malfunction" in the code-switching survival apparatus, resulting in a full disclosure of the conditions regarding their relationship status accelerated further through the technological public sphere. Sylvester is reminded of limitations their being operates and responds with a literal apology during the interview. Rivers, on the other hand, a straight, white, cisgendered female, puts forth an aloofness. While she is accepting, perhaps supportive, of Sylvester's union, she simultaneously intensifies the violent outing of Sylvester through further inquiring about the identity of their partner. Rivers pushes even further with knowledge that Cramner's parents' possible non-awareness of his queerness, with taking it upon herself, in light of Sylvester's uncomfort, to direct her words to Cramner's parents on live television. While Sylvester's response articulates the intense over laboring Black Queer bodies must do to survive a violent situation, Rivers intensifies the outing without significant threat to her being. Rivers is able to operate based on the privileges afforded to being a Straight, White, cisgendered female. Furthermore, Rivers' handling of the situation depicts the need of nuanced meanings of consent that must be engaged for anyone situating themselves in any formulation/semblance of allyship and/or accompliceship with marginalized communities. Sylvester in their interaction with Rivers, is placed in a situation in which the decision of consenting to whether to or not further discuss the details of their union with Carnmer is completely usurped. Thus, Sylvester, while comfortable in disclosing the family business to Rivers on less public formats, is placed in a predicament of being forced to publicly deal with the anxiety of not being in control of telling their family business. The already violent climate of being uncloseted at the time this interview was conducted, is an additional challenge to Sylvester's Black Queer joy. Through Rivers' angling of the inquiry, a violent emotional space is created which plunges Sylvester into experiencing the murder of their spirit. While Sylvester experiences Black Queer joy their union with Cranmer, it is a public sphere charged with heteronormative violence which Sylvester indicates, through their actions in the interview that their Black Queer joy must be suppressed to assure the safety of their union and selves. The last selected piece of the interview captures Sylvester's opposition to Rivers referring to them as a drag queen.

In this latter part of the interview starting at 7:19 Rivers makes what flippant and reckless reference to Sylvester as a drag queen.

> Rivers: What did your family say when you wanted to be a drag queen?
>
> Sylvester: I'm not a drag queen.
>
> Rivers: Well, you are sometimes

In this segment Rivers is met with opposition from Sylvester when she refers to them as a drag queen. My observation of this interaction is not an indictment on the term or embodiment of the drag queen denotation. The analysis is rooted both in the words and Sylvester's affect in response to Rivers' use of drag queen in reference to their embodiment. Thus, when Rivers asks Sylvester about the response from their family when they "wanted to be a drag queen?"

Sylvester gracefully, yet promptly corrects Rivers. However, Rivers counters, denouncing with the instance that Sylvester is a drag queen. In this moment Rivers wields a series of hegemonic apparatuses that shut down the possibility for her and the broader public to gain nuanced understandings of Sylvester understands their identity. Additionally, Rivers very problematic interaction in this moment yields raises the issue of meanings of consent.

Hegemonically, Rivers in her positionality as a White cisgendered straight female, assigns the label, drag queen, to Sylvester, according only to what she sees as opposed to listening and affirming Sylvester's realness. In this label assignment, Rivers creates a series of rigid binaries rooted in male/female and gay/straight which again forces a severe weight on Sylvester's shoulders to further exist is a binary of being heard or being silenced. In the case of this interview segment, Sylvester is silenced and furthermore denied a discursive platform to be, to explain the complexities of their understandings of self which queer all, and more, of the binaries Rivers imposed in the interview. Thus Sylvester, is relegated to a realm of survival through the imposition of Rivers' binaries. Altogether, Sylvester's realness is denied. It is a denial based in a series of spirit murders done at Rivers' public reduction of Sylvester's realness in her denotation of them as a drag queen after multiple corrections. Her disregard for Sylvester's consent, even after the slip regarding their partner and marital status is a grey area of not telling the family business is broached. The closet Sylvester's and Carnmer's relationship is intended as a space of their collective protection. Thus, Sylvester's incidental telling of the family business during the interview was not shame based. Rather, their reaction of shock dealt with the unattended disclosure which left them and Cranmer exposed to possible violence from anti-Queer collectives.

In the following section, I move to the twenty-first century with New Orleans, Louisiana bounce artist Big Freedia. Similar to my interests with Sylvester, I address how Freedia frames their realness and the imposition of fatigues being put forth in the interviews.

That Wiggle Tho': Big Freedia on realness

Black queerness is series of intersections that have brought me elation in first learning to love my body, embodiment, and uniqueness of learning to build relationships. I also realize that this joy brought on by Black queerness is not something exclusive to me as further articulated in my aforementioned example with Madonna. In the sentiment posted in memes calling attention to how the world loves Black culture but needs to focus on loving the creators of this culture, Black people. I would further amend this claim to infer that while the world loves Black/Chocoltized Queer joy culture, there is a dire need to love the creators as well, Black/Chocoltized Queer folx. In their similar context of New Orleans bounce artist Big Freedia globally joys through her demand that one "release [their] your wiggle" there needs to be the inverse reflexivity for the consumers to get open Freedia's and overall Queer Black folx need to be protected through establishing infrastructures of equity. Furthermore, as cultural expressions and productions of Black queerness are consumed, and/or neighboring communities are joyed, I ask what might those in the spectrum of White queer communities to heteronormative Black communities do to move themselves from mere cultural consumer to accomplice? In this part of the chapter discussion I go back to Big Freedia's 2014 song and video, "Explode."

In examination of protests in New Orleans and the broader Louisiana area, reclamation/and creating liberative spaces has always been at the core of protest. The space is both conceptual and material. Some instances to note are: the Congo Square gatherings of enslaved communities to engage in the acts of selling products and spiritual communing. While these gatherings were instituted by the Municipal court to circumvent desire for enslaved folx to revolt, in these gatherings enslaved Black communities gathered and publicly dreamed and re-imagined liberative possibilities together. Liberation in these contexts existed as the possibility and responsibility of dreaming liberation to fuel Black radical hope. This collective dreaming was a manifestation of the reclamation and protest. The materiality of the Black radical liberative dreaming is realized in the 1795 Point Coupee revolt 100 north of New Orleans. This stands as an example in which the liberative dreaming and re-imagination materialize through the actions of revolt. The 1795 Point Coupee revolt of enslaved Black folx stands as one early bloody examples of radical dreaming which moved enslaved folx and accomplices to action. These constituencies understood in their move to action that their lives were in line for ancestral ascendance (Hall, 1992). Regarding radical Black joy, while often presented as a smiles, laughter, and dance, it is important to see these instances of enslaved folx, confined to conceptual and material spaces as engaging joy as politics spatial reclamations. I would be remiss if I did not address one more precursory moment in radical Black joy and spatial in New Orleans which is related to the masking Indian communities.

The Black masking Indian nations of New Orleans are often referred to as Mardi Gras Indians. However, I defer to referring to them masking as Indian tribes, communities, and/or nations. Looking at some of the discourses raised in preference of one label over another, the rationale being that the most visible and sonic public displays of these nations cultures is on Mardi Gras day, therefore designating them as Mardi Gras Indians. However, some members within these nations would resist the label as Mardi Gras Indians, being that it designates them as only seasonal. Furthermore, many members would be quick to remind both insiders and outsiders that being a Black masking Indian is a way of life and community building which is always present and emerging.

Attending to the reclamation of public spaces, Black masking Indians stand as some of the many instigators of resistance through reclamation of public space and place. One of the treats to their culture has been the raising of the prices for parade permits. Being that many of the members in the nation are situated at economic disadvantage, having the money to gain these permits it a challenge. Therefore, there is the element of coming together and parading through public spaces without (with the added tension of refusing to permits which is the resistance). Parallel to the resistance ethos discussed regarding Black folx in spaces in New Orleans and the broader Louisiana conceptual and physical spaces and in considering resistance as a continuum of tensions which re-manifest in events of differing time spaces, Big Freedia is a beacon of these resistance practices of Queer Black joy. I will now shift to addressing points of the resistance through Big Freedia's 2014 song and video "Explode" along with discussing segments of an interview with did on the popular radio show the "Breakfast Club Power 105.1."

In video monologue Big Freedia says,

> My music, it makes me feel good about what I do, and the culture that I represent. People get confused by if I—am he or she. I am more than just Big Freedia. I am more than just Queen Diva. I am more than just Freedie Ross. I am me. I am the ambassador. Rrepresentin' for New Orleans and for bounce music. So many things in my head sometime, it just all makes me wanna explo[de]. (Ross, 2014)

As Big Freedia makes this statement, they shift from an inside industrial décor to the outside on a rooftop. The rooftop brings them in closer proximity to skyscrapers and towering over the streets of New Orleans. This part of the video shows Big Freedia alone. The monologue can be understood as series of mantras, whereby Big Freedia proclaims their necessity of their presence in elevating indigenous cultural New Orleans constituencies of: Queerness, the artistic repressions, and overall New Orleans folx.

Post Big Freedia's monologue, the rest of the video depicts their collective spatial transgressing New Orleans city streets, a laundry mat, and a night club. These are spaces in which Big Freedia and collective infiltrate and reclaim and thus engage in the acts of joying those spaces. Through these collective spatial transgressions, Big Freedia et al. can be understood as joying the public sphere locally, nationally, and transnationally through the imposition of Queer Black joy simultaneously "throwin' shade" on attempts on the fatigues which only allow for a damaged centered narrative of Queer Black folx (Tuck, 2009). Similar to addressing the shape shifting through outfit shifts Sylvester utilized, I will address the Big Freedia's shapeshifts through outfit changes.

Freedia's shapeshifts evolve around three main outfits. In the first they are wearing a black coat with tales tuxedo inspired outfit. In both the coat and tales, there are red accents on the lapels of the coat and along the side seams of the pants with thigh high boots. The look of this outfit resembles a militaristic appearance. Further observation of Freedia's spatial placement as towering over the public and soaring with the skyscrapers combined with the monologue starting the video is presents an individual who is in control of their life. While the primary meaning of the song is about encouraging the blowing off of stress. The urging to explode is an encouragement to release the tension one experiences in the day-to-day life hustle. However, in one way of viewing the collective of Freedia, the elevated space, and the militaristic influences outfit is as a re-imagining of authority. The re-imaging authority figure with Freedia in the position of power is then liberation the public the command to "explode" as the modus operandi of the moment. Freedia in this moment in their city of New Orleans in the grand Toussaint L'Overtuian protagonist leading the tensed-up community towards liberative dreaming through commanding the public to free themselves. However, the enslavement Freedia is asking the public to counter is dismal reality of the day in and day out. The shift accompanying this outfit is white buttondown shirt accessorized with an off white/cream scarf. In the second, they are wearing black and white horizontal stripes with bedazzled handcuffs each attached to the opposing beltloops. In connection with this Freedia's lyrical content, the horizontal stripes and the cuffs can be perceived as a having a carceral sentiment. Furthermore, there is a parallel in to the images of chain gangs throughout Louisiana, especially in regard to further carcerally re-imagined spaces as seen with Angola prison which originally was a plantation (Meiners, 2016). I am no way emphasizing that Freedia is advocating prison industrial entities. Rather I am considering how to read and/or "read" Freedia's shapeshift as a leaning into and perhaps poking fun at the carceral reality Black folx are relegated. Even further, when reading the shapeshift it appears as they are poking fun at the carceralities afforded to Black folx as to say, that even while the state/nation-state deem it acceptable to victimize, violate, and support violence against Black bodies. Therefore, the shapeshift can be read as a conceptual middle finger to authoritarian regimes. The shapeshift is ancient in its mocking of the aristocracy. The ancientness of this gesture is witnessed in the Afro-Caribbean traditions of carnival further realized on U.S. soil as Mardi Gras. As the holiday relates to Catholicism, Mardi Gras is seen as the big blow out, or rather explosion, expressed through mass indulgences before the Lenten season. However, the simultaneous intention of mocking aristocracies, in this stress produced through the 9–5 job, the day to day hustle. Overall, the tensions causing the experiencer to feel any extremes of stress and/or the latter fatigue. Therefore, Freedia and crew's notion of exploding as can be read as the grand blow out of stresses, however this blowout is not rooted in anticipation of the Lenten season. Rather, the notion of the explode is based in existential foundations, whereby the celebration is left up to the individual to make the determination of when to start the stress release. Additionally, Freedia has a black button-down shirt with white hightop Nikes accented with black. In the third outfit Freedia is wearing a white button-down shirt with a black neck tie. Black pants accompany this outfit along with a black half corset. In this outfit iteration, Freedia has shifted the bedazzled handcuff accessory, originally attached to their two front belt loops, to a necklace. With attention to the shifted handcuff accessory this can be read a variety of ways. While, it may or may not be Freedia's intention, the overall inquiry I am posing is in regard to how the resistance plays on carcerality they employ in the aesthetic shapeshifts. With this inquiry, Freedia has engaged sorts of jocularity with presentations of carcerality via the direct placement of cacerlities tools, horizontal stripes and bedazzled handcuffs, directly as adornment on their body. However, it is the direct shifting of the bedazzled handcuffs to another outfit from waist adornment refashioned as necklace which is again another play on carcerality. In this instance, the handcuffs can be read as ultimate Caribbean 'toasting' moment as to say to those threatened by Freedia and crew's freedom as the callout challenge, as to say "if you gotta problem come deal." However, the implied challenge emphasizes to the naysayers of Queer Black joy that your challenge will not be met with an intense opposition.

For Big Freedia and crew, the collective re-appropriations of New Orleanian spaces along with their shapeshifting via outfit changes were modalities to re-embody counters to not telling the family business. Furthermore, Freedia's encouragement to "explode" is the ultimate communal call to dissolve the silencing of the spirit and for self and community to re-claim and be spiritually fulfilled through one another's the robust and enlivened beingness. The explosion is telling of family business variant done on the terms of the subaltern community (Spivak, 1995).

In the final segment of discussion on Big Freedia, I will conclude with an analysis of the interview conducted with them on the Breakfast Club radio show (Ross, 2020). It should be noted that that one of the historic and present issues with this radio show has been their struggle with Queer violence. Violence in the context of the Breakfast Club related to the discourses implied of acceptable beauty and Trans bodies as witnessed with Janet Mock and their praising of her Transness based upon her ability to "pass" as a cisgendered women. The violence of moments, as witnessed with Janet Mock, is the rigid equation of being trans as equating to the ability to "pass" as cisgendered. Altogether, it is the promulgation of these and many other violently anti-Queer ethos which further sustains and promotes a binary of either/or, Gay/Straight, and/or Trans/Cis. In the context of the Straight Cis governmentality situates communities as not passing at rationalized points of violence at state, nation, and on world scales (Helfenbein, 2010). However, in light of these context Freedia comes on the Breakfast Club as a beacon of unapologeticness in their Queerness, Blackness, and overall embodiments.

During course of the interview, at the 11:35 mark Freedia makes the profound statement, "I bring all walks of life together through the power of ass." Their statement is a direct affirmation of the essentiality of Queer Black joying practices. However, I will jump around additional segments of this interview consider the broader embodiment of Freedia.

In this interview, Freedia briefly discusses associations and collaborations with New Orleans bounce colleague Katey Red. In part of this discussion Freedia draws a comparison between their and Red's relationship to the Black church. Freedia situates their musical roots as starting in the Black church as a gospel singer and with the association with Red shifting from sacred to the secular intents in their musical paths. Simultaneously, it is important to consider the ways in which the queering of space has occurred in historically in Black secular musical forms. Some of the ranges being in consideration of Ray Charles' song "Hallelujah, I Love Her So" to Little Richard's "Tutti Frutti" both instances in which musical stylings of the Black church holy roller aesthetic to the more direct way Richard blurs and questions the notion of Black masculinity in his gender presentations. Similarly, the queering of sacred and secular spaces is witnessed in Freedia's Black holy roller sanctified church aesthetic re-embodied expression of twerking and antiphonality (call and response). Additionally, Freedia dispels the idea of twerking as being new in their acknowledgement of it as being rooted in the West African dance traditions of the Mapouka. Thus, the queering of the literal and conceptual spaces occurs in those of the secular/sacred, Cis/Trans, present/ancient, and nationally/transnationally. Collectively, these queering constitute the complexity of ways in which Queer Black bodies joy the space.

Big Freedia's discussion of the parallel with being singers in the Black church tradition denotes the complexity of telling the family business. While the broader discourse of the church community and Queer folx in the speculative narrative context, Freedia's telling of the family business is a deeper discussion of how the vocal aesthetics where bequeathed to them via participation in the rituals of the Black church. Overall, for Freedia, communication of Radical Black Queer joy is made possible through the connecting the vocal aesthetics of the Black Church and the West African dance traditions, as witnessed with their discussion of the Mapouka. Thus, the family business in Freedia's case is might be fraught with trauma, but then they also frame unapologetically how they have fused aesthetic traditions as a way to express Queer Black joy.

The collective: Sylvester and Big Freedia on Queer Black Joy and the 'Fatigues'

The collective analytical frameworks of racial and Queer battle fatigue are situated in conjunction to consider the ways in which the complex ways Queer Black joy simultaneously joys public spheres, is attacked/denied to Queer Black communities, co-opted, and/or works to counter violent cisheteronormative patriarchal violence. Additionally, the placement of racial and Queer battle fatigue together is in anticipation of what is untranslatable with discussion and analysis of one or another. While translation always contends with variations of untranslatability, or difference at play, not exclusively attributed to language, the untranslatability also relates to socio-cultural experiences (Derrida, 1978). Thus, if I were to frame it racial battle fatigue, I would risk not considering the complexities at play for the Queer communities and the same goes exists if I were to frame the analysis in regard to exclusively Queerness. Therefore, the combination of Racial and Queer battle fatigue is a dynamic reverberative series of transcendental spheres that do not cross. Rather they sit intimately together at the space in between is the unstable varieties of meaning for Queer Black bodies and their acts of joying the public sphere.

In witnessing how Queer Black music artists Sylvester and Big Freedia navigated/navigate worlds ascribing rationalized state sanctioned variances of violence presented possibilities to conceptualize/inquire the ways of meaning of joy, survival, and survivance translate for Black Queer communities (Story, 2020; Wright, 2015).

For Sylvester, the two instances discussed rooted in analysis of the video from their 1978 disco hit, "You Make Me Free (Mighty Real) and in their 1986 post-performance interview Joan Rivers. For the video, "You Make Me Free (Mighty Real)", while Sylvester unpacks an experience of what would be read on the surface as a hookup, through shapeshifting radical re-imaginings, realness is created and cultivated for them in the relationship with the unnamed figure. The realness for Sylvester is the acceptance and honored lines of consent in the spontaneous relationship with its realms of intimacy. In this context joy is the freedom to feel at home in the layers of self. Perhaps it sounds simple, however historic and present dismal treatments of Black Queer bodies must be acknowledged. In the context of Enlightenment thinking and its resonant constructs ascribing pathologizing Black bodies in tandem with the continual normalization/re-normalization of White cisheteropatriarical maleness, it is the national and transnational ascribing of Queerness and Blackness as illnesses. Thus, Sylvester's mantra of "You Make Me Feel (Mighty Real)" can be understood as the act of establishing Queer Black joy when Queer Black bodies are rationalized as a disease, or as Dubois would say, "a problem" on national and transnational scales (DuBois, 1903/1994). Additionally, in this mantra, Sylvester articulates the fatigues through the implication of the binary between realness and fakeness. While Sylvester's 6 total shapeshifts throughout the video are presented in video, they indirectly show awareness of ending up on the side of the binary which situates them as a problem.

Inversely, the designation of Queer Black bodies is an extended continuum of applying fatigues to Queer Black communities through the implications of surveillance. Altogether, the historic and present pathologizing of Queer Black bodies as "a problem" translates to a nuanced realization of "double-consciousness" with additional linkages to an internalized locus placing the sole goal on baseline survival, the dregs, of living which is fatiguing and spiritually lynching (DuBois, 1903/1994).

The instance of Sylvester and Joan Rivers presents another nuanced context to process the meanings of Queer and Racial Battle fatigue in the cultivation of allyships and accompliceships (Gershon, 2020). While Rivers is supporter, fan, and friend of Sylvester, the intensification of the outing Sylvester's male partner's identity on national television is problematic. Sylvester accidentally, reveals their partner is Rick Cramner, however awareness they have done this, quickly expresses fear through prompt self-surveillance. Rivers in response centers in on Sylvester's disclosure and pushes the inquiry further without considering Sylvester's discomfort. Rivers takes it upon herself to solidify the outing. This exchange is a point in which Rivers could have reacted more supportive in respecting and cultivating lines of consent. Additionally, Rivers, later in the interview, refers to Sylvester as a drag queen which they object to, however Rivers in insistent on entrenching them in that identity.

While Rivers sees herself as "cuttin' up" with a good friend, she dismisses simultaneous problematic publicization and repression of Sylvester she has engaged. In this interaction, Sylvester finds themselves violently outed and denied complex understandings of their identity. Thus, Queer and Racial fatigue in this occurrence functions as a repressive/outing surveilling in which Sylvester is not the determiner in the explanation of self. Rather, it is Rivers armed with a violent cisheteronormative hegemony which makes the final determination.

Moving a few decades forward Big Freedia emerges in 2014, with the song and video "Explode." Additionally, in 2020 they are interviewed in the radio program "The Breakfast Club," a space which in prior settings has been a violently cisheteronormative space.

The 2014 video and song "Explode" present a collective of queering of New Orleans public and private spaces through dance, movement, and overall joy. With the monologue of the video Freedia discusses the distaste for the ways in which binaries touch and move across their body. Further elaboration from Freedia about how these binaries are mapped on to their body in: he/she and Big Freedia, Queen Diva, or Freedie Ross. However, for Freedia, the biggest problematic is the entrapment in one entity because they understand themselves as much more expansive. Furthermore, Freedia understands themselves and crew as a representative of overall New Orleans bounce music culture. However, in the finality of the monologue, Freedia says, "So many things in my head sometime, it just makes me wanna explo[de]." The statement acknowledges distinct frustrations along with attempting to reconcile the mounting tensions of self in response to lived experience. While explode, in Freedia's context is the dance and unapologetic Queer Black joy, the explode can also be read as shape shifts expressed via outfit spatial variations engaged throughout the video.

The implications of Queer Battle fatigue emerge directly from the forced binary of either/or regarding Freedia's construction of self. However, Racial Battle fatigue emerges in addressing the spaces Freedia engages of New Orleans. Historically and presently, New Orleans is space in which the complexity of racial disparity has been recreated through accessibility and inaccessibility to public space through city infrastructures (i.e.-interstates, gentrification, public parks.). It is these reformulations of points of access rooted in race which creates Racial Battle fatigue in regard to how Black bodies are unable and/or able to navigate public spaces (Buras, 2015; McKittrick & Woods, 2007).

Conclusion: Queer Black Joy and the lesson

My situating of musical and interview discourses from the late Sylvester and Big Freedia is in acknowledgement of how their grit and demand beyond baseline survival was bequeathed to them from Queer Black communities. Furthermore, Sylvester and Big Freedia are the products of Queer Black joy. The lessons they received are simultaneously the ones they gifted to the broader public sphere. However, what does it mean to enjoy the expressions and products of Queer Black joy without love for the community? The inattentiveness to this inquiry is where Queer and Racial battle fatigue infiltrate.

Looking at the cultural influence of Sylvester and Big Freedia there is the extensive economic and aesthetic contributions they bequeath nationally and globally through the Queer Black expressions of joy in their music and broader community building. While Sylvester utilized disco to do this work, Big Freedia does this similar work through the bounce genre. The musical and interview segments analyzed from each artist depict the variances of Queer Black joy. These instances mark the ways in which Queer Black joy is feared in the violent territories of cisheter-patriarchal, anti-Black, and heteronormatively violent contexts of the interviews. Both Queer and

Racial Battle fatigue are at play in through Sylvester's and Big Freedia's encounters with major media sources.

Neoliberally, the violence of Queer and Racial Battle fatigue points to the premise of how Sylvester and Big Freedia are acceptable as producers of culture while being damned to the closet. Or, rather a love of the culture produced by the marginalized individuals and communities simultaneously in absence of loving, respecting, and supporting the equitable treatment those principal producers. Thus, for cisgender straight communities while the tokenization of having a Queer Black acquaintance and/or consuming Queer Black expressions might be seen as provocative, an approval of violence via the negation of violence which has/was done to Sylvester and Big Freedia and broadly to Queer Black communities nationally and globally. While the popularity of the Sylvester and Freedia, to some, presents the neoliberalist illusion of strides toward liberation, as a global community there must be a long slow drink of reality regarding the incurring violence towards Black Queer folx. Altogether, what is it to consume Queer Black expressions absent of acknowledging the fatigues endured?

Sylvester and Big Freedia problematize Enlightenment notions of knowledge residing on the laurels of Cartisian ethos and the rigid institution. The centralization of these artists challenges notions of knowledge as exclusively developed through the Enlightenment. Furthermore, Sylvester's and Freedia's artistic voices articulate the ways in which apparent and subversive resistance can occur, countering the varieties of the "ivory tower" through refusal to allow their voices and communities to silenced. However, when the institutional critique is re-positioned the discourse of addressing both Queer and Battle fatigue as a barometer to further gauge which knowledges are allowed to exist within settler colonial institutions. Inversely, settler colonial institutions are given poetic license to terrorize communities within their confines as well as surrounding communities. Historic to the present, marginalized folx knowledges are quickly dismissed, erased, while readily being consumed. Therefore, centralization of Sylvester and Freedia is an extension regarding the complexities of knowledges in play absent of the neoliberal gazes deployed by the institution.

For the institution as related to the "ivory tower," the look outside of the "traditional academic" setting and to the lives lived by Sylvester and Big Freedia points back to the bloodiness of the institution's hands, both literally and conceptually. Thus, the "ivory tower" position comes, to some in these spaces relishing the entitlement, to negate acknowledgement its proclivity to produce violence. However, when looking at the radicalness of Queer Black joy embodied through Sylvester and Big Freedia, it is this sense of joy radiating from Black Diasporic resistance saying to the settler colonialist and its specters, "whatever you do, you will kill my spirit" in collaboration with the succinctness of Kendrick Lamar ala "Bitch don't kill my vibe" (Lamar, 2012). Furthermore, understanding Sylvester and Big Freedia as being products of a much broader community centralized in Black Queer joy illuminates the greed of institutional control, but as with any violent captor, for all the bloodshed and spirit murdering conducted through institutions crusades, the acts are rooted in the fears of how the liberated infused with Black Queer joy. Therefore, when analyses of Queer and Racial Battle fatigues are addressed in qualitative research, the additional resonance to consider is how institutional violence is based in a continuum of colonialist fear around the inability to ever fully control the spirit of Queer Black joy and overall desire. Altogether, Black Queer joy, when considered as a lens qualitative research inquiry, is a dynamic multimodal transdisciplinary series of knowledges which nuances the analysis and equity building project in response to the resistance and eradication of Queer and Racial Battle fatigue.

Note

1. In this discussion I use they/them/their for both Sylvester and Big Freedia in response to both the complex, gender fluid, and non-binaried ways they frame gender for themselves.

Authors Notes

Big shoutout to my sister, friend, chosen family, and confidant Tracy P. Beard for blessing me with the inquiry, "when are you going to write about Black joy?" It was this inquiry which was vital in framing the discourse as I did. The inquiry was the self-reflexive point to remind me that I am worthy to write, discuss, and get lost in Queer Black joy, even when the nation-state tells my community and I opposite.

Disclosure statement

No potential conflict of interest was reported by the author(s).

ORCID

Reagan Patrick Mitchell http://orcid.org/0000-0002-0119-9029

References

Brown, A. (2019). *Pleasure activism: The politics of feeling good*. AK Press.
Brown, A. (2017). *Emergent strategy: Shaping change, changing worlds*. AK Press.
Browne, S. (2015). *Dark matters: On the surveillance of blackness*. Duke University Press.
Buras, K. (2015). *Charter schools, race, and urban space: Where the market meets grassroots resistance*. Routledge.
Derrida, J. (1978). *Writing and difference*. University of Chicago Press.
DuBois, W. (1903/1994). *The souls of black folk*. Dover Publications, Incorporated.
Foucault, M. (1977). *Discipline & punish: The birth of the prison*. Random House.
Gershon, W. (2020). Allies, accomplices, and aggressions: The pernicious nature of queer battle fatigue. *Journal of Lesbian and Gay Studies*, *26*(2), 226–229.
Hall, G. (1992). *Africans in colonial Louisiana: The development of Afro-Creole culture in the eighteenth century*. Louisiana State University Press.
Helfenbein, R. (2010). Thinking through scale: Critical geographies and curriculum spaces. In E. Malewski (Ed.), *Curriculum studies handbook: The next movement* (pp. 304–317). Routledge.
James, S. (1978). *You make me feel (mighty real)* [Video File]. https://www.youtube.com/results?search_query=sylvester+you+make+me+feel
Kelley, R. (2002). Freedom dreams: The black radical imagination
Kelley, R. (1994/1996). *Race rebels: Culture, politics, and the black working class*. The Free Press.
Lamar, K. (2012). Bitch, don't kill my vibe. [Recorded by Kendrick Lamar]. On *good kid, m.A.A.d city*. Interscope Records.
Love, B. (2019). *We want to do more that survive: Abolitionist teaching and the pursuit of educational freedom*. Beacon Press.
McKittrick, K. & Woods, C. (Ed.). (2007). *Black geographies and the politics of place*. South End Press.
Meiners, E. (2016). *For the children: Protecting innocence in a carceral state*. University of Minnesota Press.
Miller, S. (2012). *Afrosurreal manifesto: Black is the new black*. Epicenter Press.
Moten, F. (2003). *In the break: The aesthetics of black radical tradition*. University of Minnesota Press.
Pickens, T. (2019). *Black madness: Mad blackness*. Duke University Press.
Rivers, J. (1986). *Someone like you*. [Video File]. https://www.youtube.com/watch?v=FNS7VM5oTRU
Ross, F. (2020). *Big freedia talks New Orleans bounce history, drake, beyonce, being loud, proud + more*. [Video File]. https://www.youtube.com/watch?v=AQh4oq6YGyY
Ross, F. (2014). *Explode*. [Video File]. https://www.youtube.com/watch?v=Pa5IV_3fVfk
Sharpe, C. (2016). *In the wake: On blackness and being*. Duke University Press.
Smith, W. A., Allen, W. R., Danley, L. L. (2007). "Assume the position … you fit the description": Campus racial climate and the psychoeducational experience and racial battle fatigue among African American male college students. *American Behavioral Scientist*, *51*(4), 551–578. https://doi.org/10.1177/0002764207307742

Spivak, G. (1995). *The spivak reader*. Routledge.

Story, K. A. (2020). Black femme menace: How queer battle fatigue intersects with queerness and gender. *Journal of Lesbian and Gay Studies, 26*(2), 233–236.

Szwed, J. (1997). *Space is the place: The lives and times of sun Ra*. Da Capo Press.

Taylor, S. (2018). *The body is not and apology: The power of radical self-love*. Berrett-Koehler Publishers, Incorporated.

Tuck, E. (2009). Suspending damage: A letter to communities. *Harvard Educational Review, 79*(3), 409–427. https://doi.org/10.17763/haer.79.3.n0016675661t3n15

Vizenor, G. (1994). *Manifest manners: Post-Indian warriors of survivance*. Wesleyan University Press.

Wozolek, B., Varndell, R., & Speer, T. (2015). Are we not fatigued?: Queer battle fatigue at the intersection of heteronormative culture. *International Journal of Curriculum and Social Justice, 1*(1), 186–214.

Wright, M. (2015). *The physics of blackness: Beyond the middle passage epistemology*. University of Minnesota Press.

Young, T. (2016). *Black queer ethics, family, and philosophical imagination*. Palgrave Macmillan.

STEM as a Cover: Towards a Framework for Queer Emotions, Battle Fatigue, and STEM Identity

Mario I. Suárez, Andrea M. Hawkman, Colby Tofel-Grehl, Beth L. MacDonald, Kristin Searle, David F. Feldon, Taryn Sommers and Evelynn Foley-Hernandez

ABSTRACT
This study seeks to understand the daily violence endured by queer youth. We use Queer Battle Fatigue, Ahmed's cultural politics of emotion, and STEM identity theories to make meaning of youth's experience. We draw from audio recordings and transcriptions of 15 queer youth over the course of a summer and fall LGBTQ + maker camp in a rural town in the Intermountain Western part of the United States. Findings show that the maker camp environment provided queer campers casual conversations about microaggressions and violence endured at school. In this context, STEM served as a cover (concealed goals) in three ways: emotion, validation/advice, and safety. This particular environment provided them recognition and validation of both their STEM and queer identities, allowing the group to be able to casually mention these instances of violence they had endured.

Increasingly, research suggests that students' interest in and identification with Science, Technology, Engineering, and Mathematics (STEM) fields, as well as deep STEM learning, develop across time and settings (Ito et al., 2013; National Research Council, 2015). Young people spend only about 20% of their waking hours in school. Thus, informal STEM learning opportunities, those opportunities to engage with STEM skills and concepts outside of a classroom setting, play a crucial role in helping young people to develop interest in and identification with STEM and STEM career pathways. This is especially true for female-identified and minoritized youth, who may feel more of a connection to informal STEM learning activities (Tan et al., 2013; Polman & Miller, 2010). Successful informal STEM programs tackle issues of youth engagement, responsiveness to youth interests, and connection to other aspects of youths' lives in ways that in-school STEM activities typically do not (National Research Council, 2015). Further, such programs are typically embedded in communities and are often facilitated by adults or older youth in the community, thus establishing STEM role models (National Research Council, 2015). STEM role models are important because research suggests that developing an identity compatible with STEM is equally as important as exposure to and participation in STEM activities (Aschbacher et al., 2009; DeWitt & Archer, 2015; Tan et al., 2013; Wang & Degol, 2013). In considering identities compatible with STEM, we engage Kim et al.' (2018) definition of STEM identity as a "[S]ocially based identity grounded in the extent to which individuals see themselves and are accepted as a member of a STEM discipline or field (p. 591)." To that end, there is a need to create meaningful and integrated STEM learning experiences that provide foundational knowledge, prepare young people to become informed citizens, and seed their interest in and awareness of professional opportunities in STEM.

Making activities in informal STEM learning contexts have shown particular promise for supporting a range of STEM identities and practices while providing space for creativity, personal expression, and community engagement (Calabrese Barton & Tan, 2018; Halverson & Sheridan, 2014; Kafai et al., 2014; Peppler et al., 2016a, 2016b; Sheridan et al., 2014). In spite of this promise, makerspaces are frequently spaces where cisgender, white, middle- and upper-class youth are able to practice merging STEM education and creativity through traditional electronics and robotics projects (Brahms & Crowley, 2016; Buechley, 2013). The problem is exacerbated for STEM spaces that are often uninviting for queer identities (Cooper et al., 2019). Miller et al. (2020) refer to this phenomenon as "bro/dude culture," which can be a daunting and intimidating educational environment for queer[1] students who fall outside of a cisgender and/or heteronormative binary and who might not necessarily adhere to traditionally positivistic views presented in many STEM disciplines (Miller et al., 2020; Strunk & Hoover, 2019). In this study, we refer to makerspaces "as a uniquely American activity focused on technological forms of innovation that advance hands-on learning and contribute to the growth of the economy" (Vossoughi et al., 2016, p. 207). Thus, recent research focuses on factors that impact the recruitment and retention of queer students into STEM field in college, who are retained at lower rates than their non-queer counterparts in part due to negative self-concepts regarding their STEM identity and contributions to the field (Hughes, 2018). Helping queer students develop their STEM identities while affirming their sexual orientation and/or gender identity could contribute to increasing the pipeline to STEM careers and majors for queer students in college.

There is a growing body of research that studies queer people's STEM identity development (e.g. Mattheis et al., 2020; Yoder & Mattheis, 2016). Mattheis et al. (2019) developed a model of the internal and external factors influencing queer STEM identity development. These include defining one's gender identity, forming a STEM identity, and navigating the relationship between personal and professional identities in work and school contexts. For young people who may still be trying to define their gender identities, navigating when and where to express that identity and how to do so in heteronormative spaces is especially challenging. Thus, it is essential that we develop makerspaces where queer youth feel safe to define their sexual orientation and gender identity, form STEM compatible identities, and navigate between them across contexts (Freeman, 2018; Masters, 2018; Moorefield-Lang & Kitzie, 2018). These spaces should be diverse in terms of not just participants, but also activities, presenting queer youth with a variety of options regarding what it means to be a STEM professional. Though these activities should not be tailored specifically for queer youth as they benefit all youth, the reality as presented in the research shows that the experiences of queer and non-queer youth in STEM are drastically different. Moreover, through diversifying makerspaces, non-queer youth will also experience STEM learning situated in contexts that reflect the complexities of real life and will be encouraged to understand that queer people exist, and should exist, in all spaces and professions.

Here, we report on a series of maker camps developed for queer youth in the rural, Intermountain Western region of the United States (U.S.). Though the intent of the project was to increase STEM self-efficacy and engagement for queer youth as part of a larger project, once the campers felt safe, they started having casual conversations with their peers and instructors about personal challenges due to their gender identity and/or sexual orientation. These instances spoke to the aggressive and violent experiences they have endured in their small, rural community. As such, this study reports on the students' recollections of micro- and macro-aggressions endured in their daily lives, provided through the context of an informal STEM makerspace.

While we understand that these negative encounters can occur in everyday environments, considering their existence within STEM-identified spaces can instruct educators and researchers on how best to account and respond to them in similar contexts, given the intentionality given to this space by the research team and camp instructors.

Literature review

In order to better understand the micro- and macro-aggressions encountered daily by queer youth seeking to engage in informal STEM spaces, we review literature on (1) queer people in rural America, (2) experiences of queer youth in STEM spaces, and (3) informal STEM experiences for minoritized youth.

Queer people in Rural America

Queer people encounter different challenges given the sociopolitical context and environment in which they live, such as living in rural America in comparison to large, urban parts of the United States like New York City, San Francisco, or Los Angeles, among others. Some potential factors that contribute to the differences in experiences in rural communities is the level of education, access to resources, and usually low socioeconomic status of the community (Shelton & Lester, 2016; Stone, 2018), which negatively impact queer youth living in those areas (Palmer et al., 2012). These factors are particularly important when considering the experiences of queer youth. Rural communities are more static both in terms of the community culture and the structures of those communities. For example, research has documented that LGBTQ+ people of all ages in rural areas report negative experiences, largely in part due to lower levels of education and socioeconomic status and high levels of conservative religions that create a hostile environment for queer people (Palmer et al., 2012). Thus, factors such as external supports, access to resources, and community perspectives make the experiences of rural queer youth very difficult. For instance, in examining the number of LGBTQ+ pride organizations (as listed on www.lgbtqcenters.org) the state where the maker camp took place has one registered pride organization which happens to be located a major city almost two hours away. Conversely, New York State registers 24 discrete organizations, the bulk of which are in New York City. This points to the concentration of LGBTQ+ support organizations and services within urban spaces. With the lack of supports and services for LGBTQ+ youth (Palmer et al., 2012), the experiences of queer rural youth are fundamentally different than those of their urban counterparts.

Some of the most pervasive threads in the literature on queer people in rural spaces are those of isolation, harassment, lack of support and access to resources, and community connectedness (Paceley, 2020; Shelton & Lester, 2016; Swank et al., 2012), often due to cultural homogeneity (Swank et al., 2012). Based on the 2010–2011 GLSEN National School Climate Survey (Palmer et al., 2012), 97% of K-12 students in rural areas reported hearing homophobic remarks in school, with minimal intervention from faculty/staff (13%) or peers (6%). Additionally, over a third of queer students in rural areas reported missing school as a result of feeling unsafe and felt less connectedness to their schools, while only 11% reported learning about queer issues at school. A later study found similar results (Kosciw et al., 2015).

In rural areas, experiences of queer individuals vary depending on sociopolitical context of the location (i.e. "Deep South" vs. Midwest), as the Deep South (e.g. Alabama, Georgia, Louisiana, Mississippi, North Carolina, South Carolina, Texas) is deeply rooted in overt racism since prior to the Civil War. For example, Hall et al. (2018) studied the experiences of queer youth in rural North Carolina using photovoice, a method that centers the participant through the use of photographs. Hall et al. had Gay Straight Alliance members take pictures of what they wished others knew about their lives as part of the queer and ally community in that rural town; then proceeded to have a gallery exhibit which was presented to adults, with 20 who participated in the study. The findings showed that the adults who participated sensed the same isolation, judgement, hostility, and rejection from family and friends that queer youth expressed feeling in their small town. Moreover, the exhibit allowed for adults to visualize themselves in such a hostile environment. While progress had been made, the adults in the study noted that there was more work to be done and prompted them to be more involved in supporting these youth. Forstie (2018) also found that some of these same feelings were shared in a study of 25 queer women living in a rural Midwest town. In studying queer friendships, Forstie (2018) found when lesbians in that Midwest town felt isolated, they longed to have friendships with other queer women who could understand their experiences. Findings suggested that queer folks could potentially empathize more with similar relationships. On another hand, some queer women expressed what Forstie referred as "post-lesbian ambivalence" (or identity-blind) sentiments, meaning that the participants did not care whether their friends were queer or not. Shelton and Lester (2016) add that discrimination and racism are exacerbated for queer people of color in rural contexts.

Though isolation and need for queer friendships can be important for rural queer people, the literature also reveals positive relations between queer people. One of the first studies of queer youth took place in rural Kentucky and studied technology use as a form of finding community (Gray, 2007). Gray's documentation of their participants included AJ, a transman who talked about his transition in detail on a website in hopes of inspiring others like him to be their true selves. While most of the website's guestbook comments were from friends and family members, the comments also revealed rural and international audience who read AJ's journey. Gray found that queer youth connected in a small, rural town by meeting at the local Wal-Mart for several hours, as it could be used as a runway when dressing in drag. The level of support these youth received either from online connections or in person connections helped them become resilient to the small-town harassment and threats they experienced. Findings also indicated that these online and in-person connections created liberating experiences that they were able to share. A study by Swank et al. (2012) comparing 285 queer people from rural and urban areas found that even when those in rural areas reported greater levels of minority stress, they also reported lower levels of discrimination. Additionally, those participants with higher income felt more connected to their queer community and felt less discrimination. A quantitative study of 151 rural queer youth in California found that having support and an affirming schooling environment (i.e. teachers, staff, administration, peers) improved feelings of safety (De Pedro et al., 2018). However, De Pedro et al. (2018) surprisingly also found that having a Gay Straight Alliance negatively impacted safety, attributing it to possible inconsistent attendance and homophobia prevalent in rural areas. These studies summarize some of the hardships that come with living in rural contexts for queer people.

Queer youth in STEM spaces

President Obama's administration launched a report titled *Engage to Excel* in 2012 as a call to increase the pipeline for STEM professionals and in particular, engaging minoritized youth in STEM. In hopes of engaging minoritized populations (e.g. Latinx, Black, LGBTQ+), some scholars have called for a decolonization of STEM. Efforts to decolonize STEM include shifts in fundamental STEM epistemologies and structures that leverage curricula and testing development in schools. For instance, in mathematics education, Gutiérrez (2017) termed the phrase *mathematx*, which is "a way of seeking, acknowledging, and creating patterns for the purpose of solving problems (e.g. survival) and experiencing joy" (p. 12). For Gutiérrez, *mathematx* is different from ethnomathematics in that it embraces and comes from indigenous and decolonized epistemological ways of knowing, it embraces a "both/and" perspective, and rejects binaries created by

Western epistemologies. Similarly, Rands (2019) refers to this notion of challenging heteronormativity in mathematics as *mathematical inqueery*.

Research addressing STEM engagement, self-efficacy, and academic achievement of queer students focuses primarily in higher education (Brinkworth, 2016; Butterfield et al., 2018; Cech & Rothwell, 2018; Hughes, 2018; Leyva, 2016; Linley et al., 2018; Miller et al., 2020). Though these studies have been crucial in understanding the terrain that queer students encounter once they arrive at a university, it is important to understand the K-12 contextual factors that play a role in the STEM pipeline for queer youth. One of the themes that run through research in this area is the primarily heteronormative, cisnormative nature of STEM. For example, Leyva (2017) conducted a literature review of mathematics education research on achievement and participation of students. He found that achievement was usually assessed quantitatively and engaged in binary operationalization of gender, which often privileges White, heterosexual, cisgender males. Studies that addressed participation as an outcome used qualitative methods, and the more recent ones engaged in intersectional analyses. Heybach and Pickup (2017) echo these limitations in STEM research by asserting that diversity in STEM typically focuses on improving access for cisgender, heterosexual women.

In spite of navigating an environment that is not entirely conducive to STEM learning for queer youth, some research exists that identifies positive outcomes. One of the first quantitative and longitudinal studies to examine sexual minority youth in STEM used the Add Health data from 1994 to 2002 (Gottfried et al., 2015). Gottfried et al. (2015) analyzed the number of advanced STEM courses taken by high school sexual minority students. These data were then compared to their heterosexual counterparts. Findings showed that these two groups' STEM course enrollment were not significantly different from each other. Fischer (2013) examined relationships between six queer youths' mathematical identity and queer identity at a large east coast city. Fischer found that some of the factors that contributed to a positive queer identity consisted of having a Gay Straight Alliance, supportive teachers and schooling environment, extracurricular after-school support, and support from family and friends, thus reinforcing the need for these in STEM contexts.

With a surge in the maker movement and makerspaces, there have been some of these spaces that have targeted queer youth's engagement in STEM. Masters (2018) asserts that maker spaces are perfectly situated to include minoritized populations as an "equalizer", though only a handful actually do. Moorefield-Lang and Kitzie (2018) specifically address seven questions in creating maker spaces that can also be safe spaces for queer youth. Among them, they assert that in order for maker spaces to also be safe spaces, they must be queer-inclusive in terms of curriculum, rules, accountability, and accessibility. Given these findings, it is distressing to learn that far few of these spaces exist across the United States (Riley et al., 2017), as resources and accessibility vary from region to region. One example that has been presented at the American Geophysical Union annual meeting is that of a program called Queers in STEM (QSTEM) in Los Angeles, where queer students have participated in camp-like STEM experiences (Ulrich et al., 2019). These findings provide contexts for supportive environments in STEM that paved the way for the creation of the makerspace environment provided in this study.

Informal STEM experiences for minoritized youth

In opposition to the dominant view of making "as a uniquely American activity focused on technological forms of innovation that advance hands-on learning and contribute to the growth of the economy" (Vossoughi et al., 2016, p. 207), a number of scholars have put forth equity-oriented frameworks for making. These frameworks require us to critically attend to educational injustice and pedagogy, acknowledge and value the making practices found in diverse communities in the present moment and historically, and remain conscious of the sociopolitical values of making (e.g. Barajas-López & Bang, 2018; Vossoughi et al., 2016). Drawing on equity-oriented approaches to making, a number of scholars have documented the outcomes of equity-oriented making activities for minoritized youth (e.g. Barajas-López & Bang, 2018; Calabrese Barton & Tan, 2018; Searle et al., 2019; Tzou et al., 2019). These activities have emphasized the use of original technologies that utilize low-tech materials (e.g. clay) alone or in conjunction with high-tech materials (e.g. circuits), and technology hacking (e.g. remixing code). These scholars also address heritage and language grounded in cultural connections and equity issues of consequence to the participating youth. For instance, Calabrese Barton and Tan (2018) documented how two girls spent eight months creating a light up, heated jacket after identifying safety while commuting as an experienced faced by youth in the community. Throughout the research on equity-oriented approaches to making is a goal of connecting youths' existing identities to the development of STEM-compatible identities. Findings from these studies suggest that these connections develop most effectively when students develop personally meaningful projects, engage with authentic audiences, and when researchers broaden conceptualizations of STEM to allow multiple points of STEM access.

Central to the work presented here are the ways in which making practices provide opportunities for self-expression and personalization that are often not afforded to youth in other STEM contexts. Youth make projects that express aspects of their identities, such as a light up, musical tote bag made by a student from Jamaica with a light indicating his home town and Bob Marley playing (Kafai et al., 2014) or a clay incense burner in the shape of an otter made by an Indigenous youth in the Pacific Northwest (Barajas-López & Bang, 2018).

Theoretical frameworks

This study blends three theories to frame this study: Queer Battle Fatigue (QBF) (Wozolek et al., 2015), cultural politics of emotion (Ahmed, 2014), and STEM identity (Carlone & Johnson, 2007) to better understand how experiences of queer students in a rural town in the U.S. Intermountain West influence their perceived societal norms related to possible STEM identity construction.

Queer battle fatigue

Queer Battle Fatigue (QBF) is a framework coined by Wozolek et al. (2015) to explain exhaustion queer people and their allies experience (Gershon, 2020) when enduring daily acts of societal (micro)aggressions and ontological aggressions. Born as an extension to Racial Battle Fatigue (RBF; Franklin et al., 2014; Smith et al., 2011, 2016), QBF is distinctly different from RBF in its intentional fluidity (i.e. queer). This fluidity prevents constraints to the framing of dynamic identities in relation to societal values and behavioral norms under examination. Wozolek et al. (2015) assert QBF often evidences itself in verbal dialogue describing (micro)aggressions as explicit or implicit and not small in nature. Moreover, queer people describe fatigue when encountering ontological aggressions, which result due to preconceived societal structures that suggest how groups of people should be engaged regularly. When encountering (micro)aggressions and ontological aggressions, queer people are left exhausted from picking and choosing battles, resulting in their resilience and/or resistance to these aggressions.

Aggressions queer people experience take many forms. For example, ontological aggressions can be manifested through queer-friendly (or the lack of) policies with trans youth unable to go to the restroom that aligns with their gender identity or other schooling practices (Mayo, 2020; Miller et al., 2020). Macro-aggressions and micro-aggressions also show up in casual encounters with peers at school for a Latinx trans man who was being friendly and called a "whatever" (Suárez, 2020), or with a self-identified Black Femme Professor who is undermined in class by a so-called

White cisgender feminist female (Story, 2020). These implicit, yet important events can affect a queer person significantly. Given, possible negative effects, findings also evidence queer people developing resilience and resistance in response to these aggressions. For instance, González (2020), a Latinx lesbian Professor who identifies as "fat, butch, [and] feminist" learned to see her imposter syndrome feelings as her "armor" and "intersectional chainmail" (p. 237). QBF can be disrupted through dialogue around societal categories and values related to aggressions queer people experience (Wozolek et al., 2015). In this paper, we consider how these particular disruptions to QBF may occur when queer youth, enrolled in a STEM camp, engage in this type of dialogue.

Cultural politics of emotion

The field of STEM has a reputation of being dry and emotion-less (i.e. positivist), an emotion that is reproduced, according to Ahmed (2014), culturally over time. Ahmed (2014) writes that "norms surface *as* [sic] the surfaces of bodies; norms are a matter of impressions, of how bodies are 'impressed upon' by the world, as a world made up of others. In other words, such impressions are effects of labor; how bodies work and are worked upon shapes the surfaces of bodies (p. 145)." In reference to queer people, Ahmed explains that feelings of (dis)comfort in a heteronormative society may, over time, influence queer people to assimilate to the norms of a certain culture. However, with this assimilation comes a sense of queering, which results from the "disturbances" created in not being part of the norm. For example, being that a family has historically been viewed as a marriage between a man and a woman with the sole purpose of biological reproduction, referring to a queer couple as a "queer family", according to Ahmed, "interrupt[s] one ideal image of the family" (p. 153). In this case, being that STEM is referred to as an emotion-less field, we hypothesize that queer students may "queer" STEM in the sense that they may adopt more affective ways of exploring their queer and STEM identities.

STEM identity

One's STEM identity can also be shaped with particular ontological frames, as determined by white, masculine values negotiated in science (Carlone & Johnson, 2007). Essentially, Carlone and Johnson (2007) describe identity as encapsulating "[I]ndividual agency as well as societal structures that constrain individual possibilities" (Brickhouse, 2000, p. 286 as cited in Carlone & Johnson, 2007, p. 1188). In particular, STEM identity, which can be measured quantitatively or qualitatively, consists of individuals' feelings of: *competence, performance*, and *recognition*. Competence refers to individuals' feelings of success when engaging in STEM content. When individuals display signs of STEM proficiency in socially acceptable ways, they are said to evidence performance. Finally, recognition refers to one's own view when developing fluency or expertise in STEM. Carlone and Johnson (2007) explain that these three aspects of STEM identity interact with other aspects of one's identity (e.g. socioeconomic status, race, gender identity, sexuality), and do not exist in a vacuum. Quite often, people of color and females evidence values that are at odds with those associated with science communities, preventing many from identifying as competent, from performing in acceptable ways, and from recognizing their own fluency and expertise. Given, such constraints, Carlone and Johnson (2007) explain that individuals have life-long opportunities to develop STEM identities, as identity is not predetermined or fixed. In fact, findings suggest that one's science identity is shaped by developing social structures and communities of practice aligned with values and behavioral norms of those underrepresented in STEM (Carlone & Johnson, 2007; Tan et al., 2013). Thus, for this STEM maker camp, we were particularly interested in how the intersection of an affirming STEM environment through the intentional curriculum design and professional development provided to the research team and instructors, contributed to their STEM competence, performance, and recognition, since STEM identity has not been used to explore experiences of queer students in STEM.

We frame this study in the intersection of QBF, cultural politics of emotion, and STEM identity to better understand how particular communities of practices (STEM identity) aligned with values expressed by queer youth (cultural politics of emotion), attending our maker Summer and Fall camps, removed aggressions and constraints (QBF) to their individual possibilities as they developed dialogue centered on reliance and resistance. See Figure 1 for a description of each of the theoretical frameworks and how we hypothesize the intersection of these at play in the context of this STEM maker camp. Based on the review of literature, it may be possible that having an intervention such as this camp for queer youth may provide a safe environment where students are able to speak about their experiences as queer individuals with their peers. To that end, this study asks:

> In what ways can a queer youth and allies STEM maker camp help queer youth navigate their queerness and STEM identity? What role (if any) did this space serve for the participants' exploration of their STEM identity, QBF, and expression of emotions?

Method

Researchers' positionalities

We are a group of university faculty and research assistants housed within a college of education at a research institution located in the rural Intermountain West. Within our research team, individuals embody identities across the LGBTQ+ spectrum, while some members of the team are

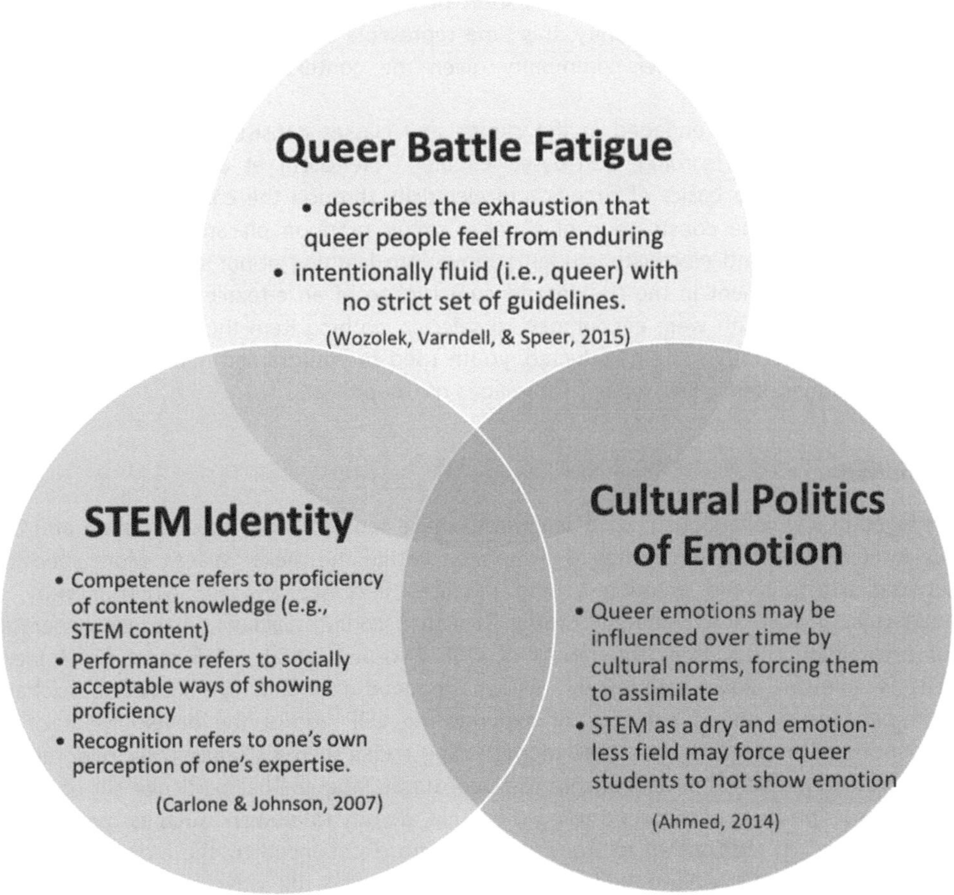

Queer Battle Fatigue
- describes the exhaustion that queer people feel from enduring
- intentionally fluid (i.e., queer) with no strict set of guidelines.

(Wozolek, Varndell, & Speer, 2015)

STEM Identity
- Competence refers to proficiency of content knowledge (e.g., STEM content)
- Performance refers to socially acceptable ways of showing proficiency
- Recognition refers to one's own perception of one's expertise.

(Carlone & Johnson, 2007)

Cultural Politics of Emotion
- Queer emotions may be influenced over time by cultural norms, forcing them to assimilate
- STEM as a dry and emotionless field may force queer students to not show emotion

(Ahmed, 2014)

Figure 1. Description of theoretical frameworks.

also pursuing allyship to the queer community. Throughout the research process, we individually and collectively reflected on our identities, knowledges, and experiences relating to queerness, STEM, and emotion as a way to make sense of our positionality throughout the study. This reflective process afforded queer members of the team the ability to process their own experiences with queer battle fatigue in academic and social spaces and provided ally members of the team an opportunity to critically interrogate their cisnormative and heteronormative privilege.

Context of the STEM maker camps

We draw from audio recordings and transcriptions of 15 queer youth over the course of multi-session summer and fall LGBTQ+ maker camps, instructor reflective journals, and researcher field notes. In advance of the maker camps, instructors and researchers participated in LGBTQ+ allyship training, provided by a university-sponsored queer resource center. The camps were open free of charge for youth (ages 10–17) who identified as LGBTQ+ or allies. Participants were recruited from nearby schools, the local LGBTQ+ resource center, social media, and by word of mouth within the community. All camps took place at the local library in a rural town in the U.S. Intermountain West. Each program (Summer and Fall) lasted approximately 10 hours. The Summer program lasted for five consecutive days for two hours per session. The Fall program was after school and consisted of seven sessions (once a week), each about one and a half hours in length. Each session in both programs introduced the youth to a STEM concept (e.g. circuitry, e-textiles) through a project (e.g. pronoun nametags, mask making). While ten hours of contact time might on the surface appear a short period of time, for youth with no opportunity to safely gather as a queer community, this time represents a significant magnitude increase in time together within the queer community given the context of this rural town with little resources.

The project curriculum engaged in the camps and classes consisted of a three-level faded scaffolded approach to learning craft-based circuits (Tofel-Grehl et al., 2017). Students first engaged in learning the basics of circuits and electricity through the construction of paper circuits, culminating in the construction of a paper circuit pronoun placard. After understanding the basics of circuits and electricity, students move into learning about switches and short circuits through engagement in the design and construction of an e-textile bracelet. For the final project in the class, youth were encouraged to select a clothing item that they wished to make light up. With these clothing items selected, youth used pre-programed microprocessors to create light up clothing items. See Table 1 for images of the projects.

Data analysis

We engaged in a simultaneous coding scheme to make sense of how queer emotion and battle fatigue interacted with STEM identity development within the maker spaces. More specifically, we utilized structural and emotion coding practices informed by QBF, STEM Identity, and Ahmed's cultural politics of emotion. Through structural coding (Saldaña, 2016) we generated a set of preliminary codes from the tenets of QBF (Wozolek et al., 2015) and STEM Identity (Carlone & Johnson, 2007) frameworks. As we engaged the data, we identified exchanges wherein participants shared evidence of experiencing QBF and/or the development of their STEM identities. For example, data were tagged using codes such as "implicit microaggressions", "explicit microaggressions", in relationship to queer battle fatigue. That particular set of excerpts from the transcripts were then coded using the STEM identity framework, such as "performance", and "recognition", in relationship to the situation being experienced by the individual. Through this dual layer attribute coding (Saldaña, 2016), we identified the ways participants expressed concerns related to QBF alongside the development of their STEM identities.

Table 1. Class/Camp curriculum examples.

Project	Description	STEM concepts/ applications	Example
Identity Name Tags	This project helps youth learn each other's names and pronouns in the class/camp context. The name tags help folks be mindful of each other's identities.	This project ensures participants learn how to construct basic circuits to make LEDs light up as part of the artistic design of the name tag.	
E-textile Bracelets	These bracelets provide an opportunity for youth to make an artifact that reflects their identity in any way they choose.	This project reinforces the construction of basic circuits that light up multiple LEDs integrated in the bracelet.	
Pre-programmed Clothing Project	This project requires the design and construction of an item of clothing incorporating a computational circuit.	Students engaged in designing and constructing computational circuits with preprogrammed microprocessors that allowed them to integrate technology and science within a wearable object.	

Note. Examples drawn from queer maker camp.

Drawing upon Ahmed's (2014) concept of the cultural politics of emotion, we simultaneously examined the data in consideration of the ways in which queer emotionalities functioned within the space. Through emotion coding (Saldaña, 2016), we made sense of the ways that queer participants utilized the STEM camp as a space to process feelings they encountered as queer youth in a rural community (e.g. joy, dissonance, frustration, uncertainty). By combining structural and affective coding practices we were able to make sense of the fluidity through which queer emotionality is expressed in relation to QBF and STEM identity. Coding was iterative and flexible, while also providing members of the research team the ability to draw on our shared conceptual framing. We met before, during, and after the coding process to ask and answer questions, ensure clarity of code interpretation, and generate consistency. Once simultaneous coding was complete, the codes were analyzed and grouped into themes in order for us to generate understanding of how the space served to explore participants' STEM identity, QBF, and expression of queer emotions.

Findings

Findings show that by providing queer campers an inclusive STEM environment, they more readily discussed their experiences at school vis-à-vis STEM identity's *competence, performance,* and *recognition,* as campers' STEM and queer identities developed positively, while also developing resilience to microaggressions (Wozolek et al., 2015). For instance, instructors affirmed and enforced chosen names and pronouns, which made campers feel safe to openly talk about microaggressions related to their queerness (e.g. being misgendered at school). One of the most evident results from this study was how secondary these youth's STEM identities were to these youth. We uncovered that through framing this camp within STEM skill development, queer youth participants utilized the space to engage their queerness directly and openly, sometimes represented through emotional episodes. However, in the majority of the instances mentioned in the next couple sections, students initiated all interactions with adults through one or all of the STEM identity forms. That is, before mentioning a difficult experience they encountered to adults, they often sought recognition or affirmation of their competence and/or performance in the STEM activity they were working on at that time. In this sense, STEM functioned as a cover for their queerness in this conservative rural community. Though STEM was the end product and way to get to this maker space, it served a secondary purpose. In this context, STEM served as a cover in three ways: emotion, validation/advice, and safety. Though presented as separate themes, they all worked in tandem with each other as evidenced in some of the vignettes featured below. All names of the youth have been changed to maintain anonymity.

Within the context of this study, we recognize that our STEM camp afforded youth with a cover for their engagement with the group. As noted earlier, the camp was listed for LGBTQ + youth and their allies. The decision to include allies was an intentional one. Because of the highly religious and conservative nature of the community in which this work was conducted, we recognize that not all youth who might benefit from participating in such an affinity group might be out. Thus, youth who engaged in our camp had an automatic explanation beyond their sexuality and gender for engaging in our camp. With that as context, we explore how youth as a group with common identity and interest explored the emotions around their experiences within the safe, constructed space of our LGBTQ + camps. Here, we briefly discuss each of the three acts of cover the STEM spaces provided.

STEM as a cover for emotion

A STEM maker camp, as a more socially acceptable activity in rural, conservative and highly religious town in the U.S. Intermountain West, allowed students to express their emotions and experiences with bullying and harassment in school and their everyday experiences. Here, campers were able to be honest and blunt about their experiences with bullying and harassment from peers at school, family members, and teachers.

QBF helped give a name to the fatigue these students are experiencing, such as with Charlie, who visibly broke down in one of the camps about wanting to live stealthily as a man (Camp Transcript, 7/18/19). As Charlie struggled to express himself, overwhelmed with the weight of the emotions he felt, his classmates and teachers rallied around him and tried to empathize, as they saw he was noticeably distraught. The group engaged in a concerted and organized effort to support Charlie both in their physical and verbal engagement with him, apparent by jokes and laughter they engaged in, as evidenced by the brief conversation below between Christina, one of the camp instructors, Charlie, the distraught queer student, and a concerned peers, Aubrey, Vincent, and Wren.

> Christina: Yeah, it's hard. Yeah, it's hard finding like good folks in [the name of the town] sometimes
>
> Charlie: Yeah
>
> ...
>
> Christina: How do you feel? How do you feel in this group?
>
> Charlie: It's nice
>
> Christina: It's nice, good. Cause I know, like I know martial arts like I can take care of it
>
> *Laughing*
>
> Vincent: I'm learning fencing so I can take care of it
>
> Researcher: Wait who's a fencer?
>
> Christina: Who's a fen...I think they are yeah
>
> Aubrey: We are totally doing it

Wren: Fencing sounds so fun, but I don't

Christina: Do you like carry a mini sword in your pocket

Vincent: No, I wish

Wren: Would you use fencing as self-defense?

Vincent: I haven't like fully started yet, like we are trying to figure out the coach situation, but like I kinda know how to fence

...

Charlie: Cause I used to have like growing up my hair was super long, and I didn't really like it but my dad wanted me to keep it that way and then my mom finally let me cut it when like back here somewhere and I loved it so much. I think it was like fifth grade I completely chopped it off and then I was like it is too short, and then I grew it to like here. And then when I came out it was like right here, but I guess because I had just barely come out it was kinda like.

Christina: Oh yeah, we all did that, where it's like oh we just came out, we have to make ourselves look hyper one way like. You wanna like fit the stereotype, you wanna be like I am this stereotype respect me

Aubrey: I came out as bi and I shaved the back of my head

Wren: I wore nothing but like flanels for the longest time

Laughing

Christina: We all done that. And now you're gonna grow it out to like shoulders?

Charlie: Yeah probably, somewhere around there it's shaggy

Christina: Nice!

Charlie: I liked having my hair like around that or at least like being able to put it up like in a bun, it's always so nice

Christina: Yeah like those man buns are pretty good

Charlie: Yeah I know, that's what I wanna do. Now that I'm on T it will be easier for me, you know to pass better

Christina: Oh yeah totally

Charlie: So now I can do it and hopefully it will be okay and I won't have to break down and cut it off

After his initial breakdown, Christina, the class instructor, pulled him aside to talk through the heavy and complex feelings he was experiencing; Charlie was able to tell the instructor about his inability to experience consistent and meaningful gender affirmation in his current home situation. The depth of Charlie's pain was evident in his rubbing of the self-harming scars visible on his arms. Charlie's teacher spent the next hour listening and affirming his perception, his feelings, and his experience as a trans man living in a highly rural religious community. Charlie's classmates also worked to support him. Christina, the teacher, wrote the following in their reflective journal after the incident.

> He [Charlie] was in the middle of explaining his experience on T (he is a trans man). I validated and supported, asking how I could help and giving options for new sensory environments or activities. After a few minutes, I asked him to finish what he was saying about T. He started talking about how he wants to be "stealth" and a couple of his friend groups have been spreading that he is trans and that everyone knows and then transphobia comes out. He really wants to be stealth. Me and another participant (a cis girl) validated and acknowledged his feelings and experience. He calmed down and things became chill again. (Instructor Reflective Journal, 7/18/19)

Upon his return to the larger group to work on his projects, Charlie's peers, youth he had not met prior to that week, enveloped him in a palpable nest of care. Each member of his table group checked in on him to make sure he could catch up on the project, threading his needles for the e-textile project, gathering his supplies, and helping him debug short circuits in his work.

While their help was STEM focused, the group successfully supported and validated Charlie through his despair and back to present moment wherein he was able to engage in the community of affirmation built by his peers and teachers. This space made a conscious attempt to not reproduce the same type of actions that inhibit students' emotions, thus queering the space (Ahmed, 2014).

STEM as a cover for affirmation and advice

Secondly, students felt that their queerness was validated and affirmed in this space, while still engaging them in exploring their STEM identities simultaneously. Participants sought validation regarding their experiences as it relates to QBF. Specifically, participants communed over shared queer microaggressions they experienced at school and home. It was evident that through these exchanges, participants found solace from each other and camp instructors.

In feeling affirmed, campers sought advice on how best to navigate situations that were uniquely queer and rife with exposure to QBF. For example, during a session in the Fall 2019 maker camp, one participant, Jim, was struggling with how to support a queer friend (not participating in the camp) who was in the midst of a gender identity crisis (Camp Transcript, 11/5/19). Within the camp, Jim sought advice from Christina, the camp instructor, a trans person herself and community leader. In one instance, Jim waited until the end of the class to ask for advice.

Jim: Also, I don't know if this is the right place to get advice on this, but whenever a friend texts you at 3:00 a.m. and they're either about to say something really funny or they're having an issue—and one of my friends, while I was on the debate trip—I was just getting to sleep. They texted me. I look up and check my phone, and they're having a bit of a gender identity crisis, and I don't know how to help them. It feels just like they're going to ignore it, and I feel that's [background noise 01:37:58] —

Christina: Tell them that you hear them and ask them what they want your role to be in that situation.

[Crosstalk and background noise]

Christina: Does that make sense?

Jim: Yeah. I don't know. They've been having mental health issues for a while, and then this actually makes a lot of sense and would explain a lotta stuff they said they've been feeling over the past couple years.

Christina: Yeah, totally.

Jim: It feels really rough for them.

Christina: Yeah. I would say just tell them that you're [background noise] in the situation [background noise] want your role to be.

Jim: Yeah. It's just like, every time they talk about it, and I'm like, "All right, what can I do now? What do you want me to do? How can I help you?" It just turns into, "No, I'm going to ignore it."

Jim: Interesting. Maybe, if you [background noise], hey, I hear you. This is one. What do you think? I don't know. Maybe just work on their reassurance and validation instead of like a, "You tell me what to do."

Researcher: Recognize that it takes people different timeframes to figure that stuff out. I know somebody who's my age who just came out as [name of person] and just started transitioning. It took her 40-plus years to get to a point where she was comfortable doing that in her life.

Jim: Yeah. No, it's really rough to watch 'cause I'm like, "Oh—"

Youth also noted how refreshing and novel it was for adults and peers to work towards mindfulness about their pronouns. As Ace reflected on during the summer camp both staff and campers made a conscious effort to use the correct pronouns for all community members. When someone misgendered another person accidentally, all community members worked together to consistently correct pronouns; there was a community effort to affirm identities through both action and reaction. Ace noted that they had never had an experience where so many people paid close attention to their pronouns and affirm their identity.

Ace was so comfortable in the STEM camp that they opted to attend camp one day in a full cosplay costume that allowed them to express their feminine persona without ceding their non-binary identity.

The following exchange occurred between Ace, Christina, the camp instructor, and a peer.

Ace: Three people noticed me today.

Christina: What?

Ace: Three people noticed me, like, noticed my character! And I was like YES!

Other student: Oh like they knew who it was?

Christina: Nice!

Other student: That's awesome!

Ace: Like, Junko, from Danganronpa, and I'm like, yes!

Christina: That's good! That sounds like it'd be very validating.

Ace: Mhmm.

Christina: Cool.

Ace: Love when that happens, and you're like yay!

Christina: Like … you understand, thank god

Despite sharing their struggle to gain recognition for their non-binary identity, Ace felt safe enough within the constructs of their STEM maker camp as to explore gender neutrality. For them, being engaged in a STEM space that supported all identities allowed them to drop the typically necessary rigidity of portraying themselves as non-binary.

STEM as a cover for safety

Thirdly, students felt a sense of safety in this space that was not often experienced at school or around the town. Due to the lack of queer-identified spaces within their rural community, students suggested that they often felt unsafe—whether it be in school or when attempting to find "safe" spaces to exist in their community. They casually mentioned feeling unsafe in a very manner-of-fact way.

Though not specifically related to gender identity and/or sexuality safety, the students mentioned casual things they encountered in their everyday life related to safety. For example, in one instance the students mention seeing meth pipes on their way to the queer maker camp at the town's library, and immediately went right back to working on their STEM assignment, as evidenced in the following interaction between Ty and Brandi below.

Ty: Oh, guess what I found on the way walking over here?

Brandi: What?

Ty: I found a heroin needle in the bushes walking over here.

Brandi: Someone left a used meth pipe in my neighbor's yard. I live in the most boring part of town.

Another aspect of safety that students experienced in the classes was the ability to explore their gender identity in a safe and STEM focused way. The selection of a clothing project as the summative project for the program was intentional. By having kids create clothing-based projects wherein the focus was incorporating STEM into the clothing, youth were afforded a unique opportunity to select clothing for any gender. In order to support students in this, the camp procured dozens of clothing that would typically be deemed "masculine" and "feminine" as well as many items that did not reflect society's normal gender expectations. These clothing items were presented to the class as theirs to use as they saw fit. Youth were eager and excited to create items that were choosing. One camper, identifying as male, selected a pink shirt and sewed a computational circuit on to it. When queried he noted he was making the t-shirt for his brother. However, upon follow up discussion, he noted the shirt was going to be for him. With barriers broken and a secure community, youth proceeded in their work on the STEM projects. In this way STEM was a cover for more safely exploring gender identity.

A final aspect of safety came in the form of a discussion with one of the researchers regarding safety in locker rooms and the hesitation that Vale, a trans male, felt in signing up for gym class at school, which another student joined into about halfway through the conversation (Camp Transcript, 10/22/19).

> Vale: Oh, I have him [referring to a teacher] next semester, but joke's on all of them. I get to take online gym 'cause I don't feel safe in the locker rooms. I don't know if I'd be allowed or at least safe in the locker rooms at school, so I'm probably gonna take online gym 'cause that's an option 'cause I still have to get gym credits unless I can get a parent to sign off. Usually, you have to have a health condition that makes it so you can't. I don't know. My mom was like, "Well, we go to the gym all the time, so I'll just get you on online gym." Besides, I thought gym class was pretty useless myself. I'm hoping I can do that for the—I think I need two more gym credits.

When asked what the school could do to make it safer for him to go to gym, Vale responds:

> Vale: I'm not sure about the locker room situation 'cause it's not even the—it would mostly be the boys, I guess, that would be a concern 'cause—
>
> Peer: 'Cause guys can be schmucks.
>
> Vale: Guys can be schmucks. Also there's an issue with privacy. Some may not feel comfortable around me, and people would also, probably, try to peek 'cause there are some real pervs in this school.

The identities designed in this space became more visible as campers' STEM identity was accepted and recognized as competent (Carlone & Johnson, 2007). As students participated in maker activities and completed maker projects, they demonstrated their abilities to complete STEM tasks in meaningful ways within the queer space afforded to them. Finally, we posit the nature of the STEM curriculum (e.g. creating pronoun nametags and masks with circuits and e-textiles) afforded campers multiple entry points and allowed for personal and meaningful content engagement.

Discussion

This study sought to better understand ways in which STEM makers spaces can intentionally serve to foster and affirm queer youth's STEM and queer identities. While the development of STEM identities was central to design of the camps, participants engagement with each other evidenced the reality that queer identities and safety were integral to their experience, often overpowering their STEM identity. In this context, STEM served as a cover in three ways: emotion, validation, and safety. By this, we first mean that a STEM maker camp, as a more socially acceptable activity in rural, conservative and highly religious town in the U.S. Intermountain West, allowed students to express their emotions and experiences with bullying and harassment in school and their everyday experiences. Here, campers were able to be honest and blunt about their experiences with bullying and harassment from peers at school, family members, and teachers. QBF helped give a name to the fatigue these students are experiencing, such as with Charlie who visibly broke down in one of the camps about wanting to live stealthily as a man. This STEM space made a conscious attempt to not reproduce the same type of actions that inhibit students' emotions often apparent in STEM environments, thus queering the space

(Ahmed, 2014). Secondly, students felt that their queerness was validated and affirmed in this space, while still engaging them in exploring their STEM identities simultaneously. Thirdly, students felt a sense of safety in this space that was not often experienced at school or around the town. They mentioned feeling unsafe taking classes like gym class, and even walking around the park and seeing meth pipes. In a way, we attribute these findings to the privilege afforded to a primarily cisnormative and heteronormative field like STEM, a field that provides enough monetary support to have such a maker space where queer youth and their allies could come together without the need for performance. Additionally, we attribute the support that the students felt to the amount of training, sensitivity, and awareness that the instructors and research team had gone through before the camps started.

We think this study has the potential to contribute to the literature on queer studies and to STEM literature. As was mentioned prior in the literature, STEM has a reputation of being a very dry field where emotions must be regulated in order to be successful (Rice et al., 2019; Rozek et al., 2019). The findings from this study show that STEM teachers need not affix themselves or their classes to just teaching content. One can still teach about culturally responsive topics (e.g. pronouns, identity beads, masks we wear) while teaching STEM concepts without having to sacrifice one or the other.

The findings add significantly to the gap created by the use of the three theoretical frameworks often used in isolation. While QBF and the cultural politics of emotion are often used to put the experiences of queer people in context, they do not expand to STEM environments. Additionally, STEM identity as a framework has not been used to explore the experiences of queer students. This study breaches the gaps created by those frameworks in the literature. Being that the majority of the research on queer students in rural spaces take place in non-STEM environments, and most of the STEM education research does not address the needs of queer students, this research is uniquely suited to help STEM practitioners and researchers seeking to understand how best to meet the needs of queer students within their classrooms and in their research.

Implications for practitioners

The findings of this study highlight some implications that could be relevant to educators and their administrators. Specifically, for STEM educators, though this study took place in an informal context, it provides a vision of the potential of what could be possible when STEM is embedded in a social justice-oriented curriculum. That is, it is not necessary to separate social justice and STEM content. Both can be taught simultaneously, even in the most rural and conservative towns. Additionally, it is crucial for administrators to recognize the importance in supporting their teachers who are trying to implement similar programs and curriculum in their schools, as this type of work cannot be done in a vacuum. Upon reflecting on the work that this research team has embarked on in STEM, we recognize how crucial holding each other accountable is. For example, when someone in the research team or one of the camp staff misgendered a student, others came in and constantly corrected that person, while change does not happen overnight. It took a very conscious effort, constant training and awareness, and a lot of reflection to provide such a space for the queer youth who attended this camp.

Note

1. For the purposes of this manuscript, we use the term "queer" to mean anyone who identifies as lesbian, gay, bisexual, intersex, transgender, gender nonbinary, nonconforming, among other non-cisnormative or heteronormative categories.

Disclosure statement

No potential conflict of interest was reported by the author(s).

ORCID

Mario I. Suárez http://orcid.org/0000-0001-6008-1664
Andrea M. Hawkman http://orcid.org/0000-0002-4937-2468
Colby Tofel-Grehl http://orcid.org/0000-0002-4270-4060
Beth L. MacDonald http://orcid.org/0000-0002-5561-2026
Kristin Searle http://orcid.org/0000-0002-3465-4366
David F. Feldon http://orcid.org/0000-0003-3268-5764

References

Ahmed, S. (2014). *The cultural politics of emotion* (2nd ed.). Edinburgh University Press.
Aschbacher, P. R., Li, E., & Roth, E. (2009). Is science me? High school students' identities, participation and aspirations in science, engineering, and medicine. *Journal of Research in Science Teaching*, *47*(5), n/a–582. https://doi.org/10.1002/tea.20353
Barajas-López, F., & Bang, M. (2018). Indigenous making and sharing: Claywork in an Indigenous ST EAM program. *Equity & Excellence in Education*, *51*(1), 7–20. https://doi.org/10.1080/10665684.2018.1437847
Brahms, L., & Crowley, C. (2016). Making sense of making: Defining learning practices in MAKE magazine. In K. Peppler, E. R. Halverson, & Y. B. Kafai (Eds.), *Makeology: Makers as learners*. (Vol. 2, pp. 11–28). Routledge.
Brinkworth, C. S. (2016). *From chilly climate to warm reception: Experiences and good. practices for supporting LGBTQ students in STEM* [Unpublished doctoral dissertation], Claremont Graduate University. CGU Theses & Dissertations. https://doi.org/10.5642/cguetd/97
Buechley, L. (2013, October). *Thinking about making. Keynote address at FabLearn conference*. Stanford University.
Butterfield, A. E., McCormick, A., & Farrell, S. (2018). Building LGBTQ-inclusive chemical engineering classrooms and departments. *Chemical Engineering Education*, *52*(2), 107–113. https://journals.flvc.org/cee/article/view/105856/101502
Calabrese Barton, A., & Tan, E. (2018). A longitudinal study of equity-oriented STEM-rich making among historically marginalized communities. *American Educational Research Journal*, *55*(4), 761–800. https://doi.org/10.3102/0002831218758668
Carlone, H. B., & Johnson, A. (2007). Understanding the science experiences of successful women of color: Science identity as an analytic lens. *Journal of Research in Science Teaching*, *44*(8), 1187–1218. https://doi.org/10.1002/tea.20237
Cech, E. A., & Rothwell, W. R. (2018). LGBTQ inequality in engineering education. *Journal of Engineering Education*, *107*(4), 583–610. https://doi.org/10.1002/jee.20239

Cooper, K. M., Brownell, S. E., & Gormally, C. (2019). Coming out to the class: Identifying factors that influence college biology instructor decisions about revealing their LGBQ identities in class. *Journal of Women and Minorities in Science and Engineering*, 25(3), 261–282. https://doi.org/10.1615/JWomenMinorScienEng.2019026085

De Pedro, K. T., Lynch, R. J., & Esqueda, M. C. (2018). Understanding safety, victimization and school climate among rural lesbian, gay, bisexual, transgender, and questioning (LGBTQ) youth. *Journal of LGBT Youth*, 15(4), 265–279. https://doi.org/10.1080/19361653.2018.1472050

DeWitt, J., & Archer, L. (2015). Who aspires to a science career? A comparison of survey responses from primary and secondary school students. *International Journal of Science Education*, 37(13), 2170–2192. https://doi.org/10.1080/09500693.2015.1071899

Fischer, D. J. (2013). *Out 4 math: The intersection of queer identity and mathematical identity* [Unpublished doctoral dissertation], Drexel University, Philadelphia, PA. iDEA: Drexel Libraries E-Repository and Archives. http://hdl.handle.net/1860/4178

Forstie, C. (2018). Ambivalently post-lesbian: LBQ friendships in the rural Midwest. *Journal of Lesbian Studies*, 22(1), 54–66. https://doi.org/10.1080/10894160.2017.1309901

Franklin, J. D., Smith, W. A., & Hung, M. (2014). Racial Battle Fatigue for Latina/o students: A auantitative perspective. *Journal of Hispanic Higher Education*, 13(4), 303–322. https://doi.org/10.1177/1538192714540530

Freeman, J. (2018). LGBTQ scientists are still left out. *Nature*, 559(7712), 27–28. https://doi.org/10.1038/d41586-018-05587-y

Gershon, W. S. (2020). Allies, accomplices, and aggressions: The pernicious nature of Queer Battle Fatigue. *GLQ: A Journal of Lesbian and Gay Studies*, 26(2), 226–229. https://doi.org/10.1215/10642684-8141760

González, M. M. (2020). Queer Battle Fatigue, or how I learned to stop worrying and love the imposter inside me. *GLQ: A Journal of Lesbian and Gay Studies*, 26(2), 236–238. https://doi.org/10.1215/10642684-8141802

Gottfried, M., Estrada, F., & Sublett, C. (2015). STEM education and sexual minority youth: Examining math and science coursetaking patterns among high school students. *The High School Journal*, 99(1), 66–87. https://doi.org/10.1353/hsj.2015.0018

Gray, M. L. (2007). From websites to Wal-Mart: Youth, identity work, and the queering of boundary publics in Small Town. USA. *American Studies*, 48(2), 49–59. https://www.jstor.org/stable/40644068

Gutiérrez, R. (2017). Living mathematx: Towards a vision for the future. *Proceedings of the 39th Annual Meeting of the North American Chapter of the International Group for the Psychology of Mathematics Education*. Association of Mathematics Teacher Educators. https://files.eric.ed.gov/fulltext/ED581384.pdf

Halverson, E. R., & Sheridan, K. M. (2014). The maker movement in education. *Harvard Educational Review*, 84(4), 495–504. https://doi.org/10.17763/haer.84.4.34j1g68140382063

Hall, W. J., Witkemper, K. D., Rodgers, G. K., Waters, E. M., & Smith, M. R. (2018). Activating adult allies from a rural community on lesbian, gay, bisexual, transgender, and queer student issues in school using photovoice. *Journal of Gay & Lesbian Social Services*, 30(1), 49–63. https://doi.org/10.1080/10538720.2017.1408517

Heybach, J., & Pickup, A. (2017). Whose STEM? Disrupting the gender crisis within STEM. *Educational Studies*, 53(6), 614–627. https://doi.org/10.1080/00131946.2017.1369085

Hughes, B. E. (2018). Coming out in STEM: Factors affecting retention of sexual minority STEM students. *Science Advances*, 4(3), 1–5. https://doi.org/10.1126/sciadv.aao6373

Ito, M., Gutiérrez, K., Livingstone, S., Penuel, B., Rhodes, J., Salen, K., Schor, J., Sefton-Green, J., & Watkins, S. C. (2013). *Connected learning: An agenda for research and design*. Digital Media and Learning Research Hub. http://eprints.lse.ac.uk/id/eprint/48114

Kafai, Y., Fields, D., & Searle, K. (2014). Electronic textiles as disruptive designs: Supporting and challenging maker activities in schools. *Harvard Educational Review*, 84(4), 532–556. https://doi.org/10.17763/haer.84.4.46m7372370214783

Kim, A. Y., Sinatra, G. M., & Seyranian, V. (2018). Developing a STEM identity among young women: A social identity perspective. *Review of Educational Research*, 88(4), 589–625. https://doi.org/10.3102/0034654318779957

Kosciw, J. G., Palmer, N. A., & Kull, R. M. (2015). Reflecting resiliency: Openness about sexual orientation and/or gender identity and its relationship to well-being and educational outcomes for LGBT students. *American Journal of Community Psychology*, 55(1–2), 167–178. https://doi.org/10.1007/s10464-014-9642-6

Leyva, L. A. (2016). An intersectional analysis of Latin@ college women's counter-stories in mathematics. *Journal of Urban Mathematics Education*, 9(2), 81–121. https://doi.org/10.21423/jume-v9i2a295

Leyva, L. A. (2017). Unpacking the male superiority myth and masculinization of mathematics at the intersections: A review of research on gender in mathematics education. *Journal for Research in Mathematics Education*, 48(4), 397–433. https://doi.org/10.5951/jresematheduc.48.4.0397

Linley, J. L., Renn, K. A., & Woodford, M. R. (2018). Examining the ecological systems of LGBTQ STEM majors. *Journal of Women and Minorities in Science and Engineering*, 24(1), 1–16. https://doi.org/10.1615/JWomenMinorScienEng.2017018836

Masters, A. S. (2018). How making and maker spaces have contributed to diversity & inclusion in engineering: A [non-traditional] literature review. *2018 CoNECD—The Collaborative Network for Engineering and Computing Diversity Conference, American Society for Engineering Education.* Paper #23113. https://www.asee.org/public/conferences/113/papers/23113/view

Mattheis, A., Arellano, D. C., R, D., & Yoder, J. B. (2020). A model of queer STEM Identity in the Workplace. *Journal of Homosexuality, 67*(13), 1839–1863. https://doi.org/10.1080/00918369.2019.1610632

Mayo, C. (2020). Visitor. *GLQ: A Journal of Lesbian and Gay Studies, 26*(2), 218–220. https://doi.org/10.1215/10642684-8141718

Miller, R. A., Vaccaro, A., Kimball, E. W., & Forester, R. (2020). It's dude culture": Students with minoritized identities of sexuality and/or gender navigating STEM majors. *Diversity in Higher Education, 14*(3), 340–352. https://doi.org/10.1037/dhe0000171

Miller, S. J. (2020). Gender identity complexities turn. *GLQ: A Journal of Lesbian and Gay Studies, 26*(2), 239–242. https://doi.org/10.1215/10642684-8141816

Moorefield-Lang, H., & Kitzie, V. (2018). Makerspaces for all: Serving LGBTQ makers in school libraries. *Knowledge Quest, 47*(1), 46–50. https://scholarcommons.sc.edu/libsci_facpub/211/

National Research Council (2015). *Identifying and supporting productive STEM programs in out-of-school settings.* Washington, DC: The National Academies Press. https://doi.org/10.17226/21740

Paceley, M. S. (2020). In their words: A found poem on the experiences of rural LGBTQ youth. *Qualitative Inquiry, 26*(3-4), 407–408. https://doi.org/10.1177/1077800418810980

Palmer, N. A., Kosciw, J. G., & Bartkiewicz, M. J. (2012). *Strengths and silences: The experiences of lesbian, gay, bisexual and transgender students in rural and small town schools.* GLSEN. https://www.glsen.org/sites/default/files/2019-11/Strengths_and_Silences_2012.pdf

Peppler, K., Halverson, E., & Kafai, Y. B. (2016a). *Makeology: Makerspaces as learning environments.* (Volume 1). London: Routledge.

Peppler, K., Halverson, E., & Kafai, Y. B. (2016b). *Makeology: Makers as learners.* (Volume 2). London: Routledge.

Polman, J. L., & Miller, D. (2010). Changing stories: Trajectories of identification among African American youth in a science outreach apprenticeship. *American Educational Research Journal, 47*(4), 879–918. https://doi.org/10.3102/0002831210367513

Rands, K. (2019). Mathematical inqueery: Queering the theory, praxis, and politics of mathematics pedagogy. In C. Mayo and N. Rodriguez (Eds.), *Queer pedagogies* (pp. 59–74). Springer. https://doi.org/10.1007/978-3-030-27066-7_5

Rice, K. G., Montfort, A. K., Ray, M. E., Davis, D. E., & DeBlaere, C. (2019). A latent change score analysis of emotion regulation difficulties and evaluative threat in STEM. *Journal of Counseling Psychology, 66*(2), 158–169. https://doi.org/10.1037/cou0000325

Riley, D. M., McNair, L. D., & Masters, S. (2017). MAKER: An ethnography of maker and hacker spaces achieving diverse participation. *American Society for Engineering Education, 2017,* 443. https://vtechworks.lib.vt.edu/handle/10919/82443

Rozek, C. S., Ramirez, G., Fine, R. D., & Beilock, S. L. (2019). Reducing socioeconomic disparities in the STEM pipeline through student emotion regulation. *Proceedings of the National Academy of Sciences of the United States of America, 116*(5), 1553–1558. https://doi.org/10.1073/pnas.1808589116

Sheridan, K., Halverson, E. R., Litts, B., Brahms, L., Jacobs-Priebe, L., & Owens, T. (2014). Learning in the making: A comparative case study of three makerspaces. *Harvard Educational Review, 84*(4), 505–531. https://doi.org/10.17763/haer.84.4.brr34733723j648u

Saldaña, J. (2016). *The coding manual for qualitative researchers* (3rd ed.). Sage Publications.

Searle, K., Tofel-Grehl, C., & Breitenstein, J. (2019). Equitable engagement in STEM: Using e-textiles to challenge the positioning of non-dominant girls in school science. *International Journal of Multicultural Education, 21*(1), 42–61. https://doi.org/10.18251/ijme.v21i1.1778

Shelton, S. A., & Lester, A. O. S. (2016). Risks and resiliency: Trans* students in the rural south. In S. J. Miller (Ed.), *Teaching, affirming, and recognizing trans and gender creative youth* (pp. 143–161). Palgrave. https://doi.org/10.1057/978-1-137-56766-6_8

Smith, W. A., Allen, W. R., Danley, L. L. (2016). Assume the position … you fit the description": Psychosocial experiences and Racial Battle Fatigue among African American male college students. *American Behavioral Scientist, 2016,* 742. https://doi.org/10.1177/000276427307742

Smith, W. A., Hung, M., & Franklin, J. D. (2011). Racial Battle Fatigue and the miseducation of Black men: Racial microaggressions, societal problems, and environmental stress. *The Journal of Negro Education, 80*(1), 63–82. https://www.jstor.org/stable/41341106

Stone, A. L. (2018). The geography of research on LGBTQ life: Why sociologists should study the South, rural queers, and ordinary cities. *Sociology Compass, 12*(11), e12638–15. https://doi.org/10.1111/soc4.12638

Story, K. A. (2020). Black femme menace: How Queer Battle Fatigue intersects with blackness and gender. *GLQ: A Journal of Lesbian and Gay Studies, 26*(2), 233–236. https://doi.org/10.1215/10642684-8141788

Strunk, K. K., & Hoover, P. D. (2019). Quantitative methods for social justice and equity: Theoretical and practical considerations. In *Research Methods for Social Justice and Equity in Education* (pp. 191–201). Palgrave Macmillan. https://link.springer.com/chapter/10.1007%2F978-3-030-05900-2_16

Suárez, M. I. (2020). Bye girl, or bye boy, or whatever you are.": A Latinx transgender man's experience with Queer Battle Fatigue in Texas. *GLQ: A Journal of Lesbian and Gay Studies, 26*(2), 230–232. https://doi.org/10.1215/10642684-8141774

Swank, E., Frost, D. M., & Fahs, B. (2012). Rural location and exposure to minority stress among sexual minorities in the United States. *Psychology and Sexuality*, *3*(3), 226–243. https://doi.org/10.1080/19419899.2012.700026

Tan, E., Calabrese Barton, A., Kang, H., & O'Neill, T. (2013). Desiring a career in STEM-related fields: How middle school girls articulate and negotiate identities-in-practice in science. *Journal of Research in Science Teaching*, *50*(10), 1143–1179. https://doi.org/10.1002/tea.21123

Tofel-Grehl, C., Fields, D., Searle, K., Maahs-Fladung, C., Feldon, D., Gu, G., & Sun, C. (2017). Electrifying engagement in middle school science class: Improving student interest through e-textiles. *Journal of Science Education and Technology*, *26*(4), 406–417. https://doi.org/10.1007/s10956-017-9688-y

Tzou, C., Suárez, E., Bell, P., LaBonte, D., Starks, E., & Bang, M. (2019). Storywork in STEM-art: Making, materiality, and robotics within everyday acts of Indigenous presence and resurgence. *Cognition and Instruction*, *37*(3), 306–326. https://doi.org/10.1080/07370008.2019.1624547

Ulrich, R. N., Friedman, H., Marvin, H., Voss, M., O'Riordan, A., Engels, J., Patel, A., Valliere, J., & Billingsley, J. (2019). Queers in STEM: Creating spaces for LGBTQIA2+ in STEM. *AGU Fall Meeting Abstracts*, *33*, 54U. http://adsabs.harvard.edu/abs/2019AGUFMED33G1054U

Vossoughi, S., Hooper, P. K., & Escudé, M. (2016). Making through the lens of culture and power: Toward transformative visions for educational equity. *Harvard Educational Review*, *86*(2), 206–232. https://doi.org/10.17763/0017-8055.86.2.206

Wang, M., & Degol, J. (2013). Motivational pathways to STEM career choices: Using expectancy-value perspective to understand individual and gender differences in STEM fields. *Developmental Review*, *33*(4), 304–340. https://doi.org/10.1016/j.dr.2013.08.001

Wozolek, B., Varndell, R., & Speer, T. (2015). Are we not fatigued? Queer Battle Fatigue at the intersection of heteronormative culture. *International Journal of Curriculum and Social Justice*, *1*(1), 1–35.

Yoder, J. B., & Mattheis, A. (2016). Queer in STEM: Workplace Experiences Reported in a National Survey of LGBTQA Individuals in Science, Technology, Engineering, and Mathematics Careers. *Journal of Homosexuality*, *63*(1), 1–27. https://doi.org/10.1080/00918369.2015.1078632

Curricula of Oppressions: Queering Elementary School Norms and Values

Boni Wozolek and Samantha Antell

ABSTRACT
Troubling longstanding histories of teaching elementary school with an asexual approach for fear of children losing their innocence, this paper argues that schools and teacher preparation programs should be explicit about the inclusion of LGBTQ+ voices and perspectives from early childhood forward. Using a narrative inquiry study that foreground the experiences of a 19-year-old college student reflecting on queer-bias at an early age and the exhaustion he endured from various forms of exclusion, the implications for this paper are significant in that they consider not only how curriculum studies should be central to all teacher preparation but also how elementary curricula should be queered.

> In third grade we had to write a story and I wanted to write mine about gay ants. My teacher said I couldn't do that. My classmate Travis wanted to write a potty humor story. He wasn't allowed to do that. Derek wanted to write about some violent TV show he saw with his parents—you can't do that. My classmates were told they couldn't draw pictures of fecal matter or guns. I was told I couldn't draw bugs holding hands.

Elementary schools remain places of perceived innocence and asexuality (Meiners, 2016; Payne & Smith, 2014). They are spaces where, while dialogue on sexual orientation is silenced, gender identity and expression are often cemented within normalized cisgender ideas and ideals (Robinson, 2013). From teachers who are expected to present within narrow cishetero ways of being, knowing, and doing (Kissen, 1996), to a lack of dialogue on the multiplicity of family structures a student might experience at home (Dor, 2018), primary grades are constantly and continuously a place where cis-hetero patriarchal norms and values are engendered and maintained. For example, while policies like dress code disproportionately impact and sexualize girls and, specifically, girls of color (Morris, 2016), these policies are often overlooked for events like Halloween parties where young girls' outfits are sexualized at an early age (Boas, 2016), and in the curriculum where even children's literature is sexualized (Tribunella, 2008). Similarly, hyper masculine ideals for boys are also often encouraged from an early age (Pascoe, 2011). As a result, youth tend to learn fixed over fluid gender possibilities with normalized anti-queer ontoepistemologies (Barad, 1999). Although national dialogues have recently begun to consider the necessity of LGBTQ+ voices across the curriculum (Biegel, 2018; Casemore, 2010), the elementary school disciplines remain largely untouched by decisions enacted through national concerns (Blackburn et al., 2016).

The purpose of this paper is to examine the narrative of a 19-year-old bisexual white male in order to think about how young ontoepistemologies are formed and informed through the silencing of LGBTQ+voices across the forms of curricula found in elementary schools. Specifically, this paper thinks about how one's ways of being and knowing are influenced not just by what is taught, through what is referred to as the "formal" or "official" curriculum, but by the implicit and explicit messages found within the enacted, hidden, and null curricula. This is significant because while studies cited for the determination of educational policy tend to focus on the formal curriculum (O'Connor et al., 2007; Skinner & Kuenzi, 2015), all forms of curriculum are central to reinforcing sociopolitical structures (Apple, 1993; Gershon, 2017a; Jackson, 1968). Take, for example, the vignette above, which not only underscores the marginalizing practices of the teacher who categorizes queer ants along with guns and feces but, as we argue below, is an example of the enacted and hidden curricula that were always already at play throughout schools.

To explicate the entangled nature of the participant's narrative as it intra-acted, to borrow from Barad (2007),[1] with the body of the curriculum, this paper has interspersed narrative blocks with questions of methodology, literature, and analysis. The purpose of nesting these narrative blocks is to create a kind of polyphonic text (Bakhtin, 1981) that opens a queer space of being and knowing (Halberstam, 2005) to disrupt normalized privileging of academic over participant knowledges (Gershon et al., 2009). This is also, as qualitative researchers have noted (e.g. Geertz, 1973; Pierre, 2014; Schneider & Wright, 2021), important in terms of disrupting the crisis of representation. However, as anthropologists have long argued (e.g. Foley, 2010; Geertz, 1973; Nespor, 1997; Tatum, 2003) and queer scholars of color have more recently stated (Bailey & Miller, 2016; Brockenbrough, 2015; McCready, 2012), it is impossible to completely be free of this kind of privileging. Keeping this tension in mind, we argue that it is important to consider how one might further entangle texts in general but, specifically, to work against marginalization through qualitative educational research.

This paper begins by discussing the methodology before turning to literature that is resonant with the analysis. The participant's narrative, while possibly read as one story, is discussed at length after these sections. The analysis of Ivan's[2] story is concluded with several findings that are relevant to schools, systems of schooling, and, more broadly, to educational research. It is also important to pause and note that the analysis of Ivan's narrative, like any findings, are based in the context of one's experiences. Too often the acronym "LGBTQ+" has become a way to not only think with or about the queer community as a whole but it has also been used to think about individuals. For example, in a 2020 news article that discussed gaps in protection for LGBTQ+people under the Civil Rights Act of 1964, NBC News wrote that "it's still an open question whether employers can fire *an LGBTQ person* for religious purposes [emphasis added]" (The Associated Press, para. 4). We would like to attend to two points here. First, we acknowledge that a person might identify across the LGBTQ+spectrum; meaning that one can be trans, questioning, and asexual or one might only identify with one part of the community, such as those who are cisgender lesbians. Even if a person identifies across questions of queerness, that person still holds a specific identity that should be recognized. By identifying a person as "LGBTQ", rather than referring to that person's identity, can be understood as both an erasure of how one identifies and a flattening of the queer community. Given the ongoing homo and transphobias that are harmful to queer people and communities, being specific when possible can be understood as one way to honor someone's distinct ways of being, knowing, and doing with/in queerness.

Second, it is important to note that Ivan's story is spoken from the position of a bisexual, white, cisgender man. Ivan's experiences reflect those of his childhood and, while queer, might not necessarily align with people who share a similar identity as a bisexual person but do not share his experiences across questions of race, class, or gender. The findings here are meant to explore how one might queer the elementary curriculum but it is equally important to think about how such findings might be considered with culturally sustaining pedagogy (e.g. Paris,

Hearing narratives: narrative inquiry as method

> Being gay floated around as this nebulous concept that was never brought up in formal context. If it was ever brought up in school, it was by a student, and usually to a student. I remember the closest my class had to a bully brought a dictionary to us and was like, "Look for the word gay. Look for the word homosexual. Can you believe that's in the dictionary? That that's here? At school???"

As Clandinin and Rosiek (2006) argue: "We live storied lives" (p. 37). Narrative inquiry has been a significant methodological tool in qualitative research for (re)claiming stories and listening to silenced voices. From women and girls (Reynolds & Taylor, 2005), to critical race dialogues (Marin, 2014), and queer(ed) narratives (Endo et al., 2010) to critical dis/ability studies (Smith & Sparkes, 2008), telling stories through narrative inquiry has been significant in unpacking experiences across contexts, spaces, places, and histories.

Oliveros (2005) writes that process of listening, what she calls *deep listening*, is one of intention and care. Although Oliveros' work primarily focuses on the intimacy of listening to music, her ideas on how we might listen are resonant across forms of qualitative research. Although there are several methods that call for intimacy in the relationship between participant observer and participant (e.g. Behar, 1996; Denzin & Lincoln, 2011; Gershon, 2017b; Pink, 2013), this study focused on the vulnerability and intimacy found within narrative inquiry (Clandinin, 2006) that is often evoked through deep listening. The purpose of this method is to think deeply about the phenomenon (Clandinin & Rosiek, 2006; Connelly & Clandinin, 1990) of anti-queer violence present in elementary schools that germinates into physical and emotional harassment often discussed in middle schools, high schools, and universities.

Like all narratives, queer(ed) stories are entangled with sociopolitical and cultural contexts that run through the narrator who experienced the phenomenon. Afterall, bodies are never formed or informed in a vacuum. They are always already intra-acting with other bodies and their ways of being, knowing, and doing. Listening deeply to queer narratives is central to unpacking the resulting socioculturally constructed identities, to interrupting normalized oppression, and to engendering "spaces of belonging" (Kraus, 2006, p. 108) within cishetero places for queer people and groups.

The narrative presented in this paper was collected from a 19-year-old out bisexual white male, and it speaks to those aspects of identity not as discrete and fixed in their definitions but as inter-woven and complex. For example, while he is often assumed by others to be male and gay based on dichotomous interpretations of expression, Ivan's orientation is bisexual with a preference toward men and his gender expression more fluid than rigid. In a similar complexity, Ivan is empowered by his white cisgender male identity but, pertaining to this paper's narrative as example, was disempowered by his identity as a queer person in a community with conservative parents and community members. This included anti-queer sentiments prominent in his household that similarly lurked in his public school.

As described in the section below, there are more than one form of curriculum at work that give implicit and explicit messages to students in schools. Specifically, Ivan's narrative attends to the phenomenon of anti-queer curricular violence in elementary schools. Attending to the narrative is important for at least the following reasons. First, feelings and subjective experiences are often given less weight than what can be measured quantitatively. While there are several scholarly arguments that focus on the importance and necessity of narratives, schools continually cleave to deterministic practices that tend to be rooted in quantitative evidence (Au, 2016). In other words, schools continue to value experiences that can be objectively observed by the eye, measured, or proven.

Second, diverse narratives are important in contributing to—and often interrupting—collective memories. Winfield (2007) argues that collective memory are the sociohistorical understandings that inform how we move in contemporary contexts. She continues by explaining that the examination of narratives as they are aligned with, or in tension to, collective narratives, is especially important in schools as it can reveal the extent to which "what we say we do is congruent with what we actually do" (p. 20). In terms of marginalized people and groups, when the narratives of the oppressed are dismissed or discounted, a collective memory that normalizes dehumanization often condones and overlooks dire patterns such as Black mothers' high maternal mortality rate and women's continued victimization to sexual violence (Collins, 2002). Like these examples, Ivan's narrative carries not only his personal history as a member of the LGBTQ+ community, but it also adds to the collective history of queer communities that can interrupt cishetero collective memory.

Finally, as with qualitative research in general, and specifically as it is noted throughout narrative inquiry, there is always a tension between the narrator and the researcher. As scholars like Riessman (1993), Clandinin and Rosiek (2006), and Endo et al. (2010), to name a few, have argued, we tend to research experiences that speak to our lives. In the interest of transparency, this is also true in the case of this study. Specifically, both authors of this paper share questions and concerns of anti-queer violence in schools. Wozolek, for example, not only teaches how the forms of curriculum are central to normalized violence from the schoolroom to their broader communities (Woodson, 1933), but as an out bisexual woman of color, she found herself struggling with similar pejorative messages about queerness from a young age. Further, in her work as a Genders and Sexualities Alliance advisor in the Midwest, she witnessed first-hand how the curriculum constantly and continuously silenced LGBTQ+ students in school. Similarly, Antell is drawn to this research as a college freshman studying elementary education and as a queer person. Her impulse to keep her queer identity quiet despite feeling the safety of white middle class privilege raised questions about how schooling can silence LGBTQ+ voices, and how that silencing can be especially violent toward students unshielded by high racial or economic privilege.

Curricula of silence

> Because it was alphabetical, I was always behind him in the lunch line. And he, my second-grade classmate, whenever we were in line, we were always so close. And because of that I was like, "Ah, god you're such a good friend—I love you so much—you're such a GOOD FRIEND. Good. Friend. I didn't realize what I was feeling was a childhood crush because that was, again, I didn't even realize I was missing the terminology for it. As a child I was just genuinely locked into the idea of "this is my best bro. I love this guy. Wow, you're like my brother."
> At that time most of my friends were girls. And it was that thing that kids—and you know what? adults, too—would do where they would tease you for having a crush. I would always get really upset because it felt like, "that's not right; I don't like her I just, like, like her, you know?"
> Then later in fourth grade I remember "dating" a girl. And we broke up. I was dev-astated I was performative, dramatic; I went over the top. It was a very strong response to something that didn't matter. I didn't know enough about what relationships mean to actually feel it that much.

Deciding what knowledge is of most worth (Spencer, 1859) is a sociocultural construction that is centered in political ideas and ideals (Apple, 1993; Jackson, 1968; Rist, 1973; Winfield, 2007) which are too often based in the white cishetero patriarchy. As a result, marginalized people and groups are disproportionately impacted by the decision to value dominant knowledges. Since schools and systems of schooling are places that are meant to reinscribe norms and values (Anyon, 2000; Watkins, 2001), communities like people of color (e.g. Tatum, 2003; Woodson, 1933), LGBTQ+ individuals (Quinn & Meiners, 2009), and those with dis/abilities (Erevelles, 2011), to name a few, frequently face oppressions across contexts—from the classroom to the corridor (Metz, 1978) to less local communities. The purpose of this section is to explore the forms of curriculum that have, as Gershon (2017a) argues, become "critical in the selection of knowledge deemed socially valuable" (p. 7) in ways that specifically impact queer and questioning youth. This is significant because as queer youth continue to feel unsafe at school, it is important to consider the sociocultural constructions at school that continue to silence LGBTQ + ontoepistemologies.

For queer and questioning youth, schools are spaces where indelible silencing—both the process of being silenced and learning how to silence oneself—occurs (Sedgwick, 1990; Wozolek et al., 2017). By *silencing* we are attending to two facets that are often central to the absence of voices in and across schools: the mass number of students who engage in self-harm or those who die by suicide (Wozolek, 2018), and to the constant funneling of queer youth into the school-to-prison pipeline (Meiners, 2016). The mechanisms that encourage such silencing exist in multiplicity in schools; from a curriculum that is absent of queer voices, to schools that are not designed to have queer inclusive facilities like locker rooms or bathrooms, to handbook policies and procedures that have a disproportionately negative impact Black, Brown, Indigenous, and queer youth. While there are many ways to think about silencing, from questions of curricular noise and silencing in the classroom (Gershon, 2017b) to the spirit murdering that silences voices over time in schools (Love, 2019), here we focus on how the forms of curriculum—formal, enacted, hidden, and null—are entangled in ways that propagate violent forms of silencing across every aspect of the school day for minoritized youth.

Regardless of the statistics that continue to show how such silencing impacts minoritized youth, schools remain reactive—and sometimes, sadly, indifferent or encouraging—to silencing rather than proactive in terms of dismantling normalized bias such anti-queer bias. While it can be argued that such (in)action serves to maintain the cishetero status quo, it can also be said that schools and their faculty are ill-equipped to facilitate the interruption of sociocultural violence. In an era of neoliberal reform where standardized testing is more significant than establishing a school culture based in equity and access (Ross & Gibson, 2007), it is of little surprise that teachers, counselors, and administrators are under prepared to examine school culture. Specifically, while the formal curriculum (Apple, 1993; Page, 1991), or intended lessons taught in schools, is often the bulk of dialogue in teacher preparation programs across the country, the other forms of curriculum (hidden, null, and enacted) tend to be left to the margins; a move that serves to further marginalize youth in K-12 schools.

Beginning with what is possibly most familiar form of curriculum, the formal curriculum lives in textbooks, state standards, and teachers' lesson plans. It is the content presented in classrooms and knowledge intended to be taught. The formal curriculum is imbued with bias, often leaving out voices of marginalized people and groups. For example, as you read this, ask yourself how many white, male scientists you can easily list versus scientists of color or female scientists of color. This exercise usually yields diminishing returns with each subsequent iteration. In terms of queerness, the formal curriculum is controlled by heterosexual, cisgender perspectives (Elia & Eliason, 2010) that render straightness as not just dominant but default, and conversely queerness and non-normative gender expression as unnatural and the Other (Evans, 2013; Pascoe, 2011). When that message is received by queer youth, students who identify with the dominant group are empowered while those who identify with the "Other" are silenced twice; once by the curriculum and, too often, a second time by those empowered to believe their identities are superior.

This sense of supremacy constructed by what students learn in the formal curriculum is often reified by the null curriculum, or what is explicitly not taught (Eisner, 1985). Returning to Spencer's (1859) question, "What knowledge is of most worth?", it is equally significant to explore the knowledge that has been deemed socially inappropriate to teach. For example, while several states have recently begun to require a curriculum that is inclusive of LGBTQ + voices and perspectives, nationally only about twelve percent of students agree that the curriculum that is delivered positively portrays of LGBTQ + people (Jones & Cox, 2015). What is not taught is queerness as positive or valuable. What is often taught is queerness as synonymous with HIV/

AIDS or as a problem (Casemore, 2010). Thinking about the many ways that students are silenced or, for those with privilege, given agency, by curriculum, it is important to consider what happens when the formal curriculum explicitly teaches that a group of people is lesser in worth or, as seen by recent moves by supremacists to normalize hatred through schools, a threat. What is not taught, however, is just as detrimental as the overt messages found in the formal curriculum. Unlike those students who are empowered when figures with whom they identify show up in formal curriculum, other students see themselves missing from it (Gershon, 2017a). They experience their identity as nullified and therefore their existence as incomplete when it is not acknowledged in classrooms.

While the formal and null curriculum are central to lessons in the classroom, the hidden curriculum becomes the lessons that are implicitly learned across layers of scale in a schools or, as Mary Metz (1978) argued, the ideas that are taught from the classroom to the corridors. The hidden curriculum is therefore the means for social and cultural reproduction (Gershon, 2017a; Giroux & Penna, 1983). What makes this form of curriculum so insidious, however, is that it is literally hidden from those who enact it. It is therefore difficult, if not impossible, for administration, faculty, or students to recognize the way that dominant norms and values are maintained through the hidden curriculum. While the formal curriculum is that selected knowledge and the null curriculum is what is (un)intentionally deemed as unimportant in the selection process, the hidden curriculum is where local actors enact, engender, and maintain the knowledges taught, or absent, from the classroom. The absence of LGBTQ+ figures in curriculum reflects the dominant ideas surrounding the community as an "Other," and it legitimizes the marginalization of LGBTQ+ people as "cultural fact," reinforcing power structures that devalue their voices.

Those "cultural facts" hidden in plain sight as well as what is or is not taught through the formal and null curriculums inform classroom interactions (Gershon, 2017a; Page, 1991; Schwab, 1969). Classroom interactions between students, teachers, and their environment make up what is known as the enacted curriculum. When LGBTQ+ figures are absent from curriculum, identifying as anything outside of the assumed heterosexual, normative-gender-conforming ideal can be treated in interactions between teachers and students or between students and their peers as inappropriate, wrong, or shameful (DeWitt, 2012; Quinn & Meiners, 2009). Teachers may avoid bringing up topics focused on same-sex attraction or non-normative gender expression (Hermann-Wilmarth & Ryan, 2015). Additionally, they often censor student speech when such topics are brought up (Flores, 2014; Snapp et al., 2015). Restraints like those may be challenged by students, whose conversations may treat the subjects as secrets to be discussed out of earshot of teachers or whose physical and psychological warfare rooted in homo and transphobias may continue largely unabated. Through classroom interactions, students build conceptions about what can and cannot be talked about and where and how they can push those restraints, and they may be silenced or empowered depending on whether they find themselves permitted to exist in classrooms.

The forms of curriculum are nested and layered in ways that make them difficult to extricate from each other. What they form is an assemblage of schooling, one that forms and informs ontoepistemologies of everyone involved in systems of schooling—from students to teachers, administrators to guardians, classrooms to communities. When one recalls the words of Carter G. Woodson (1933), that there would be "no lynching if it did not start in the school room" (p. 3), it is important to recognize that Woodson is not only referring to what is enacted between bodies but what is learned through the forms of curriculum. Similarly, it is these curricular norms and values that drive the current climate described by LGBTQ+ youth as hostile and, in too many cases, physically and emotionally dangerous (Casemore, 2010). The next section presents one final part of Ivan's narrative before an analysis of the ideas presented in his story.

Ivan's narrative: the impact of normalized shame, silence, and violence

When there's this idea that this is something that shouldn't be in the forefront, and you start realizing that it is in your forefront, you feel you have to keep things under wraps. You're afraid that people will find out what's hidden; find out that you are dirty or wrong. I wasn't able to think about it at all. My friends were already trying to get dates to the dance or talking about their celebrity crushes, and I didn't feel comfortable with any of that. I was essentially going through that cooties phase people go through as kids, but as a teenager. I wouldn't say it like, halted development, because there was still development. It just turned it into this negative feeling turned inward; like you still grew it was just that growth was more of a cancer inside you than it was a positive thing.

By seventh grade I was in mental shambles. I was cutting I was... I had to go to therapy because of all that stuff. And I was speaking to my therapist about my sexuality because that was one of the main sources of that What's-Going-On feeling.

Once you have things instilled in you as This-Is-How-Things-Go as a kid, it takes a lot of mental, social effort to undo. And a lot of people don't even have to go through that level of effort to feel comfortable with their identity.

But being forced to do it to actually exist....

Analysis: understanding oppressions across the curricula

Ivan's narrative speaks to how formal, null, hidden, and enacted curricula deliver messages about what types of identities are accepted and valued. This section underscores the multiple ways that the forms of curriculum are central to engendering and maintaining cishetero norms and values, beginning in elementary school. Given that forms of curriculum impact students in ways that spill out from the classroom and into the community, it is significant to think about how one might queer elementary education (Letts & Sears, 1999) in ways that interrupt antiqueer prejudice during these formative years for our youth. This section considers how Ivan's story speaks to oppression across interactions in school through each form of curriculum before drawing conclusions about how we might resist and refuse normalized bias in elementary schools.

Hidden and enacted curricula: unpacking culture and interactions

"I was told I couldn't draw bugs holding hands."

In the opening vignette, Ivan wanted to draw a picture of ants holding hands. From his teacher's reaction, it is clear that the hidden curriculum was riddled with antiqueer ways of knowing and being. Part of what makes the hidden curriculum so harmful is that it is cognitively and emotionally hidden from those who perpetuate it. His teacher, while an active participant in an antiqueer hidden curriculum, might have been unaware of her role. This does not excuse her actions or her lack of reflexivity in the classroom, but it does explain how bias can become normalized in schools and through systems of schooling. The unabated censoring of Ivan's artistic expression, as well as linking queerness to violence and restrooms, is an example of the hidden curriculum in that people were generally not aware of the lessons being taught through suppressing Ivan's voice in ways that were normalized through everyday interactions. Both the teacher and the students seemed unaware of how censoring Ivan's want to draw ants holding hands was formed and informed in cultural ideals that demeans and dehumanizes LGBTQ+ people and groups.

Aside from Ivan's drawing being linked to violence and "potty humor", it is important to recognize that the act of affection between the ants who were perceived to be the same gender, was linked to queerness. The idea that any person or, in this case, animal, of the same gender holding hands is linked to being gay is important in terms of the hidden curriculum because it shows an association that any affection is sexual, rather than attending to any other possible reason for care between same-sex bodies. The hidden curriculum in this case is therefore as much about anti-queer ideas as it is about how one shows care, who can engage in physical affection, and it limits when such displays are marked as appropriate (Noddings, 1986). If Ivan had drawn two ants that were perceived as female, would he have faced the same resistance to his work? As scholars have noted, youth often face pressure to conform to "masculine" ways of being, knowing, and doing that often reject physical affection in ways that can be toxic to sociocultural norms and limiting for people across genders and gender identities (e.g. Ford, 2019; Halberstam, 2005; Letts & Sears, 1999).

Continuing with the ant story, the false equivalence between queerness and violence or feces also impacted youth across identities. This comparison, however, is not unusual in schools. For example, one of the few times that queerness is present in a K-12 curriculum is HIV/AIDs during health class (Brockenbrough, 2016; Casemore, 2010). Additionally, as Ivan and other queer youth have often experienced, there are frequently comparisons between queerness and deviance in schools (De Lauretis, 2017) that are learned through the hidden curriculum. By associating "gay ants" with feces or violence, Ivan and his classmates learned to categorize queerness with negative images. As a result, queerness tends to be shamed to the margins through constant and consistent lessons of "queer as deviant" or "queer as unsafe and unclean" (Meiners & Quinn, 2012; Sedgwick, 2003). These lessons continue to flow between the hidden curriculum and other forms of curriculum as they leak throughout the school and into community contexts.

Formal and null curricula: the impacts of absences

> Being gay floated around as this nebulous concept that was never brought up in formal context. If it was ever brought up in school, it was by a student, and usually to a student.

When the formal curriculum, or what educators intend to teach, leaves out queer voices and perspectives, queerness is relegated to the null curriculum, or what is (un)intentionally not taught. Queer identities, as Ivan suggests in the quote above, are seldom discussed aside from the talk that happens during side conversations in the classroom or places like the cafeteria, hallways, or schoolyard. As a result of such absences in planned and intended contexts, queer identities and bodies are shamed to secrecy; a taboo topic not to be explored in the classroom. In the case of Ivan's ant story, the words were silenced completely. In the narrative about Ivan's classmate finding the words "gay" and "homosexual" in the school's dictionary, the words became secretively spoken among peers. While teachers may avoid conversations about anything outside of cishetero norms, students have those conversations amongst themselves, often with pejorative understandings. For example, Ivan's classmate was scandalized to find "inappropriate" words in the school dictionary only because he had received the message that those words were inappropriate in the first place. This lesson was learned through the hidden curriculum but was reinforced because of an absence of queer ideas in the formal curriculum. Queerness as a necessary secret reifies an understanding that discussing LGBTQ + people and groups should be relegated to dialogues among students. When teachers neglect or reject queerness in the classroom, students across orientations and identities get the message—queerness is inappropriate and, by extension, unacceptable and unnatural.

On the other hand, heterosexuality is presented as the accepted and natural norm across curricular interactions. Think of how often straight relationships are depicted in story books, in illustrations, and even in parent communications. In early grade school, Ivan's friendships with girls were labeled as crushes by adults and his peers. While having crushes on girls was clearly seen as natural and encouraged, Ivan was discouraged to think about his relationship with boys through the same lens. With same-sex attraction coded as unnatural and different-sex attraction coded as an expectation, Ivan acted out the role expected of him and "dated" a girl. When they broke up and Ivan acted "over the top", he recognizes that he was performing straightness (Hill, 2009). Models for heterosexuality are made available in curriculum, and adherence to those models is encouraged while possibilities outside of them are either silenced (as they were in the gay ant story) or go unrecognized for what they are (as they did in Ivan's blindness to his childhood crush).

Ways of being based on gender and gender expression in the United States are always already closely tied to cisgender roles as they are imbricated with questions of sexual orientation. Without masculinity and straightness being codependent in cishetero culture, Ivan's majority female friendships would not have been perceived as fulfilling the "ladies man" heteromasculine role. A similarly disturbing expectation these models are tied to is the paradoxical expectation for children to model heterosexuality while simultaneously being asexual. Same-sex relationships tend to be hypersexualized; their emotional value and social legitimacy ultimately overlooked. Teachers may avoid bringing up possibilities outside of cishetero norms just as Ivan's teacher avoided the gay ants because they view those relationships as a threat not only to children's modeling heterosexuality, but also to their perceived asexuality.

With a heterosexual cisgender existence promoted as the only option in curriculum, any existence outside of it is effectively nullified. This nullification becomes a problem as students grow into their identities, and some find theirs voided. While Ivan's earliest story recounted here takes place in second grade, his story goes back further. Socialization, including exposure to everyday violence, starts young, and its lessons come to be accepted as normal. In elementary school, Ivan received the lesson that non-heterosexual feelings were inappropriate, unacceptable, and to be kept silent or only secretively spoken of. Later, as he came to realize his attraction to males, he experienced mental distress at not meeting what he knew as normal. He felt compelled to reject and silence it, just as he had learned from a young age.

Conclusion

> You're afraid that people will find out what's hidden; find out that you are dirty or wrong... By seventh grade I was in mental shambles. I was cutting I was... I had to go to therapy because of all that stuff.

The forms of curriculum—formal, null, enacted, and hidden—are central to how youth identities are formed and informed through schools and the broader system of schooling. In the case of queer youth, their identities are in constant and consistent tension with how they are identified by others through the forms of curriculum. The messages that exist in broad and rather pointed circulation through the curriculum disproportionately fall on queer youth and, over time, leak into community perspectives about LGBTQ+ people and groups. In other words, queer and questioning youth are negatively impacted but so are cishetero youth as both groups absorb messages about queerness.

For Ivan and countless queer youth, these lessons are significant to questions of mental health as they grapple at young ages with questions of exclusion and oppression. As the rates of self-harm and suicide continue to be indelible realities for those in the LGBTQ+ community and their allies, it is important to listen deeply to these narratives and think about how one might interrupt normalized homo and transphobias that are present in schools. Although strong scholarly dialogues about what this might mean for middle school, high school, and college students continues, we call for more focused efforts in elementary and early childhood education as central to disrupting cishetero ideas and ideals that are harmful to both queer and cishetero youth.

In addition, we call for a stronger attention to the work of curriculum theorists who have theoretically and practically focused on the forms of curriculum as a necessary tool for disrupting and dismantling normalized racism, sexism, queer-phobias, and other forms of sociopolitical exclusion. This is difficult because as neoliberal education practices pull teachers and schools of education, away from the deep examination of the forms of curriculum and toward standardization, the formal curriculum becomes the primary focus of schools and the academy. In cases like Ivan's, because teachers have not learned how to reflect on the forms of curriculum, it becomes difficult to interrupt a system of which the teacher and administrator might not be aware.

Ivan's narrative, like the stories of marginalized people across forms of oppressed identities, can give important insight into silencing that happens daily in schools. Narratives form the LGBTQ + community are as diverse as the broader community they represent and, as such, while Ivan's story does not represent all queer experiences, engaging deeply with his experiences is significant to the broader project of disrupting normalized homo and transphobias in school. These biases are central to engendering and maintaining the exhaustion that so many queer youth experiences that often lead to the self-harm and suicidal thoughts that Ivan describes. In Ivan's case, his experiences speak to a broader pattern in United States elementary schools of nullifying, stigmatizing, and silencing LGBTQ + lives in all forms of curriculum, as well as the distressing trend of that marginalization compounding into self-harm down the road. Studying close-up narratives like Ivan's and connecting the dots to broader contexts can guide dialogue and shape curricular practices that normalize and support LGBTQ + existence rather than silence it in places where the voices of the oppressed need to be heard and valued—in schools.

Notes

1. While not the focus of this paper, Barad uses the term "intra-action" to describe how bodies—both human and non-human—always act together to create agency. In this case, we are arguing that the curriculum intra-acts with students, teachers, administrators, the school itself, and the community to co-constitute agency. For more on this dialogue, see Barad's (2007) text *Meeting the Universe Halfway*.
2. All proper nouns are pseudonyms to protect the anonymity of the participant.

Disclosure statement

No potential conflict of interest was reported by the author(s).

ORCID

Boni Wozolek http://orcid.org/0000-0003-4226-1439

References

Anyon, J. (2000). Social class and hidden curriculum of work. In S. J. Ball (Ed.), *Sociology of education* (vol. 2., pp. 1250–1275). Routledge.

Apple, M. W. (1993). The politics of official knowledge: Does a national curriculum make sense? *Teachers College Record*, *95*(2), 222–241.

Au, W. (2016). Meritocracy 2.0: High-stakes, standardized testing as a racial project of neoliberal multiculturalism. *Educational Policy*, *30*(1), 39–62. https://doi.org/10.1177/0895904815614916

Bailey, M., & Miller, S. J. (2016). When margins become centered: Black queer women in front and outside of the classroom. *Feminist Formations, 27*(3), 168–188. https://doi.org/10.1353/ff.2016.0005

Bakhtin, M. (1981). *The dialogic imagination* (10th ed.). University of Texas.

Barad, K. (1999). Agential realism: Feminist interventions in understanding scientific practices. In M. Biagioli (Eds.), *The science studies reader* (pp. 1–11). Routledge.

Barad, K. (2007). *Meeting the universe halfway: Quantum physics and the entanglement of matter and meaning.* Duke University Press.

Behar, R. (1996). *The vulnerable observer: Anthropology that breaks your heart.* Beacon Press.

Biegel, S. (2018). *The right to be out: Sexual orientation and gender identity in America's public schools.* University of Minnesota Press.

Blackburn, M., Clark, C., & Martino, W. (2016). Investigating LGBT-themed literature and trans informed pedagogies in classrooms. *Discourse: Studies in the Cultural Politics of Education, 37*(6), 801–806.

Boas, E. M. (2016). Education in disguise: sanctioning sexuality in elementary school Halloween celebrations. *Sex Education, 16*(1), 91–104. https://doi.org/10.1080/14681811.2014.995294

Brockenbrough, E. (2015). Queer of color agency in educational contexts: Analytic frameworks from a queer of color critique. *Educational Studies, 51*(1), 28–44. https://doi.org/10.1080/00131946.2014.979929

Brockenbrough, E. (2016). Becoming queerly responsive: Culturally responsive pedagogy for black and Latino Urban Queer Youth. *Urban Education, 51* (2), 170–196. https://doi.org/10.1177/0042085914549261

Casemore, B. (2010). Free association in sex education: Understanding sexuality as the flow of thought in conversation and curriculum. *Sex Education, 10*(3), 309–324. https://doi.org/10.1080/14681811.2010.491629

Clandinin, D. J. (Ed.). (2006). *Handbook of narrative inquiry: Mapping a methodology.* SAGE Publications.

Clandinin, D. J., & Rosiek, J. (2006). Mapping a landscape of narrative inquiry. In D. J. Clandinin (Ed.), *Handbook of narrative inquiry: Mapping a methodology* (pp. 35–75). SAGE Publications.

Collins, P. H. (2002). *Black feminist thought: Knowledge, consciousness, and the politics of empowerment.* Routledge.

Connelly, F. M., & Clandinin, D. J. (1990). Stories of experience and narrative inquiry. *Educational Researcher, 19*(5), 2–14. https://doi.org/10.3102/0013189X019005002

De Lauretis, T. (2017). The queerness of the drive. *Journal of Homosexuality, 64*(14), 1913–1929.

Denzin, N. K. & Lincoln, Y. S. (Eds.). (2011). *The Sage handbook of qualitative research.* University of Illinois.

DeWitt, P. (2012). *Dignity for all: Safeguarding LGBT students.* Corwin Press.

Dor, A. (2018). Parent-teacher communication: The case of diverse family patterns. *Education and Society, 36*(1), 5–20. https://doi.org/10.7459/es/36.1.02

Eisner, E. (1985). *The educational imagination: On the design and evaluation of school programs* (2nd ed.). Macmillan.

Elia, J. P., & Eliason, M. (2010). Discourses of exclusion: Sexuality education's silencing of sexual others. *Journal of LGBT Youth, 7*(1), 29–48. https://doi.org/10.1080/19361650903507791

Endo, H., Reece-Miller, P. C., & Santavicca, N. (2010). Surviving in the trenches: A narrative inquiry into queer teachers' experiences and identity. *Teaching and Teacher Education, 26*(4), 1023–1030. https://doi.org/10.1016/j.tate.2009.10.045

Erevelles, N. (2011). *Disability and difference in global contexts: Enabling a transformative body politic.* Palgrave.

Evans, K. (2013). *Negotiating the self: Identity, sexuality, and emotion in learning to teach.* Routledge.

Flores, G. (2014). Teachers working cooperatively with parents and caregivers when implementing LGBT themes in the elementary classroom. *American Journal of Sexuality Education, 9*(1), 114–120. https://doi.org/10.1080/15546128.2014.883268

Foley, D. (2010). The rise of class culture theory in educational anthropology. *Anthropology & Education Quarterly, 41*(3), 215–227. https://doi.org/10.1111/j.1548-1492.2010.01084.x

Ford, C. (2019). *Boys will be boys: Power, patriarchy and toxic masculinity.* Simon and Schuster.

Geertz, C. (1973). *The interpretations of cultures.* Basic Books.

Gershon, W. S. (2017b). *Sound curriculum: Sonic studies in educational theory, method, & practice.* Routledge.

Gershon, W. S. (2017a). *Curriculum and students in classrooms: Everyday urban education in an era of standardization.* Lexington Press.

Gershon, W. S., Lather, P., & Smithies, C. (2009). Troubling the angles redux: Tales of collaboration towards a polyphonic text. In W. S. Gershon (Ed.), *The collaborative turn: Working together in qualitative research* (pp. 3–34). Sense Publishers.

Giroux, H., & Penna, A. (1983). *The hidden curriculum and moral education.* McCutchan.

Halberstam, J. J. (2005). *In a queer time and place: Transgender bodies, subcultural lives.* New New York University Press.

Hermann-Wilmarth, J. M., & Ryan, C. L. (2015). Doing what you can: Considering ways to address LGBT topics in language arts curricula. *Language Arts, 92*(6), 436.

Hill, M. L. (2009). Scared straight: Hip-hop, outing, and the pedagogy of queerness. *The Review of Education, Pedagogy, and Cultural Studies, 31*(1), 29–54. https://doi.org/10.1080/10714410802629235

Jackson, P. W. (1968). *Life in classrooms.* Holt, Rinehart & Winston.

Jones, R. P., & Cox, D. (2015). Millennial attitudes on sexuality and reproductive health: Findings from the 2015 millennials, sexuality, and reproductive health survey. Public Religion Research Institute. Retrieved from: https://www.prri.org/wp-content/uploads/2015/03/PRRI-Millennials-Web-FINAL.pdf.

Kissen, R. M. (1996). *The last closet: The real lives of lesbian and gay teachers*. Heinemann.

Kraus, W. (2006). The Narrative negotiation of identity and belonging. *Narrative Inquiry, 16*(1), 103–111. https://doi.org/10.1075/ni.16.1.14kra

Letts, W. J., & Sears, J. T. (1999). *Queering elementary education: Advancing the dialogue about sexualities and schooling*. Rowman & Littlefield.

Love, B. (2019). *We want to do more than survive: Abolitionist teaching and the pursuit of educational freedom*. Beacon Press.

McCready, L. T. (2012). Call and response: How narratives of black queer youth inform popular discourses of the 'boy crisis' in education. *International Journal of Inclusive Education, 16*(4), 391–406. https://doi.org/10.1080/13603116.2011.555094

McRuer, R. (2006). *Crip theory: Cultural signs of queerness and disability*. New York University Press.

Meiners, E. R. (2016). *For the children? Protecting innocence in a Carceral state*. University of Minnesota Press.

Meiners, E. R., & Quinn, T. (2012). *Sexualities in education*. Peter Lang.

Metz, M. H. (1978). *Classrooms and corridors: The crisis of authority in desegregated secondary schools*. University of California Press.

Morris, M. W. (2016). *Pushout: The criminalization of black girls in schools*. The New Press.

Nespor, J. (1997). *Tangled up in school: Politics, space, bodies and signs in the educational process*. Lawrence Erlbaum Associates Inc.

Noddings, N. (1986). *Caring: A relational approach to ethics and moral education*. University of California Press.

O'Connor, K. A., Heafner, T., & Groce, E. (2007). Advocating for social studies: Documenting the decline and doing something about it. *Social Education, 71*(5), 255–260.

Oliveros, P. (2005). *Deep listening: A composer's sound practice*. IUniverse.

Page, R. (1991). *Lower-track classrooms: A curricular and cultural perspective*. Teachers College Press.

Paris, D. (2012). Culturally sustaining pedagogy: A needed change in stance, terminology, and practice. *Educational Researcher, 41*(3), 93–97. https://doi.org/10.3102/0013189X12441244

Pascoe, C. J. (2011). *Dude, you're a fag: Masculinity and sexuality in high school*. University of California Press.

Payne, E., & Smith, M. (2014). The big freak out: Educator fear in response to the presence of transgender elementary school students. *Journal of Homosexuality, 61*(3), 399–418. https://doi.org/10.1080/00918369.2013.842430

Pierre, E. S. (2014). A brief and personal history of post qualitative research: Toward "post inquiry. *Journal of Curriculum Theorizing, 30*(2), 2–19.

Pink, S. (2013). *Doing visual ethnography* (3rd ed). SAGE.

Quinn, T., & Meiners, E. R. (2009). *Flaunt it!: Queers organizing for public education and justice/Therese Quinn & Erica R. Meiners*. Peter Lang.

Reynolds, J., & Taylor, S. (2005). Narrating singleness: Life stories and deficit identities. *Narrative Inquiry, 15*(2), 197–215. https://doi.org/10.1075/ni.15.2.02rey

Riessman, C. K. (1993). *Narrative analysis*. SAGE.

Rist, R. (1973). *The urban school: A factory for failure*. MIT Press.

Robinson, K. H. (2013). *Innocence, knowledge and the construction of childhood: The contradictory nature of sexuality and censorship in children's contemporary lives*. Routledge.

Ross, E. W. & Gibson, R. J. (Eds.). (2007). *Neoliberalism and education reform*. Hampton Press.

Schneider, A., & Wright, C. (Eds.). (2021). *Between art and anthropology: Contemporary ethnographic practice*. Routledge.

Schwab, J. J. (1969). The practical: A language for curriculum. *The School Review, 78*(1), 1–24. https://doi.org/10.1086/442881

Sedgwick, E. K. (2003). *Touching feeling: Affect, pedagogy, performativity*. Duke University Press.

Sedgwick, E. K. (1990). *Epistemology of the closet*. University of California Press.

Skinner, R. R., & Kuenzi, J. J. (2015). *Reauthorization of the Elementary and Secondary Education Act: Highlights of the Every Student Succeeds Act*. Congressional Research Service.

Smith, B., & Sparkes, A. C. (2008). Narrative and its potential contribution to disability studies. *Disability & Society, 23*(1), 17–28. https://doi.org/10.1080/09687590701725542

Snapp, S. D., Burdge, H., Licona, A. C., Moody, R. L., & Russell, S. T. (2015). Students' perspectives on LGBTQ-inclusive curriculum. *Equity & Excellence in Education, 48*(2), 249–265. https://doi.org/10.1080/10665684.2015.1025614

Spencer, H. (1859). What knowledge is of most worth? *The Westminster Review, 16*(1), 522–532.

Tatum, B. D. (2003). *-Why are all the Black kids sitting together in the cafeteria?": And other conversations about race*. Basic Books.

Tribunella, E. L. (2008). From kiddie lit to kiddie porn: The sexualization of children's literature. *Children's Literature Association Quarterly, 33*(2), 135–155.

Watkins, W. H. (2001). *The white architects of black education: Ideology and power in America 1865–1954*. Teachers College Press.

Winfield, A. G. (2007). *Eugenics and education in America: Institutionalized racism and the implication of history, ideology, and memory*. Peter Lang.

Woodson, C. G. (1933). *The mis-education of the Negro*. Tribeca Books.

Wozolek, B. (2018). In 1800 again: The sounds of students breaking. *Educational Studies, 54*(4), 367–381. https://doi.org/10.1080/00131946.2018.1473869

Wozolek, B., Wootton, L., & Demlow, A. (2017). The school-to-coffin pipeline: Queer youth, suicide and resilience of spirit. *Cultural Studies, Critical Methodologies, 17*(5), 392–398.

Embodied failure: Resisting Gender and Sexuality Erasures in K-12 Schools

Darla Linville

ABSTRACT
This paper presents the initial data from a larger project, considered through the lens of failure from the perspective of Halberstam's *The Queer Art of Failure* (2011) as a way of resisting hegemonic narratives about success and how it is culturally defined. As suggested by Halberstam's use of failure, the limitations or undesirable elements of failure reside in rigid institutional definitions of success. As such, I will examine the failure of adults and institutions in queer and trans youth lives, and how uncreative and limiting rules and roles within schools require queer and trans youth to experience failure. By contrast, queer and trans adults as collaborators and accomplices to youth recognize the failure that has shown up for queer and trans youth in institutions, and redefine failure and success in solidarity with youth. Using an understanding of failure as a particularly queer epistemology and ontology, I look at this reframing of failure as resistance to institutions, such as schools, where young people are often blamed for their failure. This blame contributes to the violence young people experience in schools.

Failure is a concept that appears in many discussions of education: failing schools, failing students, the failure of education to fulfill its mission of providing social mobility, especially for Black, Indigenous, and Latinx students, as well as some other people of color (Hmong, Philippinx, and others often categorized as Asian), and students from households without economic means and power, as well as students with disabilities. In popular discourse, these discussions of failure often omit that schools are places intended for some students to fail (Patel, 2016a). In fact, this failure is required in order to accomplish the sorting function of schools (Spring, 2019), to determine which students are smart, qualified, and worthy of higher education and lucrative jobs, and which students are not, usually because of a failure or flaw within that student or community. In this analysis, I consider failure from the perspective of Halberstam (2011), and the text *The Queer Art of Failure*, as a way of examining failure as resistance to hegemonic narratives about success and how it is culturally defined. "Success in a heteronormative, capitalist society equates too easily to specific forms of reproductive maturity combined with wealth accumulation" (Halberstam, 2011, p. 2). This ideology of success also operates in school curricula (both intentional and implicit) through the economic goals of acquiring training and skills that lead to good jobs, as well as through the social goals of creating school rituals that foster heterosexual coupling (Lesko, 2001; Pascoe, 2007)

There are material and spiritual consequences of requiring some students – those with disabilities, Black, Indigenous, and other students of color (BIPOC), and those who do not conform to heteronormative or cisnormative identities – to bear the burden of resisting hegemony, and therefore the failure. Interrogating the normative values transmitted by schools and adults' roles in setting youth up for failure by adhering to those values, in contrast to out-of-school settings where queer and trans youth thrive, allows for an examination of how failure is created. Using Halberstam's (2011) understanding of failure as a particularly queer epistemology and ontology, I look at adults as collaborators and accomplices to youth, in situations where they achieve solidarity with youth, and how that creates less failure for queer and trans young people. The failure is in institutions that reject youth, even though it is often framed as failure on the part of young people, and as a consequence, contributes to the violence young people experience in schools.

When failure shows up for queer and trans youth in schools

Educators and other adults often do not resolve the harassment and bullying, discourses of discrimination and stereotype, or lack of welcome that youth encounter in schools. They often claim they are unable to change the structures in which youth exist and, in the short term, to make spaces for all the identities and bodies in which youth live, love, and attend schools. Youth and adults live and work in schools, neighborhoods, and families in which they may confront racism, classism, ableism, sexism, cissexism, and heterosexism. Adults often blame these oppressions on the culture of the community, that is the parents and families of the young people in the schools, and claim that making changes to school structures to address sexism, heterosexism, and cissexism, as well as racism, classism, and ableism, would not be accepted by (some in) the community, and would be viewed as "too political" or outside of the purview of school (Fields, 2008, 2012; Irvine, 2002; Loutzenheiser, 2015). Although adults may show reluctance to take action, youth resist the structures of school that deny their existence and limit their self-expression, even when these acts of resistance are punished and lead to disciplinary actions that result in loss of school days, loss of instructional time, or being labeled as uninterested in getting an education. These consequences can lead to failure for students – failing grades, suspensions, expulsions, and other marks that count against them in the present and future – and also fail to change the institutions. It is important to understand their actions as resistance to the limitations of available identities, actions, and positions, *even though* youth almost always fail to change the institution, and *almost never* are able to move the institution to recognize their resistance as something other than misbehavior. "And yet 'failure'—not smashing capitalism, overthrowing racism, undermining patriarchy, or eradicating homophobia—cannot be mistaken as the absence of resistance" (Fine et al., 2014, p. 50). The consequences of the failure are borne by the students in most instances, the least institutionally-powerful actors. Yet youth often must choose this failure rather than submit to discursive power structures that abjure their existence, that require their erasure. Adults, who are institutionally more powerful than youth in schools, can become better advocates for and collaborators with LGBTQ + youth, including those who are BIPOC and differently-abled, by learning to work in solidarity with young people in their roles as teachers, counselors, and school administrators.

Young people already understand classrooms to be "sexualized as well as gendered, spaces" (Linville, 2017, p. 378). In these classrooms, sometimes they also become spaces "where sexuality and gender can be spoken [to] allow students to examine their desires and pleasures, and adults can create a public forum for justice about sexuality and gender identity" (Linville, 2017, p. 378). In a previous study with youth researchers in New York City (Linville, 2017), I saw, in embodied ways, students' resistance to negative hegemonic discourses about sexuality and gender in schools, their strategic use of supports and role models, and the creative ways young people enacted their desires in school spaces. I am interested in theorizing about how adults can better embody the supportive roles that students need, working *for* and *with* students to restructure society in a way that is more nurturing to a more diverse society, and perhaps would not require failure from students.

Not all expressions of sexuality and gender are considered inappropriate for school, and conversely, not all kinds of gender or sexuality can be acknowledged in school, even in sex education classes. Expressions of sexuality and gender that reside comfortably in school include dating rituals such as school dances, examples in curriculum of heterosexual families, couples, or the rites of those couples such as marriage, and personal disclosures by students, teachers, administrators and staff about heterosexual families and normative gender activities and expected capabilities (Garcia, 2009; Lesko, 2001; Pascoe, 2007). On the other hand, contested discourses within sex education classes strictly limit the desires, acts, and relationships that can be discussed, often locating sexual desire in boys only, and including only heterosexual relationships (Fields, 2008; Hoefer & Hoefer, 2017). Some states have enacted laws, called "no-promo-homo" laws, that interdict mentioning non-heterosexuality, even in response to student questions (Fair, 2021; McGovern, 2012). Fear of speaking about queer and trans lives and relationships may contribute to misunderstandings about who queer and trans people are, and ignorance about students or community members (Hoefer & Hoefer, 2017; McGuire et al., 2010). Queer and trans students who are also BIPOC, poor, or who have a disability may not be recognized by adults with little experiences or knowledge of queer and trans communities, and therefore may not be identified as experiencing harassment from peers (Heck et al., 2016; Kosciw et al., 2016). Students who protest lack of recognition or protection from violence are often blamed for their own victimization (Snapp et al., 2015). In addition, adults and peers who understand sexual and gender identities as static may be hostile to queer and trans youth who understand gender as a process of always becoming (Airton et al., 2019), within which they may define themselves with different terms and pronouns at different times. Adults in schools often pathologize these changes as mental health issues, behavioral problems, or a lack of self-knowledge among young people. Queer and trans students have to navigate questions of visibility and invisibility of their identities every day and in school contexts the visibility of sexuality and gender make queer and trans erasure that much more palpable.

Where policies exist to protect queer and trans youth in schools, the policy lens and the perspectives of individual teachers and administrators may inhibit an intersectional view of student identities (Shelton, 2017) by ascribing one identity label per student. In these cases, queer youth may be seen as different from Black or students of color, meaning that Black or Brown queer or trans youth become invisible or are subject to punishment through these policies (Venzant Chambers & McCready, 2011). Queer and trans inclusive policies may be used to punish straight, queer, or trans students of color, because of stereotypes that position communities of color as more homophobic and transphobic, and because teachers and administrators may misunderstand the interactions between students or feel that harassment on the basis of gender identity or sexuality requires punishment, regardless of the circumstances of the interaction, or the identities of the students (Shelton, 2017).

Practices that may also affect queer and trans students include race or class discrimination that pathologizes family structures outside of heteronormative, blood relations (Hartman, 2019; Ziyad & DuWhite, 2020). This discrimination elides important caretakers and networks of support, unrecognized by institutions, that some communities of color and poor communities rely on (McArthur & Lane, 2019). These practices both fail to recognize community networks that are not within nuclear, heteronormative family model, self-sustaining and economically prosperous (Hartman, 2019), and may further punish students for living in the wrong place, not being able to get a guardian signature, or because a parent is unable to show up at the school when the student needs them (Morris, 2015; Patel, 2016b). Failures like these penalize students for living in families that understand how to create resilient communities and networks to survive violent and discriminatory forces of capitalist markets.

Class discrimination affecting queer and trans students also is institutionalized in schools through school funding structures that provide educational opportunities within institutions that are fundamentally different because of financial differences. Students that attend schools in low socioeconomic areas get different curricula (Anyon, 1997, 2005), follow different rules (Fine & Burns, 2003; Lipman, 2004), experience more policing (Nolan, 2011), are assumed by teachers to "not value education" or to "not be in need of an education" (Reay, 2001; White, 2020). Students in these districts more often experience education as punishment, not receiving enrichment activities and arts, but facing double periods of math and grammar as a means of bringing up scores on standardized tests. In fact, test scores comprise the only, impoverished equality that schools that serve poor students of color often aspire to (Kornhaber et al., 2014). Stereotypes and expectations that teachers, administrators, and policymakers have about lower socioeconomic status students assume failure for them, and so very little effort is made to change structures in such a way that students can achieve a different outcome. The assumption that they are not getting very far, or that where they are going they will not need an education, assumes failure from the beginning (Anyon, 2005). Queer and trans youth who are poor may experience any or all of these discriminatory, violent practices, and in addition may be less likely to be able to use parental leverage for support against homophobic and heteronormative, or transphobic discrimination. Their sexuality and gender resistance may be seen as another pathology of their family structure or poverty (Istar Lev, 2010).

Ability discrimination, which may affect queer and trans students, describes the ways that students with disabilities are always considered to be lacking something, to have to make up what they do not have in order to fit with the rest of the students in the school, of the same age, or in the same grade level (Kafer, 2013; Mitchell et al., 2014; Skrtic, 2005). The idea that all students will be in the same place academically, doing the same work at the same time, is a function of the systems that discipline and punish (Foucault (1977). Under these systems, "those labeled deficits or dis/abilities are then viewed as needing to be removed from public space remediated, rehabilitated, or redistributed into spaces less visible" (Annamma, 2016, p. 1214). The regulation of students in this way misunderstands students' abilities, and finds faults within the student, rather than finding fault within the system that claims all children should be the same.

Queer and trans youth may experience any of these kinds of violence in addition to the specific gender and sexuality performance failures that affect their school experiences. In situations where queer and trans youth are privileged in other ways (ability, class, race) they may be tokenized or held up as an example of the school or district inclusivity (Elliott, 2012). But in cases where the students' identity, behavior, or abilities already position them as a problem in schools, their queer or trans identities may be read as another way of acting out, defiance, or pathology (Elliott, 2012). In some cases, students may be punished by the very policies meant to protect them, as when fighting back against harassment and bullying results in suspension for queer youth of color (Center for American Progress, 2014) or when students with disabilities are placed in restricted learning environments, isolated from other students and denied access to educational resources (Erevelles et al., 2019).

Theorizing queer failure

If, then, queer and trans youth often experience failure resulting from institutional pathologizing and punishment of their identities, including but not limited to their sexual and gender identities, how can schools be changed to not be sites of failure, and what can educators do about it? What might a different definition of success look like? For Halberstam (2011) the failure to achieve the social markers of success is a way out of a confining system and a deliberate move to reject these markers of normativity, that provides access to creativity and freedom. Youth sometimes view themselves or are viewed by others as failing to get on the path to wealth and career, independence, and relationships. Paths that are considered out of time (Kafer, 2013) but that would otherwise be celebrated such as pregnancy, or alternative routes to the successful culmination of education such as the GED are viewed as inferior outcomes, or failures. Students with family resources can adjust to these circumstances, and mediate the effects of undervalued paths or timing, but students without resources to readjust and start over, without institutional help, are often left without access to hegemonic options for success. However, young people may also perceive limitations within the socially mandated accomplishments and timelines, and may view them as inhibiting their access to choice, creativity, or freedom.

In some instances "it is less a question of choosing failure than choosing what to do with the failure that has chosen us" (Nyong'o, 2012, cited in Johnson, 2015, p. 264). Failure can keep showing up for queer and trans bodies in schools, brown and black bodies, youth with disabilities, bodies that are marked as different and that don't conform easily to "inclusionist" (Mitchell et al., 2014, p. 301) efforts and programs that attempt to make space for "diverse" students in educational settings. Building on Nyong'o, Johnson suggests a separation between "desiring failure" and "subverting failure...a more precise typology of failure... [that] acknowledges the pleasures of failure – embodied choices to stand apart from social norms of gender, sexuality, reprocentricity, and romantic affiliations – and the distress of failures embodied in lives gone haywire, symptoms run rampant, personal lives devolving into uninhabitable havoc" (Johnson, 2015, p. 264). This distinction is useful for thinking of ways that queer and trans students resist the strictures of gender and sexuality presentation and performance in institutions like schools through expression of their desires and pleasure, and also to analyze the punishing consequences that may follow. Disciplinary codes that result in students losing days of school or dropping out, either because of the surveillance their bodies are subjected to or because of the lack of visibility under the policy structures for the harms that they are experiencing, ultimately punish students for their identities.

> Universities (and by implication high schools) squash rather than promote quirky and original thought. Disciplinarity, as defined by Foucault (1977), is a technique of modern power: it depends upon and deploys normalization, routines, convention, tradition, and regularity, and it produces experts and administrative forms of governance. (Halberstam, 2011, pp. 7–8)

These forms of discipline and punishment for not conforming often target bodies that express identities outside of gender binaries and heterosexuality. The resistance to or exit from institutions that require submission to discipline or erasure is agentic and even sometimes necessary, even when the consequences are harmful (Tuck & Yang, 2014).

Heterosexism, cissexism, sexism, "ways of seeing the world...established as normal or natural, as obvious and necessary," (Halberstam, 2011, p. 9) are systems that describe ways of doing sexuality and gender as normal, healthy, and moral, and that also describe queer, trans, and women's experiences as not normal, as departing from the norm, and sometimes as unhealthy and immoral. Classism, racism, and ableism describe habits and behaviors of middle class or white or able-bodied, as normal, healthy, and socially acceptable or even desirable, and the behaviors of other groups as delinquent, aberrant, or undesirable. In schools, children learn about behaviors that are coded to support privileged groups and ways of life that assume everyone can and wishes to conform to norms based on hegemonic ideals (Elliott, 2012, 2016), which deny the richness and pleasures of other ways of creating families, spending time, and relating to one another (Mitchell et al., 2014).

Similar to Johnson's framing of failure as either chosen or inflicted, "curricular cripistemologies" imagine the embodied experiences of "crip/queer bodies" (Mitchell et al., 2014) within the inclusionist discourses of schools. "*Curricular cripistemologies* involve the development of teaching pedagogies that deviate from core teachings by foregrounding crip/queer content as fortunate failure" (p. 303, emphasis in original). Mitchell et al. (2014) critique this approach that posits what they call "crip/queer" bodies as just like normative bodies because of the ways that it flattens out the differences, and keeps in place a mythology that it is embarrassing to be different, and that everyone would wish not to be different if possible. Instead of "the flattening out of embodied differences" (p. 301) their approach to learning views disability, and other embodied differences such as queer sexuality and gender identity, as teaching opportunities, and ways to question normative categories and the many ways they do not make space for everyone. Flattening creates a limited range of possible accommodations and praises mental and physical capacities to take advantage of accommodations to "overcome" disability (Kafer, 2013). In this flattening, crip/queer bodies who are able to be assimilated into the normative classroom and school practices or structure are considered successes, and the school considers that the work of accommodation is done. However, the burden of assimilation is put on the disabled body, and the bodies and experiences of those unable to assimilate, as well as the contributions they might make to the educational and social space, are erased (Annamma & Handy, 2019). "While social spaces superficially appear open to all who wish to navigate them, curricular cripistemologies unveil architectural, aesthetic, and moral spaces of inclusion that, paradoxically, strictly police ways of being different for the bodies they include" (Mitchell et al., 2014, p. 304). This policing of the allowed differences encoded in the discipline structure of classroom behavior is inherently violent (Annamma & Handy, 2019; Halberstam, 2011).

Students see this violence and may react with violence to the injustices they experience (Meiners, 2010). Queer failure advocates for an affective range that includes "rage, rudeness, anger, spite, impatience, intensity, mania, sincerity, earnestness, overinvestment, incivility, brutal honesty, and disappointment. [These feelings represent] the promise of self-shattering, loss of mastery and meaning, unregulated speech and desire unloosed" (Halberstam, 2011, p. 110). These feelings, and their expression, are usually not welcomed in classrooms (Annamma & Handy, 2019), are perceived as dangerous and anathema to learning or as defying the authority of teachers. Teachers often require that students repress these feelings, and reign in the self-shattering and unregulated speech, and disguise the loss of mastery and meaning.

In this exploration of failure that students with queer and trans identities experience in schools, I have tried to hold a tension between the failures that choose them (Johnson, 2015) and the agentic expressions of bodies and desires represented in queer and trans youth, as well as the refusal to submit to erasure or normalizing inclusionist practices. I want to hold a focus on reframing the failures as belonging to, or being a lack within institutions, not belonging to or being a lack within young people. I am interested in how schools might become sights of care and nurture for youth with queer and trans identities, including those young people who are BIPOC, poor, or disabled queer and trans youth. Halberstam asks,

> What kinds of reward can failure offer us? Perhaps most obviously, failure allows us to escape the punishing norms that discipline behavior and manage human development with the goal of delivering us from unruly childhoods to orderly, predictable adulthoods... And while failure certainly comes accompanied by a host of negative affects, such as disappointment, disillusionment, and despair, it also provides the opportunity to use these negative affects to poke holes in the toxic positivity of contemporary life. (Halberstam, 2011, p. 3)

The meritocratic myth of US educational institutions promises hope and socioeconomic gains for students who work hard and follow the rules of educational institutions, and blames them (or their teachers or parents) for their failures. Failure offers the possibility of questioning the "it gets better" promises of a variety of progress narratives, and to critique the structures of systems that require winners and losers.

Imagining other futures for queer and trans youth

In contemplating the ways that schools create failure for queer and trans youth, I reflected on the practices of other organizations – queer and trans youth serving organizations – that explicitly desire to serve and create successes for young people. Having worked in and with some of these organizations, I knew that their pedagogical and curricular and disciplinary practices stemmed from different ethos and assumptions about the desirability of queer and trans identities. These organizations, I thought, worked from assumptions about creating the spaces and services that queer and trans youth deserve, rather than focusing just on eliminating the most egregious violence that youth experience (and it could be argued that schools do not even do that). I began a research project to talk to adults working in out-of-school, queer and trans youth-serving organizations, with a desire to understand more completely the epistemic, ontological, pedagogical, and ethical frames with which these adults approached their work with youth. Their words and work could help direct the future-dreaming (Kafer, 2013) about what educational institutions could do to become places that were more than not-good-enough for queer and trans youth. This project is ongoing, and the narratives presented here represent initial findings.

Accessing radical dreams about educational settings, and what could be the experiences of queer and trans youth, inclusive of BIPOC queer and trans youth and youth with disabilities, requires looking in places where radical teaching and learning and conspiring with queer and trans youth are happening. Youth-serving organizations that have been established for several decades in communities with multifaceted, activist queer communities were chosen for the critical thought and dissent that it was imagined would have contributed and would continue to be engaged in the planning of youth services and activities. To solicit participation, I reached out to organizations where I had contacts or cold-called organizations that I was familiar with. I described the project and asked for an interview with an adult working directly with youth about what it means to advocate for and with youth in the organization. If the person agreed to be interviewed, I then asked them for suggestions of others who should participate. This form of snowball sampling attends to community knowledge that evaluates who can speak about an experience, an organization, or its practices.

At the time of this writing I have spoken to six adults as part of the data collection for this project. The participants all identify as queer or lesbian or gay, three identify as cis men, one as a cis woman, and two as nonbinary. They range in age from early 30s to early 50s. All of them have college degrees, and most have a masters level professional degree as well. The organizations where they work in are in four different cities. Each of the organizations works with youth outside of schools and provide mental health and health services, educational and job support, social opportunities, financial or food or transportation assistance, sex and relationship workshops, and coordination with or referral to other services that the youth need. Some of the organizations offer significantly more than this, including sleeping rooms, job placement, housing assistance, dance classes, wig and makeup lessons, hormone shots, and legal assistance. These are the tangible services and supports that these organizations offer, and these material goods are important, and often are what encourage youth to engage with the services. Adults navigate the exchange of services and spaces for data collection toward institutional goals, the ethics of trading on youth needs to compel the youth to share information that health departments want, or to participate in the fundraising efforts of the organization.

Even more vital, perhaps, are other intangible assets that these adults bring to their interactions with youth. These intangibles are harder to learn from or replicate in other settings, because of the work that they entail on the part of the adults to make the changes necessary to stay in relationship with young people, and because of the challenge that they pose to the "normalizing" goals of institutions like schools. A discussion of a few of these intangibles opens a conversation about how schools could require less failure from youth.

Youth organizations require less failure

For queer and trans youth in schools, there are many opportunities for them to "stand apart from social norms," (Johnson, 2015, p. 264) especially if they do not conform to gendered expectations as part of their self-expression and identity. As is often cited, youth most often experience bullying and harassment in schools based on gender identity and expression and sexuality because of the ways their self-presentation does not conform to gender binaries (Goodenow et al., 2016). The identities and expressions that often make school personnel view queer and trans youth as problems are what adults in out-of-school, queer-and-trans-youth-serving institutions admire and expect. How do these adults imagine queer and trans youth getting what they deserve/what is good enough?

Queer and trans youth celebrated

Adults in the youth-serving organizations presented admiration and delight when discussing the youth with whom they work. They view young people as part of their network, as the next generation of leaders, activists, and advocates, and see youth as contributing to the rich aesthetic and intellectual community. They see youth demonstrating strengths and ways of interacting that adults can learn from, especially when encountering others across differences and negotiating respect and dignity for each person. They note that youth operate from an ideology of mutual aid and care for one another, even when disagreeing.

Queer and trans youth in these out-of-school settings are valued for their queerness and transness, and for the queer and trans community that they create among themselves and with the adults in the organizations. Young people are viewed as "creative, artistic, ... and resilient," Adults noted that their creativity is present in the dances and vocabulary that they create, the strategic ways they negotiate power with institutions in their lives, and in the artwork that they produce.

> They make great programming. They're very innovative, they're nimble, they're taking advantage of all these new technologies. They're synthesizing new policies. They're synthesizing even how the beat cops in the neighborhood have changed and what the personalities of these cops are when they make decisions about where they're going to be. They're just navigating so much complex stuff, at the same time they're huge culture creators, always teaching us a new dance, always making up a new phrase that's such a good phrase! Young people are huge culture creators. I just can't get ... I mean I'm obviously obsessed with them that's why I work with them. I think they're really cool.

Adult participants described young people as expanding the boundaries of language and artistic expressions, including about sexuality, gender, relationships and desires. Their creativity, resilience, and artistry are connected to their queer and trans identities.

Adult co-conspirators appreciate the ways that youth negotiate power from marginalized positions without access to institutional power. They see youth resilience in the face of oppressive institutions and punitive policies. One program director said the youth demonstrate

> an ability to be their own person in the face of ... being true to themselves, and lines of people just telling them not to be who they are, definitely is true as well. Their maintaining a sense of humor about things is amazing too. And I guess it's not just resilience, but just to keep trying and not giving up. So resilience, and perseverance, and determination.

The lines of people may include family and peers, or school personnel, or criminal punishment systems. Within any or all of these structures youth may find their identities are unwelcome and that they are viewed as creating problems by not assimilating to heteronormativity or binary gender. Even in the face of these pressures, youth persist in claiming their identities and engage with others with humor and joy.

This resilience is appreciated even when youth resist the limits enforced by the organization and its staff. Youth refusals of staff rules is seen as another form of resilience and power negotiation that youth engage in, and that adults desire to foster in youth.

> And I think the commitment that some of the young people have to their own joy and their own right to feel good, when they push back against us for some of the boundaries we set for them, it's just inspiring to

me… They always want to be joyous and take up space, and make noise. They want to be seen. They want to be seen by each other. They want to be seen by us. They want to be validated.

These adults demonstrate a desire to learn from the youth about who they are and how they express themselves, and how they experience their city, neighborhoods, and institutions they engage with. They believe young people's narratives about their experiences, and they learn from youth's knowledge. They help develop the skills and knowledges that youth arrive with, with the expectation that these young people will soon fill the roles the adults currently hold. They know the young people are developing leaders in the community.

Scaffolded successes

In order to act as co-conspirators with youth, adults have to scaffold the learning that youth need to take those positions of leadership in the community. For many of these adults, they also learned leadership and honed their cultural criticism through mentoring by feminist, queer, or abolitionist leaders in their adolescence and early 20s and acknowledge how these experiences helped them grow into the leader they are now. The knowledge about queer and trans history in the US, about language and culture, about the politics of advocating for queer and trans existence was shared with them in community by queer elders and antiracism activists and feminist advocates. These mentors created opportunities for the participants to sharpen their arguments, practice speaking up, and strategically engage with structures of power. These opportunities for success helped the adults develop into politically-savvy, collaborative, and critical educators and leaders. These adults now create similar opportunities for youth in the organizations.

In organizations, youth volunteer, are selected, or are paid to provide workshops for other youth who attend the programs. These opportunities acknowledge the expertise of youth who have experiences and knowledge to share.

> And you're just building up their "I did it," even if at the end of the day, no, they didn't really write the curriculum or practice enough that it's, whatever. They're going to get up in front of that room, and they're going to deliver a workshop, and they've done it. And that's good enough. They get to put that on their resume, and they get to internalize a narrative of success, whether or not they did the entire process from A to B."

Internalizing a narrative of success is an important part of developing skills and learning. This process allows young people to gain confidence in their role and their knowledge, and to develop capacities and roles for themselves in the community.

Adults scaffold this learning process however, and help to cushion the risks that youth take. The same adult co-conspirator further explained the role of adults in helping a young person prepare to take a leadership or teaching role,

> You have to really be like, "Okay, we're going to get this to be enough that it's good and you feel good about it, not that I'm going to send you into a room of other teens or adults and you're going to do something that you're not going to feel good about.

This kind of critical care (McArthur & Lane, 2019) pushes the young person to do the best work that they can in the situation and with the available resources that they have at the time, models working in collaboration and asking for help, and ensures that their experience is a positive one from which they can gain confidence and also gain skills to apply to future opportunities. These successes are ones which may not be available to youth in other settings, where their knowledge, expertise, or self-presentation may be considered "inappropriate" or embarrassing.

Adults in these positions try to create opportunities for young people that they may not get in other areas of their lives. Youth may attend hearings, fundraising event, or administration meetings to speak on behalf of the programs and the young people who use them. The adults must assess the costs of attendance in relation to the rewards for the young people who engage in these events. These judgments are not easy to make, and are choices where the adults may question if they are doing enough to highlight that youth are entitled to these goods, without making themselves vulnerable or sharing their stories.

> I wish that I was doing a better job at not making them feel like they didn't have to work for it so much. Sometimes I invite a young person with me to an event, they immediately disclose their gender, they immediately disclose their history with the criminal justice system or sex work, with this random, rich, white person who they feel like they have to perform it for in order to say thank you to me... And not that they always have to share their experiences trauma, or their experiences of violence and harm, as a way of entertainment for wealthy people to feel good about giving them money... That they are at this dinner and they're going to be served the expensive lobster just like everybody else. They deserve to be here just as much as all these rich people. And you don't have to tell anybody shit about you."

Adult coconspirators desire to share the expansive experiences and opportunities that are available to youth in the organizations, but also want to shelter youth from situations that would make them more vulnerable or open them up to new or recurring traumas in exchange for the experiences.

In this way, adults in these settings ensure some successes for youth, allowing them to know the confidence that comes with achieving and to build upon those achievements, while engaging youth critical conversations about the stakes in the situation. Another adult coconspirator said it this way:

> They're very much aware when adults are shoving them into places to say something, and not knowing whether or not the thing that they said has actually contributed to change, or whether or not they're just being paraded around for a reason... As an adult, am I contributing to this experience [of tokenization] or am I actually having meaningful partnerships, and being honest about the limitations?

Adults engage in critical conversations about these opportunities and the costs associated with them, and encourage young people to make decisions about which causes they want to share their valuable insights and creativity with, and which ones ignore their input or use it to further marginalize or stereotype them. Helping to develop their agency about how to use their influence and presence in this way creates opportunities for youth to understand their success and worth. These critically reflective conversations, that adults have among themselves, and with youth, engage in an ethic of care in which the growth, learning, and safety of youth is prioritized, and as such, youth are given space and opportunity to develop their politics and ethics around issues of sexuality, gender, race, class, and ability.

Conclusion

In order to incorporate the learnings from the adult co-conspirators in out-of-school youth organizations, we need to change who institutions are answerable to (Patel, 2016a). One way to do this would be to stop viewing queer and trans youth as a problem to be managed or hidden from view or ignored in the hops that it will go away. These organizations center queer and trans youth's identities, needs, input, and representations. Schools would need to make queer and trans youth part of the community to whom the institution is responsible, accountable, answerable.

Setting up gender and sexuality sucesses as milestones for development and normativity means that students who fail at this gender and sexuality development model have their mental and physical (and sometimes spiritual) health called into question. Students may explore expressions of gender, sexualities, relationships structures, or styles, as well as trying on friend groups and interests (Bragg et al., 2018). These explorations are often viewed with suspicion by adults, who may view youth as "at risk" and as a problem (Loutzenheiser, 2015) for teachers, administrators, other students, or schools. Experiencing the identities youth claim as unspeakable and unimaginable for adults who are tasked with helping youth learn and grow, students may work to silence, obliterate, or ignore parts of themselves. Relationships are necessary for creating the conditions for learning, but students who are required by adults to deny part of their existence in the name of finding a place in schools have a constrained possibility for creating relationships. They will not trust the adults in schools to provide them what they need, to make space for them to break apart in the name of becoming open to new knowledge (Halberstam, 2011), or to care for the identities that the young person is nurturing within themselves (McArthur & Lane, 2019). The care of trusted adults is necessary to nurture queer and trans young people.

The adults in the out-of-school youth organizations attended to trust in developing the ethos of the adults working in the setting. The focus of their programming and services oriented around meeting youth needs first, before asking youth to contribute or share information that the organization needs. The adults let youth guide the content of the programming, by asking what kinds of workshops they wanted. The services provided respond to the health, mental health, educational, employment, and social needs expressed by young people. This focus allowed youth to develop a sense of safety with the adults, and to approach the goals of the organization with their own motivation to contribute, rather than being compelled. Queer and trans youth and adults could be engaged to suggest ways to make schools more inclusive, and less often sites of failure. Trust would need to be established, however, that these conversations were more than pandering. As the participant said above, youth know when they are being "paraded around" and that administrators have no real intentions of making changes based on their suggestions.

The expectations of gender and sexuality inclusion in schools often asks that LGBTQ + youth disguise or hide their differences and fit in with the normalized gender and sexuality that it is considered possible for the school to accommodate. "Of course they want to be like us, the story of institutional normalization goes, because our ways naturally enshrine that which all human beings desire" (Mitchell et al., 2014, p. 304). There are other stories of identity, relationships, families, and community that do not get told when these differences are silenced in schools. "Curricular cripistemologies, in contrast, openly advocate for the productive potential of failing normalization practices (if they were ever obtainable in the first place) because such goals entail erasing recognitions of the alternative values, practices, and flexible living arrangements particular to crip/queer lives" (p. 306). What might curricular inclusion of the productive potential of failing normalizing practices look like in schools, both in the explicit and the hidden curriculum? The adults in youth-serving organizations explicitly celebrate the community-making and culture-expanding creativity of queer and trans youth who use these organizations for support and survival. Curricular cripistemologies, like disability studies (Kafer, 2013) ask for adults in schools to also think about upending taken-for-granted beliefs about success and failure by learning from the creativity and perspectives of queer and trans youth, BIPOC youth, youth with disabilities, and multiply marginalized youth. The joy, opportunities, and healing found in learning from and with youth denied centrality and normativity may offer a largesse that enhances justice for all youth (Keenan, 2017; Miller, 2016).

The silencing of conversations about difference and elision of the variety of sexual and gender identities harms all students. It is clear how this flattening harms students who identify as queer and trans, but less acknowledged that strict gender and sexuality normativity uses ableist and racist tropes (Annamma & Handy, 2019; Somerville, 1990) to uphold definitions of privilege and marginalization.

> The crip/queer classroom produces a more meaningful system of differential values wherein shame about one's body as inadequate, medicalized, and pathological (the current terms of normalization within inclusionism) are abandoned. In their place, curricular cripistemologies insert the creative alternatives of interdependency, the politics of atypicality, and a more critical assessment of neoliberalism's founding in(ex)clusions. (Mitchell et al., 2014, p. 313)

Or as Halberstam (2011) would have us aspire to, we should resist mastery, privilege the naive or nonsensical, and suspect memorialization. In other words, we could always be seeking new understandings, encouraging and engaging even ignorant questions, and poking holes in the tidy stories that support institutions and groups in power. Challenging the bases of these inequitable valuing systems across different identities can help students see themselves in the curriculum and social structure of the school, and can also begin to expand understandings of possible existences for students.

Too often students understand themselves as excessive. It may be taken for granted that schools engage in normalizing processes, even that that is part of their function. However, these normalizing discourses create experiences of failure day after day for some students. As adults in solidarity with youth, teachers must begin to make it possible for students to bring all of their selves, bodies, and identities to schools, without fear that the classroom, the adult, or the curriculum cannot hold them.

Disclosure statement

No potential conflict of interest was reported by the authors.

ORCID

Darla Linville http://orcid.org/0000-0003-1896-1718

References

Airton, L., Kirkup, K., McMillan, A., & DesRochers, J. (2019). What is "gender expresssion"?: How a new and nebulous human rights construct is taking shape in Ontario school board policy documents. *Canadian Journal of Education*, 42(4), 1154–1182.
Annamma, S. A. (2016). Disrupting the carceral state through education journey mapping. *International Journal of Qualitative Studies in Education*, 29(9), 1210–1230. https://doi.org/10.1080/09518398.2016.1214297
Annamma, S. A., & Handy, T. (2019). DisCrit solidarity as curriculum studies and transformative praxis. *Curriculum Inquiry*, 49(4), 442–463. https://doi.org/10.1080/03626784.2019.1665456
Anyon, J. (2005). *Radical possibilities: Public policy, urban education, and a new social movement*. Routledge Falmer.
Anyon, J. (1997). *Ghetto schooling: A political economy of urban educational reform*. Teachers College Press.
Bragg, S., Renold, E., Ringrose, J., & Jackson, C. (2018). More than boy, girl, male, female: Exploring young people's views on gender diversity within and beyond school contexts. *Sex Education*, 18(4), 420–434. https://doi.org/10.1080/14681811.2018.1439373
Center for American Progress. (2014). *Beyond bullying: How hostile school climate perpetuates the school-to-prison pipeline for LGBT Youth*. Retrieved from http://www.americanprogress.org/issues/lgbt/report/2014/02/27/84179/beyond-bullying/
Elliott, K. O. (2012). The right way to be gay: How school structures sexual inequality. In E. R. Meiners & T. Quinn (Eds.), *Sexualities in education: A reader* (pp. 158–166). Peter Lang.
Elliott, K. O. (2016). Queering student perspectives: Gender, sexuality and activism in school. *Sex Education*, 16(1), 49–62. https://doi.org/10.1080/14681811.2015.1051178
Erevelles, N., Grace, E. J., & Parekh, G. (2019). Disability as meta curriculum: Ontologies, epistemologies, and transformative praxis. *Curriculum Inquiry*, 49(4), 357–372. https://doi.org/10.1080/03626784.2019.1664078
Fair, R. (2021). No Promo Homo Laws Hurt Students and Teachers. *English Journal*, 110(3), 101–103.
Fields, J. (2008). *Risky lessons: Sex education and social inequality*. Rutgers University Press.
Fields, J. (2012). Differences and divisions: Social inequality in sex education debates and policies. In E. R. Meiners & T. Quinn (Eds.), *Sexualities in education: A reader* (pp. 24–32). Peter Lang.

Fine, M., & Burns, A. (2003). Class notes: Toward a critical psychology of class and schooling. *Journal of Social Issues*, *59*(4), 841–860. https://doi.org/10.1046/j.0022-4537.2003.00093.x

Fine, M., Tuck, E., & Yang, K. W. (2014). An intimate memoir of resistance theory. In E. Tuck & K. W. Yang (Eds.), *Youth resistance research and theories of change* (pp. 46–58). Routledge.

Foucault, M. (1977). *Discipline and punish: The birth of the prison* (1st American ed.). Pantheon Books.

Garcia, L. (2009). Now why do you want to know about that?: Heteronormativity, sexism, and racism in the sexual miseducation of Latina youth. *Gender & Society*, *23*(4), 520–541.

Goodenow, C. S., Watson, R., Adjei, J., Homma, Y., & Saewyc, E. (2016). Sexual orientation trends and disparities in school bullying and violence-related experiences, 1999–2013. *Psychology of Sexual Orientation and Gender Diversity*, *3*(4), 386–396. https://doi.org/10.1037/sgd0000188

Halberstam, J. (2011). *The queer art of failure*. Duke.

Hartman, S. (2019). *Wayward lives, beautiful experiments: Intimate histories of riotous Black girls, troublesome women, and queer radicals*. W. W. Norton & Company.

Heck, N. C., Poteat, V. P., & Goodenow, C. S. (2016). Advances in research with LGBTQ Youth in Schools. *Psychology of Sexual Orientation and Gender Diversity*, *3*(4), 381–385. https://doi.org/10.1037/sgd0000206

Hoefer, S. E., & Hoefer, R. (2017). Worth the wait?: The consequences of abstinence-only sex education for marginalized students. *American Journal of Sexuality Education*, *12*(3), 257–276. https://doi.org/10.1080/15546128.2017.1359802

Irvine, J. M. (2002). *Talk about sex: The battles over sex education in the United States*. University of California Press.

Istar Lev, A. (2010). How queer! – The development of gender identity and sexual orientation in LGBTQ-headed families. *Family Process*, *49*(3), 268–290. https://doi.org/10.1111/j.1545-5300.2010.01323.x

Johnson, M. L. (2015). Bad romance: A crip feminist critique of queer failure. *Hypatia*, *30*(1), 251–267. https://doi.org/10.1111/hypa.12134

Kafer, A. (2013). *Feminist Queer Crip*. Indiana University.

Keenan, H. B. (2017). Unscripting curriculum: Toward a critical trans pedagogy. *Harvard Educational Review*, *87*(4), 538–556. https://doi.org/10.17763/1943-5045-87.4.538

Kornhaber, M. L., Griffith, K., & Tyler, A. (2014). It's not education by zip code anymore – But what is it? Conceptions of equity under the Common Core. *Education Policy Analysis Archives*, *22*(4), 4–27. https://doi.org/10.14507/epaa.v22n4.2014

Kosciw, J. G., Greytak, E. A., Giga, N. M., Villenas, C., & Danischewski, D. J. (2016). *The 2015 National School Climate Survey: The experiences of lesbian, gay, bisexual, transgender, and queer youth in our nation's schools*. Retrieved from http://glsen.org

Lesko, N. (2001). *Act your age!: A cultural construction of adolescence*. Routledge Falmer.

Linville, D. (2017). Unexpected bodies and pleasures: Sexuality and gender in schools. *Critical Questions in Education*, *8*(4), 377–399.

Lipman, P. (2004). *High stakes education: Inequality, globalization, and urban school reform*. Routledge Falmer.

Loutzenheiser, L. W. (2015). Who are you calling a problem?': Addressing transphobia and homophobia through school policy. *Critical Studies in Education*, *56*(1), 99–115. https://doi.org/10.1080/17508487.2015.990473

McArthur, S. A., & Lane, M. (2019). Schoolin' Black girls: Politicized caring and healing as pedagogical love. *The Urban Review*, *51*(1), 65–80. https://doi.org/10.1007/s11256-018-0487-4

McGovern, A. E. (2012). When schools refuse to say gay: The constitutionality of anti-LGBTQ No-Promo-Homo pulbic school policies in the United States. *Cornell Journal of Law and Public Policy*, *22*, 465–490. Retrieved from http://scholarship.law.cornell.edu/cjlpp/vol22/iss2/5

McGuire, J. K., Anderson, C. R., Toomey, R. B., & Russell, S. T. (2010). School climate for transgender youth: A mixed method investigation of student experiences and school responses. *Journal of Youth and Adolescence*, *39*(10), 1175–1188. https://doi.org/10.1007/s10964-010-9540-7

Meiners, E. R. (2010). *Right to be hostile: Schools, prisons, and the making of public enemies*. Routledge.

Miller, S J. (2016). Reading YAL queerly: A Queer Literacy Framework for inviting (a)gender and (a)sexuality self-determination and justice. In D. Linville & D. L. Carlson (Eds.), *Beyond Borders: Queer eros and ethos (ethics) in LGBTQ young adult literature* (pp. 153–180). Peter Lang.

Mitchell, D. T., Snyder, S. L., & Ware, L. (2014). [Every] child left behind: Curricular cripistemologies and the crip/queer art of failure. *Journal of Literary & Cultural Disability Studies*, *8*(3), 295–319. https://doi.org/10.3828/jlcds.2014.24

Morris, M. (2015). *Pushout: The criminalization of Black girls in schools*. The New Press.

Nolan, K. (2011). *Police in the hallways: Discipline in an urban high school*. University of Minnesota.

Pascoe, C. J. (2007). *Dude, you're a fag: Masculinity and sexuality in high school*. University of California.

Patel, L. (2016a). *Decolonizing educational research: From ownership to answerability*. Routledge.

Patel, L. (2016b). Pedagogies of resistance and survivance: Learning as marronage. *Equity & Excellence in Education*, *49*(4), 397–401. https://doi.org/10.1080/10665684.2016.1227585

Reay, D. (2001). Finding or losing yourself?: Working-class relationships to education. *Journal of Education Policy*, *16*(4), 333–346. https://doi.org/10.1080/02680930110054335

Shelton, S. A. (2017). White people are gay, but so are some of my kids": Examining the intersections of race, sexuality, and gender. *Bank Street Occasional Paper Series, 2017*(37), Article 8. Retrieved from https://educate.bank-street.edu/occasional-paper-series/vol2017/iss37/8

Skrtic, T. M. (2005). A political economy of learning disabilities. *Learning Disability Quarterly, 28*(2), 149–155. Retrieved from https://www.jstor.org/stable/1593616 https://doi.org/10.2307/1593616

Snapp, S. D., Hoenig, J. M., Fields, A., & Russell, S. T. (2015). Messy, butch, and queer: LGBTQ youth and the school-to-prison pipeline. *Journal of Adolescent Research, 30*(1), 57–82. https://doi.org/10.1177/0743558414557625

Somerville, S. (2000). *Queering the color line: Race and the invention of homosexuality in American culture.* Duke University Press.

Spring, J. H. (2019). *American education* (19th ed.). Routledge.

Tuck, E., & Yang, K. W. (2014). *Youth resistance research and theories of change.* Routledge.

Venzant Chambers, T. T., & McCready, L. T. (2011). Making space" for ourselves: African American student responses to their marginalization. *Urban Education, 46*(6), 1352–1378. https://doi.org/10.1177/0042085911400322

White, T. (2020). Demystifying whiteness in a market of "No Excuses" charter schools. In E. Mayorga, U. Aggarwal & B. Picower, (Eds.), *What's race got to do with it: how current school reform policy maintains racial and economic inequality* (2nd Ed). Peter Lang Publishing/USA.

Ziyad, H., & DuWhite, T. (2020). How "disparity" logics pathologize Black male bodies and render other Black bodies invisible. In C. A. Grant, A. N. Woodson, M. J. Dumas (Eds.), *The Future is Black: Afropessimism, Fugitivity, and Radical Hope in Education (chap. 6).* Routledge.

Illegible and Illiterate in Honduras: Research in a Transnational Setting as a Queer from the Global North

Kate E. Kedley

ABSTRACT
In this article, I examine an ongoing qualitative and ethnographic research project in a transnational, multilingual setting. I am not primarily a queer scholar, nor do I study queer issues, gender, or sexuality, as a primary focus in my research agenda or career. However, I am the primary research instrument in these projects, and I am also a person whose language, gender, and sexuality are at times, legible, while also to varying degrees, indecipherable to those around me. Some research projects are in the Central American country of Honduras, and as an academic from the Global North, there are many situations in which I was unable to settings and individuals while in the field. I use narrative inquiry to share and assess this illegibility, both on my part and on the part of people I met in the field. The data set includes fifteen years of living and traveling to Honduras to teach and to conduct research; however, it has never specifically been in LGBTI spaces or with LGBTI communities. Regardless, at the end of each day, my fieldnotes are filled with insight gleaned from my presence as a queer person and interactions within LGBTI communities. This article, and the larger research project in general, came to light because of the ways language, gender, and sexuality—specifically my own language, gender, and sexuality—challenged me in this transnational qualitative research setting.

In the spring of 2015, I walked down a footpath that ran parallel to an old United Fruit Company railroad track in La Lima, Honduras. Surrounded by waist-high grass, the footpath was dusty, with dried bicycle ruts and flattened garbage strewn about. The midday sun baked my shoulders, and in my hand, I clutched a phone and a small wad of sweaty and damp Lempiras, the Honduran currency.

I was headed home toward the barracones, which are a group of small rectangular wood homes on stilts, built originally for workers of the United Fruit Company or Chiquita Banana; I stayed there during my ethnographic dissertation research in Honduras about teachers, language education, and social movements. The family I lived with I had known and stayed with on and off for a decade, and I had spent years travelling back and forth between Honduras and the United States before conducting research there; I knew the area well.

A traditional mode of transportation in this area of Honduras is the bicycle, a remnant of old fruit company days decades ago, where workers rode their bikes, a machete wedged between the bars of the bicycle, in the early morning hours to the banana campos, and back again to their respective barracon at night. And thus, it was no surprise when a large, middle-aged man rode up behind me on a bike, and I stepped aside into the tall grass to let him pass on the path. He turned around as he passed to look at me and wobbled a bit as he pedaled forward. A few yards later he climbed off the bike and mindlessly looked through his shoulder bag. I walked past him; I heard him remount his bike; I let him pass me again. Further ahead, once again, he got off his bike, and started fiddling with his front tire.

I tensed up a bit. Honduras has one of the highest murder rates in the world, and impunity for crimes is nearly absolute, especially when directed toward women or members of the LGBTI community; over 95% of crimes go uninvestigated, let alone end in charges or conviction (Fernandez Aponte, 2018). (Throughout this paper I use LGBTI as the acronym I have seen most utilized in Honduras, which stands for lesbiana, gay, bisexual, transvesti, intersex). I had been held up at knifepoint and gunpoint multiple times, and I sensed this man was looking for a place along the footpath to do the same and take my phone and the sweaty Lempiras clutched in my hand.

He looked up at me as I approached, and smiled from the crouch by his bike tire. I offered a greeting—buenas—and kept going. But as I kept walking, he called after me.

"De donde viene?"

I turned: "Soy de los estados, y usted?"

People can generally tell I'm not Honduran, and thus wasn't originally from La Lima. I have freckled skin and light hair, and when I spoke, my Spanish was agringado, or like a gringo—a Spanish professor in the United States once categorized my Spanish as "lousy fluent," meaning I could participate fluently in any setting in Spanish, but my grammar and verb tenses were "lousy."

The man explained that he lived in one of the banana campos further down the path, and we chatted as I continued walking and he pushed his bike.

Finally, he paused and took a deep breath. "Tengo algo que decirle... pero tengo pena... y no sé si va a gustar..." He trailed off awkwardly but somewhat flirtatiously. *I have something to tell you... but I'm embarrassed... and I don't know if you'll like it...*

"Bueno, I'm heading home," I replied, motioning to the barracones... "So, if you want to say something..."

All the sudden my eyes widened as I realized what was happening. I sighed knowing the inevitable gender trouble about to happen. Was this man flirting with me because *he thought I was a woman*? Or was this man flirting with me because *he thought I was a man*?

"OK OK, espérame... solo quiero saber.... si usted ha sido..." He was bashful as he continued. "Si ha sido con un hombre..." *I just want to know... if you've ever been... if you've ever been with a man...*

Minutes before, I reminded him, when he asked if I had a family, I said I had children and at one point at I had an esposo. And thus, yes, I had "been" with a man before. He laughed and waived off my response. No no no... I mean.... have you ever, como.... Like gone *out on your wife with another man*? Like *have you ever slept with another man*?

I laughed and stumbled through a response about how my genitals were probably not what he was looking for. He responded that he was—in fact—very interested in *men who want to become women...*

Eventually, his eyes widened as he figured out that I was assigned female at birth, and not, in fact, a man who slept with other men, or the type of man he was looking to sleep with, and he rode his bike away to his barracon.

I have retold this anecdote in social settings to laughs and to discomfort. I have also thought long and hard about this incident in terms of what it means about my role as a researcher in a transnational context, and specifically what can be learned about legible and illegibile languages, genders, sexualities, and communities in research settings.

There were three levels of transnational illegibility in this interaction. First, language: my Spanish is typically understood by other speakers of Spanish without incident. However, my Spanish was in illegible in this moment, even when I was explicit in telling this person I wasn't a man (or at least not in the way he was looking for a man). I repeatedly said "Soy mujer, y tengo vagina..."; he thought I was telling him I *wanted* to be a woman, and I *wanted* a vagina. In his mind, the confusing conversation stemmed from my perceived lack of language abilities to convey my identity, perhaps heightened by my accent.

Second, this man did not believe the confusion stemmed from the presentation of my gendered body or my gender expression, regardless of my language. Because my body and my language were in conflict (to him), he assumed it was my language that was incorrect, and not the way he was reading my body. Typically, women in Honduras—lesbians included—don't wear sweaty men's gym clothes, or have a crewcut freshened up with a straight razor at the local barber. How was my body illegible? This wasn't a simple case of I am a woman, but he perceived me as a man. First, in the transnational context, I occupied a space that was generally legible in the United States. I present as masculine to varying degrees, but I do not identify as a man, nor do I identify as a gay man. I am not universally perceived to be a man in the United States, although it does happen, especially with people who are not familiar with the queer community. I was produced around certain gender hierarchies, and now I didn't seem to fit in them in Honduras.

However, this man not only thought I was a man; he also saw something that indicated I might be a man that sleeps with other men, and that there was no danger in asking. This, in a country where the levels of murder and violence against the LGBTI community is one of the highest in the world. Thus, this man assumed my sexuality as well, which was illegible even as I used language to explain it, and of which my gender expression (short hair, men's clothes) had nothing to do with.

I offer this vignette as an introduction to a constant destabilization of gender and sexuality—of both my own gender and sexuality, and of my understandings of the concepts of gender and sexuality—during an ongoing qualitative and ethnographic research project in a transnational, multilingual setting. I am not primarily a queer scholar, nor do I study queer issues, gender, or sexuality as a primary focus in my research agenda or career; I research literacy and language use in community spaces. However, because I am gender-nonconforming, and because I was frequently in spaces with other members of the LGBTI community in Honduras, this disruption to my own identity and understandings as a researcher was perpetual.

In this qualitative research project, I am the primary research instrument (Merriam, 2009), and I am a person whose language, gender, and sexuality were at times, legible, while also to varying degrees, indecipherable to those around me. Thus, the primary research instrument of this study (me!) was queered. The reverse was also true: I was frequently stymied in LGBTI spaces, confused on how to react ethically in certain situations, and unsure on how to react when I was read differently than I expected to be read. In the context of this transnational and multilingual setting, how did this impact qualitative findings in a project such as my own? What are the opportunities and barriers of queer legibility and illegibility, and should they be considered aggressive, oppressive, or marginalizing?

In this article, I share principles of Queer Theory (Butler, 1993, 1990; Halberstam, 1998) that guide this analysis, including an exploration of queer geographies (Blackwood, 2005; Brown et al., 2010; Browne & Nash, 2010). Transnational Feminist Theory (Alexander & Mohanty, 1997) is a useful framework to disrupt local and global binaries as they relate to research in Honduras, and an exploration of language, gender, and sexuality in my research there. I outline the history and the objectives of my overarching research in Honduras, including the methodology and the various themes and progress that have emerged from this research over the past decade. Before highlighting two themes from this analysis, I give a brief overview of gender and LGBTI issues in

Honduras, as I have learned from my academic and personal experiences there, and from work I do in the US and in Honduras with LGBTI Hondurans.

The overarching questions I ask in this article are: How did being illegible to others prompt me to closely examine the reverse: what I thought was illegible and didn't understand in Honduras? How does a sometimes legible (but more often, not) language, gender, and sexuality, for me as the primary research instrument, affect me a teacher, scholar, researcher, and person, and the products of my research? How are these interactions linked to Queer Battle Fatigue (QBF) (Wozolek et al., 2015) come into play in these interactions and lead to resistance, weariness, or clarity on my part or on the part of those I interact with?

To answer these questions, I use narrative inquiry and share anecdotes from my extensive qualitative and ethnographic data set. The data set includes fifteen years of living and traveling to Honduras to teach and to conduct research; however, it has never specifically been in LGBTI spaces or with LGBTI communities. Regardless, at the end of the day, my fieldnotes were filled with insight gleaned from my presence as a queer person and interactions in LGBTI communities. This article, and the larger research project in general, came to light because of the ways language, gender, and sexuality—specifically my own language, gender, and sexuality—challenged me in this transnational setting as a qualitative researcher.

Theoretical framework and literature review

This work uses my previously published research and investigations as a foundation to build from. I first examined gender and sexuality in the context of US K-12 education, when I suggested the body of a teacher is a text (Kedley, 2015) that students read, much like they might read a poem or a novel. The teacher-as-text can be more powerful than books or other classroom materials because of how frequently the teacher is engaged with and "read" by students. I discussed the subtle gendered and sexualized cues and norms students learn from teachers about identity and relationships based on how they read their teacher. I have also considered the researcher's body as a text (as the primary instrument in qualitative research) in the context of gathering transnational and ethnographic data (Kedley, 2019). In that work, I examined the ethics of being read differently in the research site, and the "gender trouble" I frequently found myself in while conducting research. There have even been times where I had simultaneous conversations in the same space where one person referred to me with masculine pronouns (él, or he) and another person answered using feminine pronouns (ella, o she). I draw primarily on my own extensive fieldnotes, interview data from hundreds of participants across the studies, and anecdotes from throughout my experiences to build these themes.

Queer theory

It was liberating for me, especially as a person who grew up (very unintentionally) residing outside the norm in terms of gender presentation, to see how gender norms and the heterosexual matrix (Butler, 1990) have shaped us, and have shaped how we are rewarded and punished based on our gender identity and presentation. Thus, learning about queer theory was transformational for me not only as an academic, but as a queer person. Our gender identities and expression are "embedded in power relations that limit and/or open up certain possibilities and not others" (Browne & Nash, 2010). Thus, much of our gender identity and gender expression is influenced by power dynamics, and a system of policing and rewards, that will vary across time and place.

Additionally, Queer Theory suggests that gender identity and sexuality are neither stable nor concrete, and that the categories of gender and sexuality are unstable and temporal (Butler, 2004; Marcus, 2005). Because ALL these categories are viewed as fluid and flexible, they apply to

ALL genders and sexualities, even ones that are not minoritized genders and sexualities. The focus is instead on heteronormativity, relationships between sexualities and genders, and the continuation or interruption of the dominant sexual order (Curran, 2006). Everyone's sexuality and gender evolves throughout time, in different contexts, or in response to cultural acceptance or rejection of sexualities and genders. It follows then, that conceptions of gender and sexuality in a transnational research setting would be unique and distinct (and sometimes in conflict with) from my own understandings (and even my own individual identity) of gender and sexuality.

Queer Theory recognizes that sexuality and sexual desire is based on many factors, such as context, interaction, preference, and availability, which result in a plethora of possible and sometimes inconsistent sexualities in an individual. If sexuality is freed from the binary, gender follows, as the concept of heterosexuality is highly dependent on the "natural" coupling of gender, meaning male and female (heterosexual), and their relative position to the opposite, homosexual (male and male, female and female). Once we question the reality of these categories and their supposed relationships to each other, other configurations within these binaries are suspect as natural. This also suggests that the queer identities produced in the United States cannot be seen as a natural and normal progression to queer liberation or freedom of gender or sexual identity.

Queer theory challenges the idea that man and woman are natural gender categorizations and offers an alternative to thinking about how these categories became normalized, and how they led to a dominance of heterosexuality in US society, and a dominance of US cultural norms abroad, including conceptions of gender and sexuality (Blackwood, 2005). Cultural and legal norms that build the categories of gender and sexuality maintain our understandings of what is normal, natural, and thus universally accepted and promoted, or what is worth resisting. This can be especially complicated because cultural, legal, linguistic, and social norms are different in different regions, decades, communities, and nations. Thus, given the transnational and multilingual research setting, questioning "naturally occurring" gender categories or even the concept of queer progress is paramount to this analysis.

Queer geographies and space

As a reminder that queerness is not a universal concept, and that conceptions of gender and sexuality vary across regions, I turn to queer geographies. Browne and Nash (2010) note that understanding "geographical variation is critical to understanding both legislated and lived experiences" of queer and LGBTI communities (p. 2). The unique context of Honduras—from banana enclaves, to maquilas or sweat shops, to migration and militarization, to violent US intervention and coup d'états—has shaped the complexities of the LGBTI communities in Honduras.

Brown (2012) reminds us to not map conceptions of gender or sexuality from the US on Honduras, and warns that "the experiences of metropolitan gay men and women are too frequently extrapolated from, globalized, and presented as the universal gay experience" (p. 1068). A transnational project, especially with a Global North researcher conducting research in the Global South, runs the risk of centering concepts of gender and sexuality that are more common in the United States or the Global North.

I have not studied gender and sexuality in Honduras as a researcher, but because of my gender identity and expression, and because of social and friendly connections in Honduras, I spent a lot of time within LGBTI spaces and interacted with LGBTI people. Brown (2012) notes that "by studying the specific relations that produce ordinary homosexualities in ordinary locations, sexualities research might move beyond the exceptional and contribute to a new sexual politics rooted in the heterogeneity of everyday social relations" (p. 1071). For example, in some senses, a homonormativity might be beneficial in Honduras or other places because it would contribute to visibility and normalization of a marginalized culture that is often otherwise met with violence.

However, in this project, dynamics of gender and sexuality will not be measured against the United States or the Global North, nor will they be looked at in terms of "progress."

Transnational feminist theory

I frequently turn to transnational feminist theories to analyze my position in the Central American country of Honduras and in multiracial and multilingual spaces in the United States. Mohanty (2003) defines transnational feminism as an analysis that connects "everyday life and local gendered contexts and ideologies to the larger, transnational political and economic structures and ideologies of capitalism" (p. 504). Information, people, technology, goods, and capital do not flow evenly through national borders, and thus an analysis using national borders as a guide (in the boundaries of the United States, or within the borders of Honduras) is incomplete and hides important understandings of transnational relationships. Each examination of gender and sexuality in Honduras is lacking unless the qualitative researcher also considers structural and globalizing forces that affect gender and sexuality.

The local and the global are connected in multi-directional ways and they are not, in fact, a binary. To illustrate, a small percentage of the global population has limited access to a large percentage of available capital, materials, and resources. National borders do not accurately describe the directionality and implications of this phenomenon. People, goods, money, and culture move throughout the world in uneven flows. For example, as a US citizen, I was legally able to travel to Honduras, and as graduate student and teacher, I had the financial means to do so. As a queer person who is white, I was relatively safe and had recourse and connections when issues arose. I crossed these and other borders without issues. However, many Hondurans who want to travel, study, or live in the US are unable to legally cross those same borders in the other direction, and most do not have the financial means to do so. The Honduran LGBTI community is especially affected by these flows, not just of conceptions of gender and sexuality, but also of money, jobs, and family structures.

Transnational feminist theory suggests that difference between groups and people should be acknowledged, but not in way that not in ways that make marginalized communities—especially those who identify as women—"in the Third World bear the disproportionate burden of difference" and let "Western" or "first-world" be seen as the norm or standard (Alexander & Mohanty, 1997, p. 18). Otherwise, "difference" is only allowed to "unfold according to external standards and within an external frame of reference" (Nagar & Lock Swarr, 2010, p. 4). Transnational feminist theory situates the complex, dynamic, and shifting identities that people embody, inhabit, and even resist (Brochin, 2018). Status quo understandings of nationhood, community, gender, race, etc. are perpetually destabilized and challenged.

In the case of this article, transnational feminist ideas are paramount to my examination of gender and sexuality in a transnational and multilingual research setting. If I were to conclude, based on my experiences with genders and sexualities in Honduras, that genders and sexualities in the Global North are correct or natural, and those in Honduras (and in the Global South) are backwards, behind, simple, or wrong, that would be an incomplete, inaccurate, and unethical conclusion. The opposite is also true: I cannot suggest that Hondurans have a more pure and natural conception of gender and sexuality, of queer community, or of a vision forward.

Instead, I must see how these gender and sexuality dynamics work out in relations of global and local power. As I analyze my queerness in qualitative research spaces, I acknowledge that I may be susceptible to see my own understandings of gender and sexuality as "normal," yet the views of others as "different." I can't blame others for their inability to see me as legible, given that we were produced in different gendered contexts. At the same, I can't blaming others for my own inability to make their context legible, since I have the privilege of travel, movement, and border-crossing. Because I intend my work to be, at its very foundation a solidarity project, understandings of "difference" cannot lead to dominance of mainstream global values and instead must actively contest inequalities.

Affidavits and amicus briefs

Finally, for this article, I draw from my experience writing amicus briefs, or expert witness testimony, for women and members of the LGBTI community who seek asylum in the United States. I am often asked to testify in these cases because I am well-versed in gender and sexuality dynamics in Honduras. I am not well-versed simply because I have studied these issues academically or I because have been told this information second-hand; I have had years of experience living in, working in, and travelling around Honduras, beginning in 2006. This literature shows that since 2011, Honduras has one of the highest murder rates in the world, and marginalized people, especially women and LGBTI-identified people, are especially vulnerable. Nearly 100% of murders in the country go unsolved and remain without any type of arrest or conviction. Of the twelve people I have known personally that have been murdered in Honduras, about half women, none of the violent deaths were investigated by police, let alone was anyone charged or convicted. A sense of distrust of government officials and police and military forces, coupled with complete impunity in terms of solving crimes, makes women (and journalists, environmentalists, lawyers, and members of the LGBTI community) subject to persecution and victimization in Honduras. A thorough investigation into the history for this impunity, its link to migration to the United States, and the overall marginalization of the LGBTI community in Honduras, supports my themes for this article, and gender and sexuality cannot be considered alone.

Methodology—qualitative educational research in a transnational setting—ethics and responsibilities

A qualitative research project is "filled with interpersonal encounters, haptic human connection, closeness, understanding and interpersonal engagement," yet there is a gap in the research to the "extent to which ethnography is a form of emotional work, or emotional labour, with its own hazards and difficulties" (Browne & Nash, 2010, pp. 31–32). To document those hazards and difficulties, I have a large (in terms of space on my computer, boxes in my house, and amount of paperwork) data set from multiple ongoing projects in Honduras that began formally in 2012. All of these projects center on critical literacy and education, and consist of a growing archive of over two-hundred interviews, hundreds of pages of fieldnotes, and boxes of photos, posters, pamphlets, and other artifacts from years in the field. I generally spend my summer months in Honduras co-hosting workshops on reclaiming public space using poetry and literacy (from violence and state oppression), in a publicly engaged scholarship project. Thus, the work is continuous and ongoing.

Part of the emotional work and relationships built into my own ethnographic, qualitative studies are linked to my own gender and sexuality, which I have written about before (Kedley, 2015, 2019). Browne and Nash (2010) suggested that "one of the challenges of the craft of ethnographic writing is finding a way of clearly articulating what the often-hidden work of ethnography involves. Integral to this task is an account of what goes on within the field *and* within the ethnographer" (p. 38). Thus, in order to articulate the "often hidden work" in my own project, I focused on how my own illegibility and my own inability to read others affects the dynamics of relationships, interactions, and qualitative educational research broadly.

This qualitative project is interpretive, and I use narrative inquiry, vignettes, and analysis to present the data. I selected pieces of data through a process of sorting and coding, ongoing and throughout the years, and use what I have decided is important and relevant based on the topic of the piece and the goals of my study, in addition to other unseen forces that influence my selection, including power structures. Critical research "goes beyond the interpretation of people's understandings of their world" (Merriam, 2009, p. 9) and researchers conducting critical research "frame their research questions in terms of power—who has it, how it's negotiated, [and] what structures in society reinforce the current distribution of power." Because language and the ways people use language contribute to unequal hierarchies of power, and to constructions of identity, a central component of this research project is to explore the power dynamics surrounding my own queerness in this qualitative transnational project.

Narrative inquiry and learning from Testimonio y Sistematización

Throughout this article, I use narrative inquiry (Merriam, 2009) by offering stories, anecdotes, and vignettes, pulled from fieldnotes and memories of my years in Honduras. A complication of ethnographic research work, even as it inhabits multiple literary genres and travels through academic disciplines, is how culture is to be represented and who gets to tell stories about cultures. Given the intersection of research and historical colonization, tensions are heightened when academic researchers from "Western" and "First World" countries direct their ethnographic gaze towards subjects in the "Third World," representing a cultural other in their texts. Feminist and critical ethnographic research brought forth new sets of challenges including continued cultural othering and representations of people in relation to whiteness and other dominant class and gendered structures. Feminist literature and research was critiqued as predominantly white and middle-class and as denying intersections that women of color, lesbians, and working-class women inhabit. Two genres of information sharing, that I encountered in Honduras and that have origins in Latin America, guide my research and the products of my research: Testimonio and Sistematización.

I encountered Testimonio as a genre of sharing information that represents radical challenges to the ethnographic problem of cultural otherness, authorship, insider/outsider status, and literary form (Yudice, 1996). Testimonio has a long literary history in Latin America, and a formal history spanning six decades. The Testimonio originated in Cuba, and *The Autobiography of a Runaway Slave* (Biografía de un cimarrón) is often cited as the first text of this new genre (Gugelberger, 1996, p. 8). After the Cuban Revolution in 1959, Miguel Barnet recorded the story of Esteban Montejo, a formerly enslaved Afro-Cuban, who was 103 years old at the time he narrated his story. The popularity of Testimonio grew in the 1960s when a Testimonio category was created by the Casa de las Américas, a Cuban literary and cultural award organization. However, the roots of Testimonio likely reach further back into Latin American literary history, situated among war diaries of Jose Martí and Simón Bolívar or Spanish colonial crónicas (Beverley, 1996, p. 25).

Alternatively, la sistematización is linked to the construction of meaning to help us rethink the decisions we make in the process of research, to discover what informed those decisions, and to review our behavior in creative and ethical ways. Through this process, ideally, we would discover ways to transform both individuals and society. Gonzalez and Carrillo (n.d.) suggest we prioritize the lived experiences, dreams, and vision of individuals rather than traditional research procedures and techniques. Through a process of *sistematización* it is important to read the emotions, feelings, and affect that arises from this process of research development. Jara Holliday (n.d) sees sistematización as a tool that is superior to an informative piece or record of qualitative data.

The inclusion of testimonio and sistematización have resulted in and contribute to a larger dialogue that continually redefines and reexamines what counts as a critical qualitative work and what does not. I do not suggest that either methodology or genre is free of issues of othering, but I do draw from these concepts in that sharing stories and anecdotes can disrupt dominant discourses regarding legibility, cultural other, gender, sexuality, narratives in my research. I suggest that the idea of stories, oral histories, and narratives is necessary to disrupt academic tropes about what is scientific and what is evidence, especially in transnational spaces where when something is illegible it is frequently considered backwards, uncivilized, or wrong. The testimonio genre and the method of sistematización has forced me to reconsider, in my research and in my personal life, to accept personal experience and the sharing of stories with the same import I would give other forms of communication considered more formal and authentic by the academy.

Positionality: the queer researcher as the primary instrument in qualitative research

My major area of research is literacy education, and on occasion I study gender and sexuality in the context of literacy education. I was labeled female at birth, and in many ways, I navigate the world in ways common yet unique to women. For example, my name is Kate, a name nearly universally assigned to people assigned female at birth or chosen by people who identify as women. I have also been pregnant. In some settings, I am seen first as a (white) woman, other times as a (white) man, and second, as someone who seeks out intimate relationships with other women (i.e., as a lesbian, as a person who is queer, or a man). However, my research experiences, especially those in educational research settings, have challenged the relevance of my gender and sexuality when I am the primary research instrument in a research setting. For those around me, and for the space we generate together, my gender and sexuality have complicated research projects in ways I didn't anticipate in my pre-academic life.

My childhood geography has also influenced my gender and sexuality. I grew up in rural Iowa with farm families, and short hair among adult women was standard. Women and men did farm chores—woke up early to milk, feed the chickens, drove the tractor—and this type of femininity influenced what was imaginable for my own gender expression. My own gender identity and expression was produced by this context, and the opportunities and limits I was presented with in my larger society. Thus, as a researcher, I am a white, middle-class, educated, queer-identified person, whose gender and sexuality I am reluctant to define. I know how much my identity has been shaped by social pressures; I have preferences and some sense of an internal identity of who "Kate" is, but they have often manifested themselves differently at various points in my life and when in different contexts.

A critique of queer theory suggests that the queer subject has been turned into a socially constructed and materially non-existent human. This would ignore the material and lived reality that all humans face, especially those who have been minoritized because of racial, gendered, or sexual identity dynamics. In my discussions on queerness, I utilize my own material reality as a qualitative researcher, and the material reality of people I interact with at the research site. I also look at the material realities that forge and contribute to identities in Honduras, especially as related to gender and sexuality, and relationships with me as a queer teacher and researcher from the United States in that space.

Consequently, the QBF, or everyday aggression and violence LGBTI people face in Honduras, including me, offered an opportunity for growth, and challenged me to look at the aggressions those in the LGBTI community in Honduras faced with a nuanced understanding of my role in their marginalization, as a citizen from the imperializing Global North, as a white person, and as an academic. At the end of many days—including after the interaction I shared about the man on the bike in the introduction—I was exhausted navitaging these spaces and dealing with gender confusion from other. I was anxious about meeting other people, knowing when to "correct" others' assumptions about my gender or sexuality, and generally about what clothes to wear. Conversely, Queer Battle Fatigue more often led to clarity and revelation, caused by my own gender expression and identity being embodied and materialized in simultaneously contradictory ways in the qualitative research setting.

Honduras: the local and global context

Gender and sexuality in Honduras

Perhaps Honduras is most recently globally known for its exodus of migrants to the United States, the MS-13 gang which Donald Trump spoke about, and gang violence. Since 2011, Honduras has one of the highest murder rates in the world, and marginalized people, especially women and LGBTI identified people, are especially vulnerable. Some professions—including journalists, lawyers, and activists, are also frequently victimized by violence.

I consider myself well-versed on the situation in Honduras for LGBTI identified people. This is not simply because I have studied these issues academically or I because have been told this information second-hand; I also consider myself knowledgeable on the topic of LGBTI issues in Honduras because of my experiences there, beginning in 2006.

One final point important to note about Honduras is that Honduras has a history of coups, military rule, and police corruption. In June 2009, Honduras experienced a coup d'état by the military, which resulted in a sudden and unconstitutional change in the government and threw an already weak state into chaos. The United States Department of State, under Secretary of State Hillary Clinton, and President Barack Obama, affirmed this unconstitutional change in power. What has followed in the twelve years since the 2009 coup d'état are increased rates of corruption, violence, and impunity. Nearly 100% of murders in the country of Honduras go unsolved and remain without any convictions, and gender-based violence, domestic violence, and violence against the LGBTI community is common.

Themes and analysis

The themes I suggest for further examination arose from moments of confusion, aggression, trauma, and illegibility, either on my part or on the part of those I interacted with during this qualitative research project in Honduras. I offer these themes in order to challenge what qualitative research looks like in a transnational setting, for a queer-identified and presenting person, when the Global North's conceptions of gender, sexuality, and QBF can't be necessarily mapped on to the setting in Honduras. Furthermore, given that this was an ethnographic qualitative study, many of the interactions that are relevant to the questions at hand weren't in formal research settings (such as an interview, or an observation). What issues do illegibility, microaggressions, and exhaustion bring up, especially relative to gender, sexuality, and community in transnational qualitative research? What opportunities does Queer Battle Fatigue, when experienced in this transnational setting, offer in terms of deconstruction of gender and sexual identities, and formation of new understandings?

The role of the illegible and illiterate researcher

I had been attending weekly meetings, excursions to the beach, meet-ups at local bars and billiard halls, and movie nights with various groups of women and members of the LGBTI community for years. Well before my life as a researcher, when I was a secondary teacher in Honduras beginning in July of 2006, I attended events at the Communidad Gay Sampedrano, a group composed mostly of men who identified as gay, transwomen, and lesbians around the San Pedro Sula region in the North Coast of Honduras. I soon joined another group—this one founded by and primarily consisting of lesbians—called Mujeres Sin Limites or Women without Limits. The objective of the group was to support women socially, but also logistically, educationally, and sometimes financially. Most of the women identified as lesbian or bisexual, and some were married to men because they faced a lack of financial or housing options. I attended monthly meetings, participated in health workshops and community events, accompanied members to marches and manifestations, and offered classes in English to the group. In more recent years, I communicate with leaders of various activist groups, including Diamantes in La Lima, a Lesbian-Transwomen collective in San Pedro Sula, and a small group of LGBTI-identified youth in El Progreso.

When I first started spending time in LGBTI spaces in Honduras, I felt an unfamiliarity with how the groups were organized, how the meetings were run, and the level of formality and informality at times that I could never predict. There were boxes of materials from NGOs piled in the corner, filled with handouts, pamphlets, and overhead projector sheets that sat untouched for years. There were educational materials on HIV and AIDS, on using condoms during sexual activity, and on domestic violence that where offered, but to seemingly little interest. I never had clarity in what the objective of the meetings were, or how the timing of events would play out. When group leaders asked me to teach a few classes of basic English terms, I tried to make it fun and relevant—we learned phrases terms related to sexuality, gender, and dating—and had meals of fried chicken and banana flavored pop afterwards. We went to the billiard hall or watched movies. I was a gringa formed in a country that glorifies efficiency to the point where compassion and humanity, and even common sense, are often lacking, and from a culture that limits leisure and social time in favor of long and overwhelming work hours; it was a shift to be with a group of people who efficiency was secondary to a host of other organization factors.

I inquired once, about the unopened boxes and the pamphlets; the women explained to me what could have been obvious with a little more nuance on my part. Workshops with pamphlets and overhead projection sheets and group work weren't how meetings were typically run in Honduras, and so it wasn't an authentic way of sharing information and growing together. Instead, the group wanted to focus on socializing, building community, educational formation, and learning from each other. For a group of people that intentionally avoided sexual activity with penises, the constant focus on condoms and condom use seemed like an oversight, and not what was at the top of these women's needs or interests. Honduras does have one of the highest incidences of HIV/AIDS in the Western Hemisphere, and of course HIV/AIDS can affect anyone. However, the women did not think they were the right audience for an educational focus about condom use.

Regardless, it seemed as if those who did need access to HIV/AIDS education or health care couldn't get it. Recently, a friend who is a transwoman in Honduras who is also HIV+, sent me a message about helping her pay for her monthly medication. She had been getting it through an NGO, but for some reason it was no longer accessible, and she had failed to procure any medication at other clinics or hospitals in the area. She was hoping to find a place that she could purchase it. Besides a little money to help her out, she wondered if I had any connections in Honduras that could help her get the medicine beyond just that month.

In this instance, the QBF and aggression was in the form of "Western Eyes" (Mohanty, 2003), both from the perspective of me and that of NGOs, and globalization more broadly. The use of NGOs for local support is called the "third sector"—instead of public infrastructure or private investment, development work and non-profits (or the third sector) provides resources, education, and funding through charitable or philanthropy (Corry, 2010). In Honduras, the third sector often originates from the United States, Canada, and the European Union. It has been critiqued in the past for top-down organization and diminished local input and cooperation (Buffett, 2013; Hobart, 1993; Phillips, 2004). The presence of NGOs and the third sector removes responsibility and the role of local governments in protecting and providing for its citizens.

There was a subtle but ever-present conflict between the Honduran members of the groups I interacted with, and then NGOs they were receiving funding and resources from. This manifested in ways such as the unused materials, and misunderstandings about funding. The neoliberal model of development minimizes the role and responsibility of the state, leaves individuals like my friend without the material conditions they need for survival, and a lack of knowledge of how to navigate the third sector, leaving her in a difficult if not deadly position. There are many historical reasons that fostered an explosion of development and of the third sector over the last half a century. Honduras already had a weak state due to banana companies and other US corporations, and thus private industry and third sector negotiates much of daily lives. For the purpose of this article, I offer these stories of how the current model failed to read and respond to the LGBTI community in Honduras. This doesn't mean that LGBTI organizations aren't supporting Hondurans in positive ways. But a top-down organizational factor, or an NGO whose time in Honduras runs out, leaves the Honduran LGBTI community with a void.

The reason I share these anecdotes, however, is not to critique the third sector. This critique has been done sufficiently in academic spaces and in contemporary news opinion pieces (see Buffett, 2013; Hobart, 1993; Phillips, 2004). Instead, as a qualitative researcher, we are trained to look at research settings with an objective eye, knowing that regardless, we bring our subjectivities to the work. I initially came to these spaces not as a researcher, but as a friend and member of the queer community who was doing research and teaching in other spaces in Honduras. I was at times exhausted and frustrated with accessing queer community in Honduras, and I was unable to see nuance in their struggles with resources, time, and support.

At the same time, I was also illegible to people in the LGBTI community in Honduras. As indicated in the vignette in the introduction, my gender and sexuality were constantly "misread" according to the ways of reading I had learned in the United States. I had conversations with members of the LGBTI community, especially lesbians, who coyly asked if one was activa o passiva, and then admitted they themselves were versatile. The L Word, a Showtime show about a group of lesbians and queer people in Los Angeles, California was on television in Honduras, and the women's group borrowed my DVDs and had watch parties, but then questioned the use of dildos. "Born this way" slogans, self-identification, and pronouns have been a large part of US gay and lesbian culture over the last decade or so, but in Honduras, all these topics were uniquely different. For example, in 2018, I was asked to give a small workshop to a group of young women and girls who all identified as lesbians; they wanted to share and discuss how they felt dealing with their family, facing machismo in the streets from classmates and strangers, being a couple, and causes of homophobia. Sharing pronouns in a meeting or expressing a self-defined individual gender identity was not something that happened during these years in my experience. There was less emphasis on self-identification and gender identity and expression, and more emphasis on sharing and building community.

Brown et al. (2010) remind us that "critical understandings of the complexities of sexualities across the Global South cannot be transposed from the Global North" (p. 1567). What expectation did I arrive in Honduras with, that I would be "read correctly" according to my self-identification and expression, when Hondurans were not operating with the same definitions I had been socialized in? What should I have done when my pronouns were not used, or when those both in and out of the queer community didn't have any interest in the ways I had learned gender and sexuality? Perhaps what was exhausting and impossible to me was actually just a manifestation of the imperial and exploitative relationships between the United States and Honduras, and I was perceiving these situations with my "Western Eyes" instead of recognizing the role me and my country played in fostering these differences? How does one deal with a QBF that stems not from individual actions, but instead systemic global and local relationships? The difference in perspective did not stem from a simple lack of respect. Neither was it an issue of impact (on me) vs. intent (by others). In the next section, I share how I have attempted to move forward in answering these questions, through solidarity instead of critique, and evaluate the shortcomings and opportunities of how I have done this.

Material conditions, migrants, and murder

As Roughgarden (2019) explains in a chapter called "Tomboi, Vestidas, and Guevedoche," concepts of lesbian (or gay, or queer, etc.) vary significantly across cultures and times, and the concepts and identities I understood as lesbian or gay were very different than the US culture I was socialized in. Living and conducting qualitative research in Honduras led me to see how conceptions of gender identity and sexuality that I brought with me from the United States were resisted. My inner turmoil centered around the idea of impact vs. intent. I was impacted by these settings and interactions. I was exhausted at the end of the day from trying to navigate safe spaces for my queer body, or from not understanding the LGBTI community in Honduras. But could I simply say that impact > intent, and because I was impacted negatively, it didn't matter if intent was noble, as is a common conversation in the US? What about when the intent is mixed with globalization, cultural imperialism which has resulted in real and deadly consequences for the LGBTI community in Honduras?

The more time I spent with friends in Honduras from the LGBTI community, the more I saw how a model of intent vs. impact—and a model of "respecting" individual identities—seemed lacking in depth, compared to the systemic issues that influence the lives of those in Honduras. This is not to say that pronouns or individual identify formation are not important; in a US setting they certainly are. However, I question how well they transfer to a transnational setting, and what that juxtaposition can tell us about moving forward for queer global communities and LGBTI research and researchers in transnational settings

Most of the people I knew closely in Honduras in the LGBTI community when I first arrived there in 2006 are now dead or have migrated. My dear friend Juan Carlos—a gay man—was murdered in his home in 2015, just a month after taking two days off of work to drive around and help me find teachers for my dissertation research (HRD Memorial, 2021). One of the leaders of Mujeres sin Limites also died violently—it was never determined if it was suicide or murder. The majority of other friends I knew over the years have migrated to the United States and Spain, seeking asylum or living with an undocumented status.

Over the last three years, many of my friends and acquaintances fled Honduras with tens of thousands of other migrants looking for safety in migrant caravans (see Almendral & Villasana, 2021; Kinoslain & Partlow, 2018). Soon after, Honduran friends and acquaintances began contacting me en route to the US, or once they had crossed in to the US. A transwoman contacted me from near the border in Texas asking for information about shelters, and a transman messaged about a pro bono lawyer contact. Two lesbian couples felt as if the violence and fear was too much to handle in Honduras and left with a migrant caravan. One couple became stranded in Mexico with no money, and another was picked up by US Border Patrol, separated, and detained. Being LGBTI in Honduras—in terms of identity—is often closely linked with a desperate need to relocate, flee, or migrate, and is shaped by trauma of traveling, living with an undocumented status, applying for asylum, wearing an ankle monitor, and leaving a homeland. In Honduras' case, the desperate need to flee for asylum seekers is very closely related to the United States' centuries of violence abroad, including in Honduras.

Thus, I am frequently exhausted, broke, overwhelmed, and fatigued at the situation Honduran LGBTI people face, both in Honduras and abroad, and when I am physically present in Honduras and when I'm not. I have been asked to pay for coyotes (people who smuggle migrants into the United States), find lawyers, house individuals, write amicus briefs and letters of support, and testify in court. I have watched people who were directly responsible for supporting my qualitative research in Honduras—Juan Carlos, for example—be murdered, and other members of the LGBTI community flee in desperation. My fatigue and trauma comes from watching and not experiencing. What are the responsibilities of a qualitative researcher, and fellow member of the queer community, in situations such as these? Write more? Support NGOs financially or logistically? Spread information in the United States? Stay away? What are the ethics of sending money, finding lawyers, or writing amicus briefs? Most of what I have learned about gender and sexuality—truly—stemmed from years in Honduras where contrasts with US culture highlighted nuances and differences. The familiar was certainly made strange, and the strange was made familiar.

Moving forward

I share these anecdotes, and the vignette at the beginning of this article, to complicate identities related to gender and sexuality—in individual interactions and in organizations—in a transnational research setting. The point is not to praise the Honduran LGBTI community, nor is it to critique it. Instead, I ask what the ethics are when thinking about Queer Battle Fatigue as a researcher from the Global North, when confronted with trying, frustrating, or confusing situations in the Global South. In retrospect, each time I have experienced everyday aggressions (such as gender trouble) or have faced loss (the murder of Juan Carlos) or violence (being detained at a gay bar in Honduras), those instances offered me clarity, often on the backs and the lives of Hondurans, no matter how trying it was for me in the moment.

I do not suggest that there be a hierarchy of oppressions based on national borders. For example, just because the issues are unique in Honduras relative to the US, doesn't mean we should sideline important work in the US because oppression or marginalization isn't "as bad." However, researchers, in our capacity as academics, need to think about fatigue driving us to continue for those situated in spaces outside the Global North. We must challenge what "counts" as research and seek out a radical change in what is produced through qualitative research. I spend more time researching and revising amicus briefs—and then testifying in front of an immigration judge—than I do writing peer-reviewed articles or presenting at national conferences (which come with a line on the CV or the resort-like hotel setting). Transnational studies of gender and sexualities "insist on the recognition that particular genders and sexualities are shaped by a large number of processes implicated in globalization, including capitalism, diasporic movements, political economies of state, and the disjunctive flow of meanings produced across these sites" (Blackwood, 2005). Thus, our role in qualitative transnational research settings is to attack globalization and capitalism just as much as we attack homophobic or transphobic attacks on ourselves. Research can serve as resistance to homophobia or transphobia. We also need to consider neoliberal and globalized flows of information that limit where LGBTI people in the Global South can go, but open the doors for people like me. We must continue to "queer" queer research settings by focusing on other elements, besides gender and sexuality, that marginalize and oppress in order to better serve our communities and our queer friends.

Disclosure statement

No potential conflict of interest was reported by the author(s).

References

Alexander, M. J., & Mohanty, C. (1997). Intro: Genealogies, legacies, movements. In M. J. Alexander & C. Mohanty (Eds.), *Feminist genealogies, colonial legacies, democratic futures* (pp. x–xiii). Routledge.

Almendral, A., & Villasana, D. (2021). *What's next for these transgender asylum seekers stranding in Mexico?* National Geographic. https://www.nationalgeographic.com/history/article/what-next-for-transgender-asylum-seekers-stranded-mexico

Beverley, J. (1996). The margin at the center. In G. Gugelberger (Ed.), *The real thing. Testimonial discourse and Latin America* (pp. 23–41). Duke University Press.

Blackwood, E. (2005). Transnational sexualities in one place: Indonesian readings. *Gender & Society*, *19*(2), 221–242. https://doi.org/10.1177/0891243204272862

Brochin, C. (2018). Assembled identities and intersectional advocacy in literacy research. *Literacy Research: Theory, Method, and Practice, 67*(1), 164–116. https://doi.org/10.1177/2381336918786890

Brown, G. (2012). Homonormativity: A metropolitan concept that denigrates "ordinary" gay lives. *Journal of Homosexuality, 59*(7), 1065–1072. https://doi.org/10.1080/00918369.2012.699851

Brown, G., Browne, K., Elmhirst, R., & Hutta, S. (2010). Sexualities in/of the Global South. *Geography Compass, 4*(10), 1567–1579. https://doi.org/10.1111/j.1749-8198.2010.00382.x

Browne, K., & Nash, C. J. (2010). *Queer methods and methodologies: Intersecting queer theories and social science research*. Routledge.

Buffett, P. (2013). The charitable-industrial complex. *The New York Times*. Opinion Page.

Butler, J. (1993). *Bodies that matter: On the discursive limits of sex*. Routledge.

Butler, J. (1990). *Gender trouble: Feminism and the subversion of identity*. Routledge.

Butler, J. (2004). *Undoing gender*. Routledge.

Cendales Gonzalez, L., & Torres Carrillo, A. (n.d.). *La sistematización como experiencia investigativa y formativa*. Centro de Estudios & Publicaciones. http://www.cepalforja.org/sistem/documentos/lola_cendales-alfonso_torres-la_sistematizacion_como_experiencia_investigativa_y_formativa.pdf

Corry, O. (2010). Defining and theorizing the third sector. In R. Taylor (Ed.), *Third sector research* (pp. 11–20). Springer Publishing.

Curran, G. (2006). Responding to students' normative questions about gays: Putting queer theory into practice in an Australian ESL class. *Journal of Language, Identity & Education, 5*(1), 85–96. https://doi.org/10.1207/s15327701jlie0501_6

Fernandez Aponte, A. (2018, March 7) Left in the dark: Violence against women and LGBTI persons in Honduras and El Salvador. *Latin American Working Group Education Fund*. https://www.lawg.org/left-in-the-dark-violence-against-women-and-lgbti-persons-in-honduras-and-el-salvador/

Gugelberger, G. (Ed.). (1996). *The real thing: Testimonial discourse and Latin America*. Duke University Press.

Halberstam, J. (1998). *Female masculinity*. Duke University Press.

Hobart, M. (Ed.). (1993). *An anthropological critique of development: The growth of ignorance?* Routledge.

Jara Holliday, O. (n.d). Orientaciones teórico-prácticas para la sistematización de experiencias. *Ellacuria Fundazioa*. http://centroderecursos.alboan.org/ebooks/0000/0788/6_JAR_ORI.pdf

HRD Memorial (2021). *Juan Carlos Cruz Andara*. https://hrdmemorial.org/hrdrecord/juan-carlos-cruz-andara/

Kedley, K. E. (2019). El gringuito, Mr. Kate. Transnational ethnographic fieldwork as a gender nonconforming queer. *Journal of Lesbian Studies*, no. 4, 1–16.

Kedley, K. E. (2015). Queering the teacher as a text in the English language arts classroom: Beyond books, identity work and teacher preparation. *Sex Education: Sexuality, Society, and Learning, 15*(4), 364–377. https://doi.org/10.1080/14681811.2015.1027762

Kinoslain, S., & Partlow, J. (2018). LGBT asylum seekers are first to reach the U.S. border from the caravan. Now they wait. *The Washington Post*. https://www.washingtonpost.com/world/the_americas/the-first-caravan-migrants-arrive-at-the-us-border-and-begin-the-waiting-game/2018/11/13/ceef3844-e6b7-11e8-8449-1ff263609a31_story.html

Marcus, S. (2005). Queer theory for everyone: A review essay. *Signs: Journal of Women in Culture and Society, 31*(1), 191–218. https://doi.org/10.1086/432743

Merriam, S. B. (2009). *Qualitative research: A guide to design and implementation*. Jossey-Bass.

Mohanty, C. (2003). Under western eyes' revisited. *Signs: Journal of Women in Culture and Society, 28*(2), 499–535. https://doi.org/10.1086/342914

Nagar, R., & Lock Swarr, A. (2010). Introduction. In *Critical transnational feminist praxis*. SUNY Press.

Phillips, S. D. (2004). *The myths of horizontal governance: Is the third sector really a partner?* [Paper presentation]. International Society for Third Sector Research Conference. Toronto, Canada.

Roughgarden, J. (2019). *Evolution's rainbows*. University of California Press.

Wozolek, B., Varndell, R., & Speer, T. (2015). Are we not fatigued?: Queer battle fatigue at the intersection of heteronormative culture. *International Journal of Curriculum and Social Justice, 1*(1), 186–214.

Yudice, G. (1996). Testimonio and postmodernism. In G. Gugelberger (Ed.), In *The real thing. Testimonial discourse and Latin America* (pp. 42–57). Duke University Press.

Index

Page numbers in **bold** refer to tables.

ability discrimination 92
Ahmed, S. 3, 31, 36, 62, 65
Allen, W. R. 9
Antell, Samantha 4
anthropologists of education 27
anti-queer hostilities 1
Arellano, D. C. R. D. 57

Barad, K. 2, 3, 77
Bilodeau, B. 8
Black, Indigenous, and other students of color (BIPOC) 90
Blackmon, K. 20
Black mothers' high maternal mortality rate 79
Bowen, F. 20
"The Breakfast Club" radio program 52
"bro/dude culture" phenomenon 57
Browne, K. 109, 114
Brown, G. 107, 114
Bruner, J. 10
Bucceri, J. M. 9

Calabrese Barton, A. 61
Campbell, E. 27–8
Capodilupo, C. M. 9
Carew, J. 9
Carlone, H. B. 62
Chiquita Banana 103
Civil Rights Act of 1964 76
Clandinin, D. J. 78, 79
class discrimination 92
Clifford, J. 27
Critical Race Theory 2
curricula of silence 79–81
curricular cripistemologies 93–4, 99

Danley, D. G. 9
deep listening 78
De Pedro, K. T. 59
Dixon, J. 8
Dougherty, D. S. 8

elementary schools: formal/official curriculum 76; perceived innocence and asexuality 76
Elmhirst, R. 114
Endo, H. 79
Esqueda, M. C. 59
Esquilin, M. 9
Estrada, F. 60
explicit microaggressions 64
"Explode," Big Freedia song and video 47–50

Fahs, B. 59
failure: ability discrimination 92; curricular cripistemologies 93–4; disciplinary codes 93; fear of speaking 91; heterosexism, cissexism, sexism 93; institutionally-powerful actors 90; queer and trans inclusive policies 91; queer and trans youth 94–7; race/class discrimination 91, 92; scaffolded successes 97–8; sexuality and gender 91; sexuality and gender expressions 91; youth and adults 90
Faulker, S. L. 10
Feldon, David 4
Foley-Hernandez, Evelynn 4
Forester, R. 57
formal and null curriculums 81, 83–4
Forstie, C. 59
Frost, D. M. 59

Galarte, F. J. 8
Gay Liberation Movement 30
Gershon, W. S. 79–80
GLSEN National School Climate Survey 58
González, M. M. 62
Gottfried, M. 60
Greteman, Adam 3
Gusterson, H. 27
Gutiérrez, R. 59

Halberstam, J. 89, 90, 92, 93, 99
Hall, W. J. 58
Hawkman, Andrea 4
heartache, pedagogical tool 29–31
Heybach, J. 60

Hirschfield, J. 10
Holder, A. M. B. 9
Honduras: gender and sexuality 112; illegible and illiterate researcher 112–14; material conditions, migrants and murder 114–15
Hutta, S. 114

implicit microaggressions 64

Johnson, A. 62
Johnson, M. L. 92

Kedley, Kate 4
Kim, A. Y. 57
Kimball, E. W. 57
Kim, J. H. 9, 11
Kitzie, V. 60

landscapes of schools 2
Lassiter, L. 27–8
The Lavender Vita 12–14
Leavy, P. 9
"lesbian boomer" 33
"Lesbian Week" 33
Lester, A. O. S. 59
Leyva, L. A. 60
The LGBT+Intergenerational Dialogue Project: collaborative ethnographic experimentation 27–9; COVID-19 pandemic 33; description 24; dialogues, collaborative creative work and shared dinners 25; generation after generation 25; *Gen Silent* 32; heartache, pedagogical tool 29–31; histories and experiences 25; lovesickeness 33–5; low-income and food insecure 26; participants 28; transgenerational sharing of trauma 32; youngers and elders 26
LGBTQ employees: challenges 7–8; threshold of acceptance 8; workplace discrimination issues 8
LGBTQIA2S+ communities 1
lovesickeness 33–5
Lynch, R. J. 59

MacDonald, Beth 4
Marine, S. B. 8
Masters, A. S. 60
mathematx 59–60
Mattheis, A. 57
Metz, Mary 81
Miller, R. A. 57
minoritized identities of sexuality and gender (MIoSG) 7, 9–10
Mitchell, D. T. 93
Mitchell, Reagan 3, 4
Mizock, L. 8
Mohanty, C. 108
Moorefield-Lang, H. 60
Morris, Karen 3

Nadal, K. L. 9
narrative inquiry method: anti-queer sentiments 78; (re)claiming stories and silenced voices 78; deep listening 78; diverse narratives 79; feelings and subjective experiences 78; and learning 110–11; normalized shame, silence and violence 82; unpacking culture and interactions 82–3
Nash, C. J. 109
Nicolazzo, Z. 8
"no-promo-homo" laws 91

Oliveros, P. 78
Ormerod, A. J. 8
The Other Side of Middletown 28

Pickup, A. 60
Pierce, C. 9
Pierce-Gonzalez, D. 9
Pitcher, E. N. 8
poetry 9–10
post-lesbian ambivalence, identity-blind sentiments 59
Prendergast, M. 10

qualitative methodologies 9–11
The Queer Art of Failure 89
Queer Battle Fatigue (QBF) 1–3, 9, 30, 61–2, 106; *see also* transfaculty experience
Queer Black joy: description 39; "Explode," Big Freedia song and video 40–1; freedoms and equity 40; RBF frameworks 39–40; spirit murdering 40–2; "Vogue", Madonna's 1990 song and video 40
Queer people in Rural America 58–9
Queers in STEM (QSTEM) 60
queer theory 106–7
Queer youth in STEM spaces 59–60

racial battle fatigue (RBF) 9, 39
Rands, K. 60
Rankine, C. 26
Reece-Miller, P. C. 79
Richardson, L. 19
Riessman, C. K. 79
Riley, J. 8
Robinson, Sean 3
Rodgers, G. K. 58
Rosiek, J. 78, 79
Ross, Loretta 29
Roughgarden, J. 114

Santavicca, N. 79
Science, Technology, Engineering, and Mathematics (STEM): affirmation and advice 68–9; creativity, personal expression and community engagement 57; cultural politics of emotion 62; data analysis 64–5, **65**; emotion 66–8; identity 62–3; informal experiences, minoritized youth 60–1; learning

opportunities 56; maker camps 64; micro- and macro-aggressions 57–8; researchers' positionalities 63, 63–4; safety 69–70; youth's development 57
Searle, Kristin 4
Sedgwick, E. K. 2, 29
self-knowledge 19
Seyranian, V. 57
Shelton, S. A. 59
Simmons, S. L. 8
Sinatra, G. M. 57
Smith, Marti 25
Smith, M. R. 58
Smith, W. A. 9
Snyder, S. L. 93
Sotilleo, E. A. 8
Speer, T. 8–9, 30, 61
Spencer, H. 80
spirit murdering, Queer Black joy 40–2
storytelling 28
Sublett, C. 60
success, defined 89
Sue, D. W. 9
Sullivan, A. M. 10
Swank, E. 59
Sylvester 51–2; panoptic gazes 44–7; "You make me feel, mighty real" song (1978) 42–4

Tan, E. 61
Teman, E. D. 10
Tofel-Grehl, Colby 4
Torino, G. C. 9

transfaculty experience 8, 11–19
transnational feminist theory 105–6, 108–9
transnational illegibility 105

United Fruit Company 103
US K-12 education: affidavits and amicus briefs 109; feminine and masculine pronouns 106; primary instrument, qualitative research 111; queer geographies and space 107–8; queer theory 106–7

Vaccaro, A. 57
Varndell, R. 8–9, 30, 61
"Vogue", Madonna's 1990 song and video 40

Walsh, S. 10
Ware, L. 93
Waters, E. M. 58
Westrate, Nic 3
Weton, Kath 34
Willis, D. 9
Winfield, A. G. 79
Witkemper, K. D. 58
women's continued victimization 79
Woodrum, T. D. 8
Woodson, C. G. 2, 81
Wozolek, B. 4, 8–9, 30, 61

Yoder, J. B. 57
youth-serving organizations 94
Yuen, N. 8